THE POEMS OF EMILY DICKINSON

VOLUME II

THE POEMS OF

Emily Dickinson

Including variant readings critically compared
with all known manuscripts

Edited by

THOMAS H. JOHNSON

THE BELKNAP PRESS
of HARVARD UNIVERSITY PRESS
Cambridge, Massachusetts
1 9 5 5

Distributed in Great Britain by

Geoffrey Cumberlege, Oxford University Press, London

Library of Congress Catalog Card Number 54–8631

Printed in the United States of America

POEMS

495–1176

[1862–1870]

It's thoughts – and just One Heart –
And Old Sunshine – about –
Make frugal – Ones – Content –
And two or three – for Company –
Upon a Holiday –
Crowded – as Sacrament –

Books – when the Unit –
Spare the Tenant – long eno' –
A Picture – if it Care –
Itself – a Gallery too rare –
For needing more –

Flowers – to keep the Eyes – from going awkward –
When it snows –
A Bird – if they – prefer –
Though Winter fire – sing clear as Plover –
To our – ear –

A Landscape – not so great
To suffocate the Eye –
A Hill – perhaps –
Perhaps – the profile of a Mill
Turned by the Wind –
Tho' *such* – are *luxuries* –

It's thoughts – and just two Heart –
And Heaven – about –
At least – a Counterfeit –
We would not have Correct –
And Immortality – can be almost –
Not quite – Content –

10. Gallery too rare] Vatican – too rare –

MANUSCRIPT: Early 1862, in packet 6 (H 23a).
PUBLICATION: *UP* (1935), 33. The suggested change is rejected, and
the italics are not retained. The text is arranged as three stanzas of 6, 16, 7
lines. Two words are altered:

3. Ones] one's   23. two] one

As far from pity, as complaint –
As cool to speech – as stone –
As numb to Revelation
As if my Trade were Bone –

As far from Time – as History –
As near yourself – Today –
As Children, to the Rainbow's scarf –
Or Sunset's Yellow play

To eyelids in the Sepulchre –
How dumb the Dancer lies –
While Color's Revelations break –
And blaze – the Butterflies!

10. dumb] still

MANUSCRIPT: Early 1862, in packet 6 (H 23c).
PUBLICATION: *Poems* (1896), 155, titled "Asleep." The suggested change is adopted.

He strained my faith –
Did he find it supple?
Shook my strong trust –
Did it then – yield?

Hurled my belief –
But – did he shatter – it?
Racked – with suspense –
Not a nerve failed!

Wrung me – with Anguish –
But I never doubted him –
'Tho' for what wrong
He did never say –

Stabbed – while I sued
His sweet forgiveness –   *[no stanza break]*

Jesus – it's your little "John"!
Dont you know – me?

10] Or – Must be – I deserved – it –   16] Why – Slay – Me?

MANUSCRIPT: Early 1862, in packet 6 (H 24b). The two suggested changes are in fact written into the body of the manuscript as though they were additional lines of the poem; the first between lines 10 and 11, the second as the concluding line. But the presence of "Or" before the first is a clear indication of its alternative character, and the second seems to be similar in nature.

PUBLICATION: BM (1945), 304. It derives from a transcript made by Mrs. Todd and is placed among the unfinished poems, printed as two quatrains by combining lines 1 and 2, 3 and 4, etc., and arranging the whole as two stanzas. The suggested changes are incorporated as part of the text, with the final line rendered:

Jesus, it's your little "John"! Why me slay?

A note states that "In Mrs. Todd's copy the last two words are inverted."

498

I envy Seas, whereon He rides –
I envy Spokes of Wheels
Of Chariots, that Him convey –
I envy Crooked Hills

That gaze upon His journey –
How easy All can see
What is forbidden utterly
As Heaven – unto me!

I envy Nests of Sparrows –
That dot His distant Eaves –
The wealthy Fly, upon His Pane –
The happy – happy Leaves –

That just abroad His Window
Have Summer's leave to play –
The Ear Rings of Pizarro
Could not obtain for me –

I envy Light – that wakes Him –
And Bells – that boldly ring
To tell Him it is Noon, abroad –
Myself – be Noon to Him –

Yet interdict – my Blossom –
And abrogate – my Bee –
Lest Noon in Everlasting Night –
Drop Gabriel – and Me –

1. whereon He rides] That bear Him   8. As Heaven] As Eden
4. Crooked Hills] Speechless Hills   18. ring] Come
5. gaze upon] grow along   23. in] down –
7. forbidden] denied

MANUSCRIPT: About 1862, in packet 6 (H 25a). In line 11, "happy"
is crossed out and "wealthy" substituted.

PUBLICATION: *Poems* (1896), 95–96, titled "Longing." The suggested
change for line 4 is adopted. Words in two lines are altered:

14. play] be   20. be Noon to Him] his noon could
                          bring

499

Those fair – fictitious People –
The Women – plucked away
From our familiar Lifetime –
The Men of Ivory –

Those Boys and Girls, in Canvas –
Who stay upon the Wall
In Everlasting Keepsake –
Can Anybody tell?

We trust – in places perfecter –
Inheriting Delight
Beyond our faint Conjecture –
Our dizzy Estimate –

Remembering ourselves, we trust –
Yet Blesseder – than We –   [*no stanza break*]

Through Knowing – where We only hope –
Receiving – where we – pray –

Of Expectation – also –
Anticipating us
With transport, that would be a pain
Except for Holiness –

Esteeming us – as Exile –
Themself – admitted Home –
Through gentle Miracle of Death –
The Way ourself, must come –

1. fair] new
2. plucked] slipped away –
3. Lifetime] address – / gazing – /
   fingers – / familiar notice –
6. stay] dwell
7. Everlasting Keepsake] Everlasting
   Childhood –

8] Where are they – Can you tell –
11. faint] small
12. dizzy] scanty
15. hope] guess
16. Receiving] beholding
23. gentle] curious – / *easy* –

MANUSCRIPT: Early 1862, in packet 6 (H 25b).
PUBLICATION: *FP* (1929), 101. The suggested changes for lines 3
("notice"), 6, 7, 8, 11, 12 are adopted. Stanzas 5 and 6 printed without
division, are separated in later collections. Seven words are altered:

1. Those] These
5. Those] These
9. We trust] Perhaps

14. Yet] But
21. Exile] exiles
22. Themself] Themselves
24. ourself] ourselves

500

Within my Garden, rides a Bird
Upon a single Wheel –
Whose spokes a dizzy Music make
As 'twere a travelling Mill –

He never stops, but slackens
Above the Ripest Rose –
Partakes without alighting
And praises as he goes,

[383]

Till every spice is tasted –
And then his Fairy Gig
Reels in remoter atmospheres –
And I rejoin my Dog,

And He and I, perplex us
If positive, 'twere we –
Or bore the Garden in the Brain
This Curiosity –

But He, the best Logician,
Refers my clumsy eye –
To just vibrating Blossoms!
An Exquisite Reply!

10. Fairy Gig] Microscopic Gig   18. clumsy] duller –

MANUSCRIPT: Early 1862, in packet 6 (H 26a). See poem no. 1463.
PUBLICATION: *FP* (1929), 59. The suggested change for line 18 is
adopted.

501

This World is not Conclusion.
A Species stands beyond –
Invisible, as Music –
But positive, as Sound –
It beckons, and it baffles –
Philosophy – dont know –
And through a Riddle, at the last –
Sagacity, must go –
To guess it, puzzles scholars –
To gain it, Men have borne
Contempt of Generations
And Crucifixion, shown –
Faith slips – and laughs, and rallies –
Blushes, if any see –
Plucks at a twig of Evidence –
And asks a Vane, the way –   [*no stanza break*]

[384]

Much Gesture, from the Pulpit –
Strong Hallelujahs roll –
Narcotics cannot still the Tooth
That nibbles at the soul –

2. Species] A sequel –   18. Strong] Sure –
9. guess] prove it –   19. Tooth] Mouse –

MANUSCRIPT: Early 1862, in packet 6 (H 26d).

PUBLICATION: The first twelve lines were first published in the *Out-look*, LIII (25 January 1896), 140, titled "Immortality," from a transcript made by Mrs. Todd. The same lines were also issued in *Poems* (1896), 139, without title, and appear in later collections. The suggested change for line 2 is adopted. The final eight lines are in *BM* (1945), 290, arranged as two quatrains. The suggested changes are rejected. A note accompanying these quatrains points out that they also derive from Mrs. Todd's transcript, and remarks that they may or may not be a part of "After great pain a formal feeling comes," and "This world is not conclusion" – both of which are on two sheets of the Todd transcript. Three words are altered:

6. Philosophy] Philosophies   12. shown] known
10. borne] shown

502

At least – to pray – is left – is left –
Oh Jesus – in the Air –
I know not which thy chamber is –
I'm knocking – everywhere –

Thou settest Earthquake in the South –
And Maelstrom, in the Sea –
Say, Jesus Christ of Nazareth –
Hast thou no Arm for Me?

3. chamber is] palaces –   5. settest] stirrest –

MANUSCRIPT: Early 1862, in packet 6 (H 381d).

PUBLICATION: *Poems* (1891), 184. The suggested change for line 5 is adopted.

[385]

Better – than Music! For I – who heard it –
I was used – to the Birds – before –
This – was different – 'Twas Translation –
Of all tunes I knew – and more –

'Twas'nt contained – like other stanza –
No one could play it – the second time –
But the Composer – perfect Mozart –
Perish with him – that Keyless Rhyme!

So – Children – told how Brooks in Eden –
Bubbled a better – Melody –
Quaintly infer – Eve's great surrender –
Urging the feet – that would – not – fly –

Children – matured – are wiser – mostly –
Eden – a legend – dimly told –
Eve – and the Anguish – Grandame's story –
But – I was telling a tune – I heard –

Not such a strain – the Church – baptizes –
When the last Saint – goes up the Aisles –
Not such a stanza splits the silence –
When the Redemption strikes her Bells –

Let me not spill – it's smallest cadence –
Humming – for promise – when alone –
Humming – until my faint Rehearsal –
Drop into tune – around the Throne –

9. told how] assured that	20. strikes] shakes –
13. matured] grown up –	21. spill] lose / waste –
14. told] learned / crooned	

MANUSCRIPT: Early 1862, in packet 6 (H 27).

PUBLICATION: *BM* (1945), 235. The text derives from a transcript made by Mrs. Todd. Two suggested changes are adopted:

9. assured that   21. lose

One word is mistakenly adopted:

19. splits] shakes

[386]

504

You know that Portrait in the Moon –
So tell me who 'tis like –
The very Brow – the stooping eyes –
A-fog for – Say – Whose Sake?

The very Pattern of the Cheek –
It varies – in the Chin –
But – Ishmael – since we met – 'tis long –
And fashions – intervene –

When Moon's at full – 'Tis Thou – I say –
My lips just hold the name –
When crescent – Thou art worn – I note –
But – there – the Golden Same –

And when – Some Night – Bold – slashing Clouds
Cut Thee away from Me –
That's easier – than the other film
That glazes Holiday –

          11. note] mind

MANUSCRIPT: About 1862, in packet 33 (H 179a).
PUBLICATION: *UP* (1935), 88. The suggested change is rejected. In line 7 "we" is italicized. One word is altered:

          9. Moon's] morn's

505

I would not paint – a picture –
I'd rather be the One
It's bright impossibility
To dwell – delicious – on –
And wonder how the fingers feel
Whose rare – celestial – stir –
Evokes so sweet a Torment –
Such sumptuous – Despair –

I would not talk, like Cornets –
I'd rather be the One   [*no stanza break*]

[387]

Raised softly to the Ceilings –
And out, and easy on –
Through Villages of Ether –
Myself endued Balloon
By but a lip of Metal –
The pier to my Pontoon –

Nor would I be a Poet –
It's finer – own the Ear –
Enamored – impotent – content –
The License to revere,
A privilege so awful
What would the Dower be,
Had I the Art to stun myself
With Bolts of Melody!

3. bright] fair
7. Evokes] provokes
11. the Ceilings] Horizons
12. out] by –

14. endued] upheld / upborne / sustained
21. privilege] luxury

Manuscript: Early 1862, in packet 85 (Bingham 28b).
Publication: *BM* (1945), xxxi. The suggested change for line 11 is adopted.

506

He touched me, so I live to know
That such a day, permitted so,
I groped upon his breast –
It was a boundless place to me
And silenced, as the awful sea
Puts minor streams to rest.

And now, I'm different from before,
As if I breathed superior air –
Or brushed a Royal Gown –
My feet, too, that had wandered so –
My Gipsy face – transfigured now –
To tenderer Renown –

[388]

Into this Port, if I might come,
Rebecca, to Jerusalem,
Would not so ravished turn –
Nor Persian, baffled at her shrine
Lift such a Crucifixal sign
To her imperial Sun.

2, 3. permitted so, I groped] persuaded so, I perished – / accepted so – I dwelt –

MANUSCRIPT: About 1862, in packet 85 (Bingham 29a).
PUBLICATION: The first and second stanzas are in *Poems* (1896), 92. The complete poem was first published in *New England Quarterly*, XX (1947), 22. The suggested changes are rejected in both printings.

507

She sights a Bird – she chuckles –
She flattens – then she crawls –
She runs without the look of feet –
Her eyes increase to Balls –

Her Jaws stir – twitching – hungry –
Her Teeth can hardly stand –
She leaps, but Robin leaped the first –
Ah, Pussy, of the Sand,

The Hopes so juicy ripening –
You almost bathed your Tongue –
When Bliss disclosed a hundred Toes –
And fled with every one –

5] [Her] Mouth stirs – longing –   11. Toes] Wings –
hungry

MANUSCRIPT: Early 1862, in packet 85 (Bingham 29c).
PUBLICATION: *BM* (1945), 65–66. The suggested change for line 11 is adopted.

508

I'm ceded – I've stopped being Their's –
The name They dropped upon my face

[389]   [*no stanza break*]

With water, in the country church
Is finished using, now,
And They can put it with my Dolls,
My childhood, and the string of spools,
I've finished threading – too –

Baptized, before, without the choice,
But this time, consciously, of Grace –
Unto supremest name –
Called to my Full – The Crescent dropped –
Existence's whole Arc, filled up,
With one small Diadem.

My second Rank – too small the first –
Crowned – Crowing – on my Father's breast –
A half unconscious Queen –
But this time – Adequate – Erect,
With Will to choose, or to reject,
And I choose, just a Crown –

10. name] term
12. Arc] Eye / Rim (*crossed out*)
12. whole Arc] surmise (*crossed out*)
13. one small] just one

15. Crowing] whimpering / dangling
16. half] too unconscious
16] An insufficient Queen –
18. Will] power
19. Crown] Throne

Manuscript: Early 1862, in packet 85 (Bingham 30a). Although this is a packet copy and therefore supposedly in semifinal draft, it is hardly more than worksheet draft as it stands.
Publication: *Poems* (1890), 60–61, titled "Love's Baptism." The suggested change for line 19 is adopted.

509

If anybody's friend be dead
It's sharpest of the theme
The thinking how they walked alive –
At such and such a time –

Their costume, of a Sunday,
Some manner of the Hair –   [*no stanza break*]

A prank nobody knew but them
Lost, in the Sepulchre –

How warm, they were, on such a day,
You almost feel the date –
So short way off it seems –
And now – they're Centuries from that –

How pleased they were, at what you said –
You try to touch the smile
And dip your fingers in the frost –
When was it – Can you tell –

You asked the Company to tea –
Acquaintance – just a few –
And chatted close with this Grand Thing
That dont remember you –

Past Bows, and Invitations –
Past Interview, and Vow –
Past what Ourself can estimate –
That – makes the Quick of Wo!

13. were] looked   15. dip] mix
14. touch] reach   23. estimate] understand

Manuscript: Early 1862, in packet 85 (Bingham 30b).

Publication: *Poems* (1891), 204–205. All suggested changes are rejected. "And now," which begins line 12, concludes line 11. One word is altered:

23. Ourself] ourselves

510

It was not Death, for I stood up,
And all the Dead, lie down –
It was not Night, for all the Bells
Put out their Tongues, for Noon.

It was not Frost, for on my Flesh
I felt Siroccos – crawl –
Nor Fire – for just my Marble feet
Could keep a Chancel, cool –

[391]

And yet, it tasted, like them all,
The Figures I have seen
Set orderly, for Burial,
Reminded me, of mine –

As if my life were shaven,
And fitted to a frame,
And could not breathe without a key,
And 'twas like Midnight, some –

When everything that ticked – has stopped –
And Space stares all around –
Or Grisly frosts – first Autumn morns,
Repeal the Beating Ground –

But, most, like Chaos – Stopless – cool –
Without a Chance, or Spar –
Or even a Report of Land –
To justify – Despair.

5. Flesh] Knees   7. my] two

MANUSCRIPT: Early 1862, in packet 85 (Bingham 31a).
PUBLICATION: *Poems* (1891), 222–223. The suggested changes are rejected.

511

If you were coming in the Fall,
I'd brush the Summer by
With half a smile, and half a spurn,
As Housewives do, a Fly.

If I could see you in a year,
I'd wind the months in balls –
And put them each in separate Drawers,
For fear the numbers fuse –

If only Centuries, delayed,
I'd count them on my Hand,   [*no stanza break*]

Subtracting, till my fingers dropped
Into Van Dieman's Land.

If certain, when this life was out –
That your's and mine, should be –
I'd toss it yonder, like a Rind,
And take Eternity –

But, now, uncertain of the length
Of this, that is between,
It goads me, like the Goblin Bee –
That will not state – it's sting.

16. take] taste

MANUSCRIPT: Early 1862, in packet 85 (Bingham 31b). Until 1853 Van Diemen's Land was the name of Tasmania.

PUBLICATION: *Poems* (1890), 48–49. The suggested change is adopted. Alterations were made in three lines:

8] Until their time befalls.   18] Of time's uncertain wing,
17. uncertain] all ignorant

The text of the poem is correctly rendered in *Ancestors' Brocades* (1945), 186.

512

The Soul has Bandaged moments –
When too appalled to stir –
She feels some ghastly Fright come up
And stop to look at her –

Salute her – with long fingers –
Caress her freezing hair –
Sip, Goblin, from the very lips
The Lover – hovered – o'er –
Unworthy, that a thought so mean
Accost a Theme – so – fair –

The soul has moments of Escape –
When bursting all the doors –
She dances like a Bomb, abroad,
And swings upon the Hours,

As do the Bee – delirious borne –
Long Dungeoned from his Rose –
Touch Liberty – then know no more,
But Noon, and Paradise –

The Soul's retaken moments –
When, Felon led along,
With shackles on the plumed feet,
And staples, in the Song,

The Horror welcomes her, again,
These, are not brayed of Tongue –

21. shackles] irons –   22. staples] rivets –

MANUSCRIPT: About 1862, in packet 85 (Bingham 33a).
PUBLICATION: *BM* (1945), 244-245. The text is arranged in three
stanzas of 10, 8, and 6 lines. The suggested change for line 22 is adopted.

513

Like Flowers, that heard the news of Dews,
But never deemed the dripping prize
Awaited their – low Brows –

Or Bees – that thought the Summer's name
Some rumor of Delirium,
No Summer – could – for Them –

Or Arctic Creatures, dimly stirred –
By Tropic Hint – some Travelled Bird
Imported to the Wood –

Or Wind's bright signal to the Ear –
Making that homely, and severe,
Contented, known, before –

The Heaven – unexpected come,
To Lives that thought the Worshipping
A too presumptuous Psalm –

1. Like] As –   9. Imported] imported –

MANUSCRIPT: About 1862, in packet 85 (Bingham 33b).

PUBLICATION: This poem, complete in itself, was by error attached as
the concluding part of "A something in a summer's Day," and so published
in *Poems* (1890), 82–83, and in all subsequent collections. An account of
the error is given in the note to the other poem. The suggested change is
not adopted. Four words are altered:

1. news] tale   13. come] came
7. Creatures] creature   14. the] their

514

Her smile was shaped like other smiles –
The Dimples ran along –
And still it hurt you, as some Bird
Did hoist herself, to sing,
Then recollect a Ball, she got –
And hold upon the Twig,
Convulsive, while the Music crashed –
Like Beads – among the Bog –

7. crashed] *broke*

MANUSCRIPT: About 1862, in packet 14 (H 77b).

PUBLICATION: *UP* (1935), 123; *AB* (1945), 393. For a discussion of
the confusions in the published versions of this poem, see the note following
"A happy lip – breaks sudden," (no. 353). In *UP* "crashed" (line 7) reads
"cracked"; it is correctly rendered in *AB*.

515

No Crowd that has occurred
Exhibit – I suppose
That General Attendance
That Resurrection – does –

Circumference be full –
The long restricted Grave
Assert her Vital Privilege –
The Dust – connect – and live –

On Atoms – features place –
All Multitudes that were
Efface in the Comparison –
As Suns – dissolve a star –

Solemnity – prevail –
It's Individual Doom
Possess each separate Consciousness –
August – Absorbed – Numb –

What Duplicate – exist –
What Parallel can be –
Of the Significance of This –
To Universe – and Me?

6. restricted] subjected
7. her Vital Privilege] His Primo-
   geniture
8. connect] adjust –
12. dissolve] annul

16. Absorbed – Numb] Resistless –
    dumb
18. Parallel] scenery
19. Significance] stupendousness

MANUSCRIPT: About 1862, in packet 5 (H 18a).
PUBLICATION: *FP* (1929), 111. One misreading, "full" for "free" (line
5), is corrected in *Poems* (current). All suggested changes are adopted ex-
cept for line 18. One word is altered:

3. That] The

516

Beauty – be not caused – It Is –
Chase it, and it ceases –
Chase it not, and it abides –

Overtake the Creases

In the Meadow – when the Wind
Runs his fingers thro' it –
Deity will see to it
That You never do it –

1. be] is   6. Runs] puts

MANUSCRIPT: About 1862, in packet 5 (H 18b). The fourth line stands
apart from both stanzas.

PUBLICATION: *Saturday Review of Literature*, V (9 March 1929), 751;
FP (1929), 57. The text is arranged as a ten-line stanza; in later collections,
as two quatrains. The suggested change for line 1 is adopted.

517

He parts Himself – like Leaves –
And then – He closes up –
Then stands upon the Bonnet
Of Any Buttercup –

And then He runs against
And oversets a Rose –
And then does Nothing –
Then away upon a Jib – He goes –

And dangles like a Mote
Suspended in the Noon –
Uncertain – to return Below –
Or settle in the Moon –

What come of Him – at Night –
The privilege to say
Be limited by Ignorance –
What come of Him – That Day –

The Frost – possess the World –
In Cabinets – be shown –
A Sepulchre of quaintest Floss –
An Abbey – a Cocoon –

[397]

3–4] And then He leans with all His
Might/ Upon a Buttercup –
6. oversets] overturns
11. Uncertain] indifferent –

14] The liberty to say –
Authority –
17. possess the World] obtain the
World –

MANUSCRIPT: About 1862, in packet 5 (H 18c).

PUBLICATION: *UP* (1935), 56. The suggested change for line 17 is adopted. One misreading, "dangling" for "dangles" (line 9), is corrected in *Poems* (current). Three words are altered:

8. Jib] jiff
13. come] came

16. come] came

518

Her sweet Weight on my Heart a Night
Had scarcely deigned to lie –
When, stirring, for Belief's delight,
My Bride had slipped away –

If 'twas a Dream – made solid – just
The Heaven to confirm –
Or if Myself were dreamed of Her –
The power to presume –

With Him remain – who unto Me –
Gave – even as to All –
A Fiction superseding Faith –
By so much – as 'twas real –

8. power] wisdom

MANUSCRIPT: About 1862, in packet 5 (H 149b).

PUBLICATION: *BM* (1945), 248. The text derives from a transcript of the packet copy made by Mrs. Todd. The suggested change is adopted.

519

'Twas warm – at first – like Us –
Until there crept upon
A Chill – like frost upon a Glass –
Till all the scene – be gone.

The Forehead copied Stone –
The Fingers grew too cold
To ache – and like a Skater's Brook –
The busy eyes – congealed –

It straightened – that was all –
It crowded Cold to Cold –
It multiplied indifference –
As Pride were all it could –

And even when with Cords –
'Twas lowered, like a Weight –
It made no Signal, nor demurred,
But dropped like Adamant.

14. Weight] Freight –

MANUSCRIPT: About 1862, in packet 5 (H 150b).
PUBLICATION: *Atlantic Monthly*, CXLIII (February 1929), 183; *FP*
(1929), 100. The suggested change is adopted. One word is altered:

2. upon] thereon

520

I started Early – Took my Dog –
And visited the Sea –
The Mermaids in the Basement
Came out to look at me –

And Frigates – in the Upper Floor
Extended Hempen Hands –
Presuming Me to be a Mouse –
Aground – upon the Sands –

But no Man moved Me – till the Tide
Went past my simple Shoe –
And past my Apron – and my Belt
And past my Boddice – too –

And made as He would eat me up –
As wholly as a Dew
Upon a Dandelion's Sleeve –
And then – I started – too –

And He – He followed – close behind –
I felt His Silver Heel
Upon my Ancle – Then my Shoes
Would overflow with Pearl –

Until We met the Solid Town –
No One He seemed to know –
And bowing – with a Mighty look –
At me – The Sea withdrew –

12. Boddice] Bosom / Buckle   22. One] man –

MANUSCRIPT: About 1862, in packet 5 (H 382a).
PUBLICATION: *Poems* (1891), 134–135, titled "By the Sea." The suggested change for line 22 is adopted.

521

Endow the Living – with the Tears –
You squander on the Dead,
And They were Men and Women – now,
Around Your Fireside –

Instead of Passive Creatures,
Denied the Cherishing
Till They – the Cherishing deny –
With Death's Etherial Scorn –

2.   squander on] spend upon –

MANUSCRIPT: About 1862, in packet 5 (H 382c).
PUBLICATION: *BM* (1945), 197. The suggested change is rejected. The text derives from a transcript of the packet copy made by Mrs. Todd.

Had I presumed to hope –
The loss had been to Me
A Value – for the Greatness' Sake –
As Giants – gone away –

Had I presumed to gain
A Favor so remote –
The failure but confirm the Grace
In further Infinite –

'Tis failure – not of Hope –
But Confident Despair –
Advancing on Celestial Lists –
With faint – Terrestrial power –

'Tis Honor – though I die –
For That no Man obtain
Till He be justified by Death –
This — is the Second Gain —

4. gone] claimed   10. Confident] diligent –/resolute –

MANUSCRIPT: About 1862, in packet 5 (H 22a).
PUBLICATION: FP (1929), 120. The text of stanzas 1 and 2, arranged
as five lines each, in later collections is restored as quatrains. One sug-
gested change is adopted:

10. diligent

Sweet – You forgot – but I remembered
Every time – for Two –
So that the Sum be never hindered
Through Decay of You –

Say if I erred? Accuse my Farthings –
Blame the little Hand
Happy it be for You – a Beggar's –
Seeking More – to spend –

[401]

Just to be Rich – to waste my Guineas
On so Best a Heart –
Just to be Poor – for Barefoot Vision
You – Sweet – Shut me out –

3. Sum] Love   6. little] empty – /childish
4. Decay] Fatigue – / the Lapse –   8. Seeking] Saving –

MANUSCRIPTS: The copy reproduced above is in packet 5 (H 22b),
written about 1862. A variant of stanza 3, written about 1865, is in packet
88 (Bingham 51f), presented as a poem complete in itself:

Just to be Rich
To waste my Guinea
On so broad a Heart!
Just to be Poor,
For Barefoot pleasure
You, Sir, shut me out!

A second copy of the same variant stanza (Bingham), signed "Emily.,"
was sent to an unidentified recipient; it seems likewise to have been written
about 1865, and may have been sent to Bowles.

Just to be Rich –
To waste my Guinea
On so Broad a Heart –
Just to be Poor –
For Barefoot Pleasure
You – Sir – Shut me out –

PUBLICATION: The three stanzas are in BM (1945), 160–161. All sug-
gested changes are rejected. The variant stanza, arranged as a quatrain,
is published in a footnote on page 161, following the comment: "A slightly
different version of the final stanza was sent to Samuel Bowles."

524

Departed – to the Judgment –
A Mighty Afternoon –
Great Clouds – like Ushers – leaning –
Creation – looking on –

The Flesh – Surrendered – Cancelled –
The Bodiless – begun –
Two Worlds – like Audiences – disperse –
And leave the Soul – alone –

3. leaning] placing   7. disperse] dissolve – / withdraw – /
5. Cancelled] Shifted   retire –
7. Two] the –

MANUSCRIPT: About 1862, in packet 13 (H 62b).

PUBLICATION: This was one of fourteen poems selected for publication in an article contributed by T. W. Higginson to the *Christian Union*, XLII (25 September 1890), 393, and there titled "Astra Castra." The text is identical with that in *Poems* (1890), 112, also titled "Astra Castra." All suggested changes are rejected.

525

I think the Hemlock likes to stand
Upon a Marge of Snow –
It suits his own Austerity –
And satisfies an awe

That men, must slake in Wilderness –
And in the Desert – cloy –
An instinct for the Hoar, the Bald –
Lapland's – nescessity –

The Hemlock's nature thrives – on cold –
The Gnash of Northern winds
Is sweetest nutriment – to him –
His best Norwegian Wines –

To satin Races – he is nought –
But Children on the Don,
Beneath his Tabernacles, play,
And Dnieper Wrestlers, run.

6. And] Or   7. Hoar] drear –
7. instinct] hunger   12. best] good

MANUSCRIPT: About 1862, in packet 13 (H 63a).

PUBLICATION: *Poems* (1890), 104–105, titled "The Hemlock." The suggested change for line 6 adopted. The spelling of "nescessity" (line 8) is regularized.

526

> To hear an Oriole sing
> May be a common thing –
> Or only a divine.
>
> It is not of the Bird
> Who sings the same, unheard,
> As unto Crowd –
>
> The Fashion of the Ear
> Attireth that it hear
> In Dun, or fair –
>
> So whether it be Rune,
> Or whether it be none
> Is of within.
>
> The "Tune is in the Tree –"
> The Skeptic – showeth me –
> "No Sir! In Thee!"

11. none] din –

MANUSCRIPT: About 1862, in packet 13 (H 63c).

PUBLICATION: *Poems* (1891), 125, titled "The Oriole's Secret." The suggested change is rejected.

527

> To put this World down, like a Bundle –
> And walk steady, away,
> Requires Energy – possibly Agony –
> 'Tis the Scarlet way

Trodden with straight renunciation
By the Son of God –
Later, his faint Confederates
Justify the Road –

Flavors of that old Crucifixion –
Filaments of Bloom, Pontius Pilate sowed –
Strong Clusters, from Barabbas' Tomb –

Sacrament, Saints partook before us –
Patent, every drop,
With the Brand of the Gentile Drinker
Who indorsed the Cup –

12. partook] indorsed   15. indorsed] enforced
14. Brand] Stamp

MANUSCRIPT: About 1862, in packet 13 (H 64a).
PUBLICATION: *UP* (1935), 78. The suggested changes are rejected.
The third stanza is arranged as a quatrain. In *UP* line 2 is altered to read:

And walk away

In *Poems* (current) it is further altered:

And steady walk away

In all printings one other alteration appears:

12. Sacrament] Sacraments

528

Mine – by the Right of the White Election!
Mine – by the Royal Seal!
Mine – by the Sign in the Scarlet prison –
Bars – cannot conceal!

Mine – here – in Vision – and in Veto!
Mine – by the Grave's Repeal –
Titled – Confirmed –
Delirious Charter!
Mine – long as Ages steal!

[405]

4. Bars] Bolts   9. long as] while
8] Good affidavit –

MANUSCRIPT: About 1862, in packet 13 (H 66b).
PUBLICATION: *Poems* (1890), 43, titled "Mine." The suggested change for line 9 is adopted. The text is arranged as two quatrains. The last line reads:

Mine, while the ages steal!

529

I'm sorry for the Dead – Today –
It's such congenial times
Old Neighbors have at fences –
It's time o' year for Hay.

And Broad – Sunburned Acquaintance
Discourse between the Toil –
And laugh, a homely species
That makes the Fences smile –

It seems so straight to lie away
From all the noise of Fields –
The Busy Carts – the fragrant Cocks –
The Mower's Metre – Steals

A Trouble lest they're homesick –
Those Farmers – and their Wives –
Set separate from the Farming –
And all the Neighbor's lives –

A Wonder if the Sepulchre
Dont feel a lonesome way –
When Men – and Boys – and Carts – and June,
Go down the Fields to "Hay" –

2. times] Way   15. Set separate] Put quiet –
10. noise] Sound   19. Carts] Larks –

MANUSCRIPT: About 1862, in packet 17 (H 92a).

PUBLICATION: The last stanza only was published by Mrs. Todd in *Poems* (1896), 180, altered thus:

> I wonder if the sepulchre
> Is not a lonesome way,
> When men and boys, and larks and June
> Go down the fields to hay!

The same text was reproduced by Mrs. Bianchi in *CP* (1924), 244. The first complete printing of the poem was in *FP* (1929), 196, where Mrs. Bianchi attached it as five concluding stanzas to "It will be summer eventually." The suggested change in line 19 (*larks* for *Carts*) is still retained, but several words are altered:

4. It's] At	8. Fences] meadows
5. And] When	17. A Wonder] I wonder
5. Acquaintance] acquaintances	18. Dont feel] Is not

An accompanying note reads: "The first four stanzas have never before been published. The last stanza only appeared on page 244 of the 'Complete Poems.'" The error of thinking that the two poems were one was shortly detected, and the five stanzas were deleted from later impressions of *FP*. In identical text the poem was next issued in the Centenary edition (1930), and has so remained in all subsequent printings.

530

> You cannot put a Fire out –
> A Thing that can ignite
> Can go, itself, without a Fan –
> Upon the slowest Night –
>
> You cannot fold a Flood –
> And put it in a Drawer –
> Because the Winds would find it out –
> And tell your Cedar Floor –

1. You cannot] No Man –

MANUSCRIPT: Early 1862, in packet 16 (H 92b).
PUBLICATION: *Poems* (1896), 65, titled "Power." The suggested change is rejected.

We dream – it is good we are dreaming –
It would hurt us – were we awake –
But since it is playing – kill us,
And we are playing – shriek –

What harm? Men die – externally –
It is a truth – of Blood –
But we – are dying in Drama –
And Drama – is never dead –

Cautious – We jar each other –
And either – open the eyes –
Lest the Phantasm – prove the Mistake –
And the livid Surprise

Cool us to Shafts of Granite –
With just an Age – and Name –
And perhaps a phrase in Egyptian –
It's prudenter – to dream –

1. We dream] We are dreaming
1. are dreaming] should – [dream]
2. It] They
6. truth] Fact
8. never] seldom –

10. the] it's
11. the Mistake] just [Mistake]
15. phrase in Egyptian] latin inscription –

MANUSCRIPT: About 1862, in packet 16 (H 92c). In line 3 "it" is marked for an alternative, but none is given.

PUBLICATION: *UP* (1935), 76. The suggested change for line 15 is adopted. Three words are altered:

9. Cautious] Cautions
9. jar] give
10. either] seldom

Line 11 reads:

Lest the phantasm prove the mistake just

I tried to think a lonelier Thing
Than any I had seen –
Some Polar Expiation – An Omen in the Bone
Of Death's tremendous nearness –

I probed Retrieveless things
My Duplicate – to borrow –
A Haggard Comfort springs

From the belief that Somewhere –
Within the Clutch of Thought –
There dwells one other Creature
Of Heavenly Love – forgot –

I plucked at our Partition
As One should pry the Walls –
Between Himself – and Horror's Twin –
Within Opposing Cells –

I almost strove to clasp his Hand,
Such Luxury – it grew –
That as Myself – could pity Him –
Perhaps he – pitied me –

20] He – too – could pity me –

MANUSCRIPT: About 1862, in packet 16 (H 384).
PUBLICATION: *BM* (1945), 105. The suggested change for the final line is rejected. The second stanza is regularized by incorporating the last line of stanza 1. The second half of line 3 is made a fourth line. The text derives from a transcript of the packet copy made by Mrs. Todd.

533

Two Butterflies went out at Noon –
And waltzed upon a Farm –
Then stepped straight through the Firmament
And rested, on a Beam –

And then – together bore away
Upon a shining Sea –
Though never yet, in any Port –
Their coming, mentioned – be –

If spoken by the distant Bird –
If met in Ether Sea
By Frigate, or by Merchantman –
No notice – was – to me –

12] Report was not – to me –

MANUSCRIPTS: The copy reproduced above is in packet 16 (H 86a), and was written early in 1862. Some sixteen years later, about 1878, ED attempted a redaction (Bingham 98–4A–20). It is a penciled worksheet draft set down on both sides of a half sheet of stationery. It is rare among surviving worksheets in the degree of its complication. The redaction evidently never resulted in a finished poem, but it is a fascinating document of poetic creativeness in travail:

[stanza 1]
Two Butterflies went out at Noon
And waltzed upon a Farm
And then espied Circumference
Then overtook –
And caught a ride with him –
and took a Bout with him –

[stanza 2]
Then lost themselves and found themselves
    staked   lost
    chased   caught
In eddies of the sun –
    Fathoms in
    Rapids of
    Gambols with
        of
For Frenzy zies of
    antics in
      with
Till Rapture *missed them*
        missed her footing –
          Peninsula

Gravitation chased
                    humbled –
                    ejected
                    foundered
                    grumbled
Until a Zephyr pushed them
                    chased –
                    flung –
                    spurned
                    scourged
And Both were wrecked in Noon –
                    drowned –
                    quenched –
                    whelmed –
And they were hurled from noon –

                [stanza 3]
To all surviving Butterflies
Be this Fatuity
                Biography –
Example – and monition
To entomology –

PUBLICATION: The packet copy is in *Poems* (1891), 133, titled "Two Voyagers." The suggested change is adopted. Line 2 is altered to read:

                And waltzed above a stream

The text in *BM* (1945), 72, is an editorial reconstruction of the worksheet redaction. The worksheet is reproduced in facsimile in the same volume, pages xx–xxi.

                        534
            We see – Comparatively –
            The Thing so towering high
            We could not grasp it's segment
            Unaided – Yesterday –

            This Morning's finer Verdict –
            Makes scarcely worth the toil –
            A furrow – Our Cordillera –
            Our Appenine – a Knoll –

                    [411]

Perhaps 'tis kindly – done us –
The Anguish – and the loss –
The wrenching – for His Firmament
The Thing belonged to us –

To spare these Striding Spirits
Some Morning of Chagrin –
The waking in a Gnat's – embrace –
Our Giants – further on –

3. segment] Angle   13. Striding Spirits] shrinking – /
                                  wincing natures –

MANUSCRIPT: About 1862, in packet 16 (H 88c).
PUBLICATION: The first two stanzas only are in *FP* (1929), 35. The
suggested change in line 3 is rejected. The four stanzas, reproduced from
a transcript made by Mrs. Todd, is in *New England Quarterly*, XX (1947),
31–32. One of the changes suggested for line 13 is adopted:

shrinking spirits

535

She's happy, with a new Content –
That feels to her – like Sacrament –
She's busy – with an altered Care –
As just apprenticed to the Air –

She's tearful – if she weep at all –
For blissful Causes – Most of all
That Heaven permit so meek as her –
To such a Fate – to Minister.

7. meek] faint

MANUSCRIPT: About 1862, in packet 16 (H 89a).
PUBLICATION: *UP* (1935), 132. The suggested change is rejected. One
word is altered:

7. her] she

[412]

536

The Heart asks Pleasure – first –
And then – Excuse from Pain –
And then – those little Anodynes
That deaden suffering –

And then – to go to sleep –
And then – if it should be
The will of it's Inquisitor
The privilege to die –

1. Pleasure] Blessing   8. privilege] liberty / luxury.

MANUSCRIPT: About 1862, in packet 16 (H 89b).
PUBLICATION: *Poems* (1890), 21. Of the suggested changes, only "liberty" is adopted.

537

Me prove it now – Whoever doubt
Me stop to prove it – now –
Make haste – the Scruple! Death be scant
For Opportunity –

The River reaches to my feet –
As yet – My Heart be dry –
Oh Lover – Life could not convince –
Might Death – enable Thee –

The River reaches to My Breast –
Still – still – My Hands above
Proclaim with their remaining Might –
Dost recognize the Love?

The River reaches to my Mouth –
Remember – when the Sea
Swept by my searching eyes – the last –
Themselves were quick – with Thee!

1. Whoever] Whatever   3. Make haste] Come near

MANUSCRIPT: About 1862, in packet 17 (H 90b).
PUBLICATION: *UP* (1935), 110. Neither suggested change is adopted.
Three words are altered:

1. Me] We   6. As] And
2. Me] We

538

'Tis true – They shut me in the Cold –
But then – Themselves were warm
And could not know the feeling 'twas –
Forget it – Lord – of Them –

Let not my Witness hinder Them
In Heavenly esteem –
No Paradise could be – Conferred
Through Their beloved Blame –

The Harm They did – was short – And since
Myself – who bore it – do –
Forgive Them – Even as Myself –
Or else – forgive not me –

3. could] did   9. short] brief
4. Lord] Christ   12] Else – Savior – banish Me –
5. hinder Them] Them impair –

MANUSCRIPT: About 1862, in packet 17 (H 91a).
PUBLICATION: *BM* (1945), 99. The text derives from a transcript made
by Mrs. Todd. All suggested changes are rejected. One word is altered by
a misreading from the manuscript:

10. bore] owe

539

The Province of the Saved
Should be the Art – To save –
Through Skill obtained in Themselves –
The Science of the Grave

No Man can understand
But He that hath endured
The Dissolution – in Himself –
That Man – be qualified

To qualify Despair
To Those who failing new –
Mistake Defeat for Death – Each time –
Till acclimated – to –

2] Exclusively – to save –

MANUSCRIPT: About 1862, in packet 17 (H 91b).
PUBLICATION: *UP* (1935), 143. The suggested change is rejected. Two
words are altered:

3. in] within   9. qualify] certify

540

I took my Power in my Hand –
And went against the World –
'Twas not so much as David – had –
But I – was twice as bold –

I aimed my Pebble – but Myself
Was all the one that fell –
Was it Goliah – was too large –
Or was myself – too small?

8. was myself] just myself – / only me – / I –

MANUSCRIPT: About 1862, packet 17 (H 91c).
PUBLICATION: *Poems* (1891), 56, titled "The Duel." The last line
selects from suggested changes, and reads: "Or only I too small?"

541

Some such Butterfly be seen
On Brazilian Pampas –
Just at noon – no later – Sweet –
Then – the License closes –

Some such Spice – express and pass –
Subject to Your Plucking –
As the Stars – You knew last Night –
Foreigners – This Morning –

3. Sweet] Than
4. License] Vision – / Pageant
5. Spice] Rose

6. Subject] Present
8. Foreigners] Know not You –

MANUSCRIPT: About 1862, in packet 17 (H 91d).
PUBLICATION: *UP* (1935), 58. All suggested changes are rejected.
Through a confusion of the original reading and the suggested change
for line 3, lines 3 and 4 are rendered:

> Just at noon – no later,
> Then sweet license closes.

542

I had no Cause to be awake –
My Best – was gone to sleep –
And Morn a new politeness took –
And failed to wake them up –

But called the others – clear –
And passed their Curtains by –
Sweet Morning – When I oversleep –
Knock – Recollect – to Me –

I looked at Sunrise – Once –
And then I looked at Them –
And wishfulness in me arose –
For Circumstance the same –

'Twas such an Ample Peace –
It could not hold a Sigh –
'Twas Sabbath – with the Bells divorced –
'Twas Sunset – all the Day –

So choosing but a Gown –
And taking but a Prayer –
The only Raiment I should need –
I struggled – and was There –

15. divorced] reversed   16. Sunset] Sundown –

MANUSCRIPT: About 1862, in packet 17 (H 93a).
PUBLICATION: *Poems* (1891), 202–203, titled "Following." The suggested changes are not adopted. One word is altered:

8. to] for

543

I fear a Man of frugal Speech –
I fear a Silent Man –
Haranguer – I can overtake –
Or Babbler – entertain –

But He who weigheth – While the Rest –
Expend their furthest pound –
Of this Man – I am wary –
I fear that He is Grand –

1. frugal] scanty   6. furthest] inmost –

MANUSCRIPT: About 1862, in packet 17 (H 93b).
PUBLICATION: *FP* (1929), 3. The text of stanza 2, arranged as five lines, in later collections is restored as a quatrain. The suggested changes are adopted. One word is altered:

5. weigheth] waiteth

544

The Martyr Poets – did not tell –
But wrought their Pang in syllable –
That when their mortal name be numb –
Their mortal fate – encourage Some –

[no stanza break]

The Martyr Painters – never spoke –
Bequeathing – rather – to their Work –
That when their conscious fingers cease –
Some seek in Art – the Art of Peace –

3. name] fame   8. Some] Men –

MANUSCRIPT: About 1862, in packet 17 (H 93d). The second alterna-
tive was perhaps intended for the last word in line 4, though the word is
not marked.
PUBLICATION: *UP* (1935), 26. The suggested change for line 3 is
adopted. The text is arranged as two quatrains.

545

'Tis One by One – the Father counts –
And then a Tract between
Set Cypherless – to teach the Eye
The Value of it's Ten –

Until the peevish Student
Acquire the Quick of Skill –
Then Numerals are dowered back –
Adorning all the Rule –

'Tis mostly Slate and Pencil –
And Darkness on the School
Distracts the Children's fingers –
Still the Eternal Rule

Regards least Cypherer alike
With Leader of the Band –
And every separate Urchin's Sum –
Is fashioned for his hand –

16. fashioned for] fitted to –

MANUSCRIPT: About 1862, in packet 17 (H 67b).

[418]

PUBLICATION: *BM* (1945), 93. The suggested change is adopted. The text derives from a typescript made by Mrs. Todd. It exactly follows the typescript wherein one word is altered:

13. cypherer] cipher

546

To fill a Gap
Insert the Thing that caused it –
Block it up
With Other – and 'twill yawn the more –
You cannot solder an Abyss
With Air.

5. solder an Abyss] Plug a Sepulchre –

MANUSCRIPT: About 1862, in packet 17 (H 67c).
PUBLICATION: *FP* (1929), 91. The suggested change is rejected. The last two words of line 4 are arranged as a separate line.

547

I've seen a Dying Eye
Run round and round a Room –
In search of Something – as it seemed –
Then Cloudier become –
And then – obscure with Fog –
And then – be soldered down
Without disclosing what it be
'Twere blessed to have seen –

3. Something] Somewhat –

MANUSCRIPT: About 1862, in packet 17 (H 67d).
PUBLICATION: *Poems* (1890), 124. The suggested change is rejected.

548

Death is potential to that Man
Who dies – and to his friend –
Beyond that – unconspicuous
To Anyone but God –

Of these Two – God remembers
The longest – for the friend –
Is integral – and therefore
Itself dissolved – of God –

7. integral] subsequent –

MANUSCRIPT: About 1862, in packet 17 (H 68b).
PUBLICATION: *BM* (1945), 198. The text derives from a transcript made by Mrs. Todd. The suggested change is adopted.

549

That I did always love
I bring thee Proof
That till I loved
I never lived – Enough –

That I shall love alway –
I argue thee
That love is life –
And life hath Immortality –

This – dost thou doubt – Sweet –
Then have I
Nothing to show
But Calvary –

4. never lived] did not live   7. is] be –
6. argue] offer –

MANUSCRIPT: About 1862, in packet 17 (H 68d).
PUBLICATION: *Poems* (1890), 51, titled "Proof." The suggested changes for lines 4 and 6 are adopted. One word is altered:

4. live] love

550

I cross till I am weary
A Mountain – in my mind –
More Mountains – then a Sea –
More Seas – And then
A Desert – find –

And My Horizon blocks
With steady – drifting – Grains
Of unconjectured quantity –
As Asiatic Rains –

Nor this – defeat my Pace –
It hinder from the West
But as an Enemy's Salute
One hurrying to Rest –

What merit had the Goal –
Except there intervene
Faint Doubt – and far Competitor –
To jeopardize the Gain?

At last – the Grace in sight –
I shout unto my feet –
I offer them the Whole of Heaven
The instant that we meet –

They strive – and yet delay –
They perish – Do we die –
Or is this Death's Experiment –
Reversed – in Victory?

7. steady – drifting] sudden – blinding   20. the Whole] the Half
18] The Grace is just in sight   23. perish] stagger –

MANUSCRIPT: About 1862, in packet 17 (H 95a).
PUBLICATION: *UP* (1935), 109. The suggested change for line 20 is adopted. The first stanza is arranged as a quatrain. "Horizon" (line 6) is printed correctly in *UP*; it is rendered "horizons" in *Poems* (current). One line is altered:

20. I offer] Offer

There is a Shame of Nobleness –
Confronting Sudden Pelf –
A finer Shame of Extasy –
Convicted of Itself –

A best Disgrace – a Brave Man feels –
Acknowledged – of the Brave –
One More – "Ye Blessed" – to be told –
But that's – Behind the Grave –

8] But This – involves the Grave –

MANUSCRIPT: About 1862, in packet 17 (H 95c).
PUBLICATION: *Poems* (1891), 198. The suggested change is adopted.

552

An ignorance a Sunset
Confer upon the Eye –
Of Territory – Color –
Circumference – Decay –

It's Amber Revelation
Exhilirate – Debase –
Omnipotence' inspection
Of Our inferior face –

And when the solemn features
Confirm – in Victory –
We start – as if detected
In Immortality –

MANUSCRIPT: About 1862, in packet 17 (H 96a). ED assigned no place
for the following suggested changes, but perhaps they were intended thus:

1. ignorance] impotence   7. inspection] Analysis
4. Decay] Array   10. Confirm] Withdraw

PUBLICATION: *UP* (1935), 50. The suggested changes are rejected.

553

One Crucifixion is recorded – only –
How many be
Is not affirmed of Mathematics –
Or History –

One Calvary – exhibited to Stranger –
As many be
As Persons – or Peninsulas –
Gethsemane –

Is but a Province – in the Being's Centre –
Judea –
For Journey – or Crusade's Achieving –
Too near –

Our Lord – indeed – made Compound Witness –
And yet –
There's newer – nearer Crucifixion
Than That –

9. Being's Centre] Human Centre   13. made] bore –

MANUSCRIPT: About 1862, in packet 16 (H 96b).
PUBLICATION: *BM* (1945), 260. The text derives from a transcript of
the packet copy made by Mrs. Todd. The suggested change for line 13
is adopted. One word is altered:

10. Judea] India

554

The Black Berry – wears a Thorn in his side –
But no Man heard Him cry –
He offers His Berry, just the same
To Partridge – and to Boy –

He sometimes holds upon the Fence –
Or struggles to a Tree –
Or clasps a Rock, with both His Hands –
But not for Sympathy –

We – tell a Hurt – to cool it –
This Mourner – to the Sky
A little further reaches – instead –
Brave Black Berry –

3. offers] spices – / flavors –

MANUSCRIPT: About 1862, in packet 21 (H 113b).
PUBLICATION: *BM* (1945), 89. The text derives from a transcript of the packet copy made by Mrs. Todd. The suggested change is rejected. Two words are altered:

11. further reaches] farther climbs

555

Trust in the Unexpected –
By this – was William Kidd
Persuaded of the Buried Gold –
As One had testified –

Through this – the old Philosopher –
His Talismanic Stone
Discernéd – still with[h]olden
To effort undivine –

'Twas this – allured Columbus –
When Genoa – withdrew
Before an Apparition
Baptized America –

The Same – afflicted Thomas –
When Deity assured
'Twas better – the perceiving not –
Provided it believed –

10. When] till   14. assured] pronounced –
12. Baptized] To wit   15] 'Twas blesseder – the seeing not –

MANUSCRIPT: About 1862, in packet 21 (H 116b). ED underlined the final "e" in "Discernéd" (line 7), here rendered with an accent mark. For the reference to Thomas, see John 20.29:

> Jesus saith unto him, Thomas, because thou hast seen me, thou hast believed: blessed are they that have not seen, and yet have believed.

PUBLICATION: *UP* (1935), 74. The suggested changes are rejected. In line 15 "not" is italicized.

556

The Brain, within it's Groove
Runs evenly – and true –
But let a Splinter swerve –
'Twere easier for You –

To put a Current back –
When Floods have slit the Hills –
And scooped a Turnpike for Themselves –
And trodden out the Mills –

5. a Current] the Waters   8. trodden out] blotted out – / shoved
                                                                away –

MANUSCRIPT: About 1862, in packet 21 (H 116d).
PUBLICATION: *Poems* (1890), 40. The suggested changes "the Waters" and "blotted out" are adopted. The stanza division is not retained. One word is altered:

5. Waters] water

557

She hideth Her the last –
And is the first, to rise –
Her Night doth hardly recompense
The Closing of Her eyes –

She doth Her Purple Work –
And putteth Her away
In low Apartments in the Sod –
As Worthily as We.

To imitate Her life
As impotent would be
As make of Our imperfect Mints,
The Julep – of the Bee –

8. Worthily] privately   11. imperfect] Uncomely –
10. impotent] possible   11] As brew from our Obtuser Mints –
11. make of] Brew from / Mix

MANUSCRIPT: About 1862, in packet 21 (H 117a).
PUBLICATION: *UP* (1935), 65. The suggested changes for lines 10 and
11 (*entire*) are adopted.

558

But little Carmine hath her face –
Of Emerald scant – her Gown –
Her Beauty – is the love she doth –
Itself – exhibit – Mine –

4. exhibit] enable – / embolden –

MANUSCRIPT: About 1862, in packet 21 (H 117c).
PUBLICATION: *UP* (1935), 62. The suggested reading "enable" is
adopted.

559

It knew no Medicine –
It was not Sickness – then –
Nor any need of Surgery –
And therefore – 'twas not Pain –

It moved away the Cheeks –
A Dimple at a time –   [*no stanza break*]

And left the Profile – plainer –
And in the place of Bloom

It left the little Tint
That never had a Name –
You've seen it on a Cast's face –
Was Paradise – to blame –

If momently ajar –
Temerity – drew near –
And sickened – ever afterward
For Somewhat that it saw?

8. place] stead   13] [If] Her sweet Door – ajar
11. face] cheek   16. somewhat that] whatsoe'er –

MANUSCRIPT: About 1862, in packet 21 (H 117d).
PUBLICATION: *UP* (1935), 122. The suggested changes for lines 8, 13,
16 are adopted.

560

It knew no lapse, nor Diminution –
But large – serene –
Burned on – until through Dissolution –
It failed from Men –

I could not deem these Planetary forces
Annulled –
But suffered an Exchange of Territory –
Or World –

3. Burned] Glowed   7. suffered an Exchange] Absent
                              through Exchange –

MANUSCRIPT: About 1862, in packet 21 (H 117e). ED's first letter
to Col. Higginson after learning from published accounts that he was lead-
ing a regiment in the war was written in April 1863, while he was in camp
in South Carolina. It begins (*Letters*, ed. 1931, 278):

I did not deem that Planetary forces annulled – but suffered an
Exchange of Territory, or World –

PUBLICATION: *BM* (1945), 200. The text derives from a transcript of
the packet copy made by Mrs. Todd. The suggested change for line 3 is
adopted.

561

I measure every Grief I meet
With narrow, probing, Eyes –
I wonder if It weighs like Mine –
Or has an Easier size.

I wonder if They bore it long –
Or did it just begin –
I could not tell the Date of Mine –
It feels so old a pain –

I wonder if it hurts to live –
And if They have to try –
And whether – could They choose between –
It would not be – to die –

I note that Some – gone patient long –
At length, renew their smile –
An imitation of a Light
That has so little Oil –

I wonder if when Years have piled –
Some Thousands – on the Harm –
That hurt them early – such a lapse
Could give them any Balm –

Or would they go on aching still
Through Centuries of Nerve –
Enlightened to a larger Pain –
In Contrast with the Love –

The Grieved – are many – I am told –
There is the various Cause –
Death – is but one – and comes but once –
And only nails the eyes –

There's Grief of Want – and Grief of Cold –
A sort they call "Despair" –
There's Banishment from native Eyes –
In sight of Native Air –

And though I may not guess the kind –
Correctly – yet to me
A piercing Comfort it affords
In passing Calvary –

To note the fashions – of the Cross –
And how they're mostly worn –
Still fascinated to presume
That Some – are like My Own –

2. narrow, probing, eyes] analytic eyes –

MANUSCRIPT: About 1862, in packet 21 (H 21a).

PUBLICATION: *Poems* (1896), 47–48, titled "Griefs." The suggested change for line 2 is adopted. Stanza 4 is omitted. The following alterations are made:

12] They would not rather die	22. of Nerve] above
18. Harm] cause	24. In] By
19. That hurt them early] Of early hurt, if	26] The reason deeper lies
20. Balm] pause	38] Of those that stand alone

All ten stanzas (with stanza 4 restored) were first printed in *New England Quarterly*, XX (1947), 18–19, from Mrs. Todd's transcript of the packet copy. In stanza 4, there first published, one word is altered:

16. so] too

The *NEQ* version from Mrs. Todd's transcript adopts all the alterations made in *Poems* except those in lines 12 and 24, evidently on the assumption that the alterations were adoptions selected from ED's own suggested changes. But the sole suggested change in the packet copy is that in line 2.

Conjecturing a Climate
Of unsuspended Suns –
Adds poignancy to Winter –
The Shivering Fancy turns

To a fictitious Country
To palliate a Cold –
Not obviated of Degree –
Nor eased – of Latitude –

3. Adds] gives   5. Country] Summer – / Season –
4. shivering] freezing

MANUSCRIPT: About 1862, in packet 21 (H 21b).
PUBLICATION: *FP* (1929), 86. The stanza division is not retained. The
suggested changes for lines 3 and 4 are adopted.

563

I could not prove the Years had feet –
Yet confident they run
Am I, from symptoms that are past
And Series that are done –

I find my feet have further Goals –
I smile upon the Aims
That felt so ample – Yesterday –
Today's – have vaster claims –

I do not doubt the self I was
Was competent to me –
But something awkward in the fit –
Proves that – outgrown – I see –

8. claims] form   11. awkward in] odd about –

[430]

MANUSCRIPT: About 1862, in packet 91 (Bingham 74b).
PUBLICATION: *BM* (1945), 117. The suggested changes are rejected.

564

My period had come for Prayer –
No other Art – would do –
My Tactics missed a rudiment –
Creator – Was it you?

God grows above – so those who pray
Horizons – must ascend –
And so I stepped upon the North
To see this Curious Friend –

His House was not – no sign had He –
By Chimney – nor by Door
Could I infer his Residence –
Vast Prairies of Air

Unbroken by a Settler –
Were all that I could see –
Infinitude – Had'st Thou no Face
That I might look on Thee?

The Silence condescended –
Creation stopped – for Me –
But awed beyond my errand –
I worshipped – did not "pray" –

7. stepped] stood –   18. Creation stopped] the Heavens
8. see] Reach – / touch –   paused –
12. Vast Prairies] Wide Prairies

MANUSCRIPT: About 1862, in packet 25 (H 134a).
PUBLICATION: *Saturday Review of Literature*, V (9 March 1929), 751;
FP (1929), 47. Suggested changes are adopted for lines 7, 8 (Reach), 12,
and 18. Line 12 reads "Wide prairies of the air." In line 16 "on," altered to
"at," is corrected in *Poems* (current).

One Anguish – in a Crowd –
A Minor thing – it sounds –
And yet, unto the single Doe
Attempted of the Hounds

Tis Terror as consummate
As Legions of Alarm
Did leap, full flanked, upon the Host –
'Tis Units – make the Swarm –

A Small Leech – on the Vitals –
The sliver, in the Lung –
The Bung out – of an Artery –
Are scarce accounted – Harms –

Yet mighty – by relation
To that Repealless thing –
A Being – impotent to end –
When once it has begun –

11. The Bung out – of] A leakage in   13. Yet] But
12. accounted] computed   15. end] stop –

MANUSCRIPT: About 1862, in packet 25 (H 134c).
PUBLICATION: *BM* (1945), 258–259. The text derives from a transcript made by Mrs. Todd. The suggested change in line 15 is adopted.

A Dying Tiger – moaned for Drink –
I hunted all the Sand –
I caught the Dripping of a Rock
And bore it in my Hand –

His Mighty Balls – in death were thick –
But searching – I could see
A Vision on the Retina
Of Water – and of me –

'Twas not my blame – who sped too slow –
'Twas not his blame – who died
While I was reaching him –
But 'twas – the fact that He was dead –

2. hunted] worried –

MANUSCRIPT: About 1862, in packet 25 (H 135a).

PUBLICATION: *BM* (1945), 186–187. The text derives from a transcript made by Mrs. Todd. The suggested change is rejected. The first two words of line 12 are arranged as the last two of line 11.

567

He gave away his Life –
To Us – Gigantic Sum –
A trifle – in his own esteem –
But magnified – by Fame –

Until it burst the Hearts
That fancied they could hold –
When swift it slipped it's limit –
And on the Heavens – unrolled –

'Tis Ours – to wince – and weep –
And wonder – and decay
By Blossoms gradual process –
He chose – Maturity –

And quickening – as we sowed –
Just obviated Bud –
And when We turned to note the Growth –
Broke – perfect – from the Pod –

3. own esteem] estimate   11. gradual] common
7. swift] quick   13. quickening] ripening –

MANUSCRIPT: About 1862, in packet 25 (H 135b).

PUBLICATION: *UP* (1935), 8. The suggested changes for lines 7 and 13 are adopted. In line 11, "Blossoms" reads "blossom's."

[433]

We learned the Whole of Love –
The Alphabet – the Words –
A Chapter – then the mighty Book –
Then – Revelation closed –

But in Each Other's eyes
An Ignorance beheld –
Diviner than the Childhood's –
And each to each, a Child –

Attempted to expound
What Neither – understood –
Alas, that Wisdom is so large –
And Truth – so manifold!

9] Did timidly expound –

MANUSCRIPT: About 1862, in packet 25 (H 135c).
PUBLICATION: *BM* (1945), 143. The suggested change is rejected.
The text derives from a transcript made by Mrs. Todd.

I reckon – when I count at all –
First – Poets – Then the Sun –
Then Summer – Then the Heaven of God –
And then – the List is done –

But, looking back – the First so seems
To Comprehend the Whole –
The Others look a needless Show –
So I write – Poets – All –

Their Summer – lasts a Solid Year –
They can afford a Sun
The East – would deem extravagant –
And if the Further Heaven –

Be Beautiful as they prepare
For Those who worship Them –
It is too difficult a Grace –
To justify the Dream –

12. Further] Other – / final   14. For] to –
13. prepare] Disclose   14. worship] Trust in / Ask of –

MANUSCRIPT: About 1862, in packet 25 (H 137a).
PUBLICATION: *Atlantic Monthly*, CXLIII (February 1929), 180; FP
(1929), 11. Four suggested changes are adopted:

12. final   14. To
13. disclose   14. trust in

The stanza division is not retained. One word is altered:

9. Their] This

570

I could die – to know –
'Tis a trifling knowledge –
News-Boys salute the Door –
Carts – joggle by –
Morning's bold face – stares in the window –
Were but mine – the Charter of the least Fly –

Houses hunch the House
With their Brick Shoulders –
Coals – from a Rolling Load – rattle – how – near –
To the very Square – His foot is passing –
Possibly, this moment –
While I – dream – Here –

1. could] would   12. dream] wait –
9. Rolling Load] passing load

MANUSCRIPT: About 1862, in packet 25 (H 138a).
PUBLICATION: *UP* (1935), 104. The suggested change for line 1 is
adopted. The text is arranged as two quatrains.

Must be a Wo –
A loss or so –
To bend the eye
Best Beauty's way –

But – once aslant
It notes Delight
As difficult
As Stalactite –

A Common Bliss
Were had for less –
The price – is
Even as the Grace –

Our lord – thought no
Extravagance
To pay – a Cross –

6. notes] gains   8. Stalactite] Violet –
7] As clarified

MANUSCRIPT: About 1862, in packet 25 (H 138b). A small letter "a" which appears to conclude line 7 must be a slip.

PUBLICATION: *UP* (1935), 25. The suggested changes for lines 6 and 7 are adopted. The misreading "classified" for "clarified" (line 7) is corrected in *Poems* (current).

572

Delight – becomes pictorial –
When viewed through Pain –
More fair – because impossible
That any gain –

The Mountain – at a given distance –
In Amber – lies –
Approached – the Amber flits – a little –
And That's – the Skies –

7. Approached] possessed   7. flits] moves –

MANUSCRIPT: About 1862, in packet 25 (H 138c).
PUBLICATION: *Poems* (1891), 41. Neither suggested change is adopted.

573

The Test of Love – is Death –
Our Lord – "so loved" – it saith –
What Largest Lover – hath –
Another – doth –

If smaller Patience – be –
Through less Infinity –
If Bravo, sometimes swerve –
Through fainter Nerve –

Accept it's Most –
And overlook – the Dust –
Last – Least –
The Cross' – Request –

9. Most] Best

MANUSCRIPT: About 1862, in packet 25 (H 138e).
PUBLICATION: *UP* (1935), 147. The suggested change is rejected.

574

My first well Day – since many ill –
I asked to go abroad,
And take the Sunshine in my hands,
And see the things in Pod –

A'blossom just when I went in
To take my Chance with pain –
Uncertain if myself, or He,
Should prove the strongest One.

[437]

The Summer deepened, while we strove –
She put some flowers away –
And Redder cheeked Ones – in their stead –
A fond – illusive way –

To cheat Herself, it seemed she tried –
As if before a child
To fade – Tomorrow – Rainbows held
The Sepulchre, could hide.

She dealt a fashion to the Nut –
She tied the Hoods to Seeds –
She dropped bright scraps of Tint, about –
And left Brazilian Threads

On every shoulder that she met –
Then both her Hands of Haze
Put up – to hide her parting Grace
From our unfitted eyes.

My loss, by sickness – Was it Loss?
Or that Etherial Gain
One earns by measuring the Grave –
Then – measuring the Sun –

6. Chance] Risk
8. strongest] supplest – / lithest – /
    stoutest
11. stead] place
15. fade] die
15. held] thrust

17. a] the
21. that she met] she could reach
23. hide] hold
24. unfitted] unfurnished
26–27. Etherial Gain One earns]
        seraphic gain, One gets –

MANUSCRIPT: About 1862, in packet 25 (H 139a).
PUBLICATION: A variant of the final stanza only, first noted in *AB*, 394,
is published in a letter to Samuel Bowles (*Letters*, ed. 1894, 210; ed. 1931,
199; also *LL*, 237) and there dated "Early Winter, 1862." It reads:

The loss of sickness – was it loss?
Or that ethereal gain
You earned by measuring the grave,
Then measuring the sun.

The entire poem is in *UP* (1935), 43–44. All suggested changes are rejected. Two words are altered:

12. illusive] elusive   23. parting] panting

575

"Heaven" has different Signs – to me –
Sometimes, I think that Noon
Is but a symbol of the Place –
And when again, at Dawn,

A mighty look runs round the World
And settles in the Hills –
An Awe if it should be like that
Upon the Ignorance steals –

The Orchard, when the Sun is on –
The Triumph of the Birds
When they together Victory make –
Some Carnivals of Clouds –

The Rapture of a finished Day –
Returning to the West –
All these – remind us of the place
That Men call "Paradise" –

Itself be fairer – we suppose –
But how Ourself, shall be
Adorned, for a Superior Grace –
Not yet, our eyes can see –

13. a finished Day] Concluded Day –

MANUSCRIPT: About 1862, in packet 25 (H 140a).
PUBLICATION: *FP* (1929), 55. The suggested change is adopted. One word is altered:

17. be] a

I prayed, at first, a little Girl,
Because they told me to –
But stopped, when qualified to guess
How prayer would feel – to me –

If I believed God looked around,
Each time my Childish eye
Fixed full, and steady, on his own
In Childish honesty –

And told him what I'd like, today,
And parts of his far plan
That baffled me –
The mingled side
Of his Divinity –

And often since, in Danger,
I count the force 'twould be
To have a God so strong as that
To hold my life for me

Till I could take the Balance
That tips so frequent, now,
It takes me all the while to poise –
And then – it does'nt stay –

4. feel] sound
5. believed] supposed
8. Childish] solemn –
12. mingled] under – / further

17. my life] the light
18. take the] Catch my
19. tips so frequent] slips so easy
21] It isn't steady – tho' –

MANUSCRIPT: About 1862, in packet 25 (H 140c). George F. Whicher (*This Was a Poet*, 222–223) has pointed out the verbal echo in stanza 3 of a sentence in Sir Thomas Browne's *Religio Medici* (Part 1, section 13). The sentence deals with God's unknowableness:

I know he is wise in all, wonderful in what we conceive, but far more in what we comprehend not; for we behold him but asquint, upon reflex or shadow; our understanding is dimmer than *Moses*

Eye; we are ignorant of the back-part or lower side of his Divinity, therefore to prie into the maze of his Counsels is not only folly in man, but presumption even in Angels. . .

PUBLICATION: *FP* (1929), 45. Four suggested changes are correctly adopted:

4. sound	8. solemn
5. supposed	12. under

Lines 18 and 19 are rendered thus:

> Till I could catch the balance
> That slips so easily

577

If I may have it, when it's dead,
I'll be contented – so –
If just as soon as Breath is out
It shall belong to me –

Until they lock it in the Grave,
'Tis Bliss I cannot weigh –
For tho' they lock Thee in the Grave,
Myself – can own the key –

Think of it Lover! I and Thee
Permitted – face to face to be –
After a Life – a Death – We'll say –
For Death was That –
And This – is Thee –

I'll tell Thee All – how Bald it grew –
How Midnight felt, at first – to me –
How all the Clocks stopped in the World –
And Sunshine pinched me – 'Twas so cold –

Then how the Grief got sleepy – some –
As if my Soul were deaf and dumb –
Just making signs – across – to Thee –
That this way – thou could'st notice me –

[441]

I'll tell you how I tried to keep
A smile, to show you, when this Deep
All Waded – We look back for Play,
At those Old Times – in Calvary.

Forgive me, if the Grave come slow –
For Coveting to look at Thee –
Forgive me, if to stroke thy frost
Outvisions Paradise!

2. so] now –
6. Bliss] Wealth I cannot weigh/
Right
8. own] hold
14. Bald] Blank –
20. across] it seemed

21. notice] speak to –
25. come] seem
26. Coveting] eagerness –
27. stroke] touch/greet
28. Outvisions] [Out] fables –

MANUSCRIPT: About 1862, in packet 26 (H 142a).

PUBLICATION: This poem has been published as two poems: the first three stanzas are in *Poems* (1896), 182; the last four are in *BM* (1945), 165. The poem is written on the second sheet in the packet, stanzas 1–3 on the first page, stanzas 4–7 on the second and third pages. There is no evidence, either in the manuscript or in the thought sequence, that ED intended the stanzas to be separated. Evidently by error Mrs. Todd made the separation when she wrote out her transcript of the poem, before she returned the holograph to Lavinia. The publication in *BM* derives from Mrs. Todd's transcript of the last four stanzas. Suggested changes have been adopted for lines 8, 14, 21, 25, 26, and 27 ("touch"). Line 2 is altered:

I will contented be

578

The Body grows without –
The more convenient way –
That if the Spirit – like to hide
It's Temple stands, alway,

Ajar – secure – inviting –
It never did betray   *[no stanza break]*

[442]

The Soul that asked it's shelter
In solemn honesty

1. without] outside   8. solemn] timid –
4. Temple] Closet

MANUSCRIPT: About 1862, in packet 26 (H 143b).
PUBLICATION: *Poems* (1891), 69, titled "The Shelter." The suggested
changes for lines 1 and 8 are adopted.

579

I had been hungry, all the Years –
My Noon had Come – to dine –
I trembling drew the Table near –
And touched the Curious Wine –

'Twas this on Tables I had seen –
When turning, hungry, Home
I looked in Windows, for the Wealth
I could not hope – for Mine –

I did not know the ample Bread –
'Twas so unlike the Crumb
The Birds and I, had often shared
In Nature's – Dining Room –

The Plenty hurt me – 'twas so new –
Myself felt ill – and odd –
As Berry – of a Mountain Bush –
Transplanted – to the Road –

Nor was I hungry – so I found
That Hunger – was a way
Of Persons outside Windows –
The Entering – takes away –

7. Wealth] Things   19. Persons] Creatures –
8. for Mine] to earn

Manuscript: About 1862, in packet 26 (H 143c).
Publication: *Poems* (1891), 76–77, titled "Hunger." All suggested changes are rejected. Words in two lines are altered:

6. Home] lone   8. for Mine] to own

580

I gave myself to Him —
And took Himself, for Pay,
The solemn contract of a Life
Was ratified, this way —

The Wealth might disappoint —
Myself a poorer prove
Than this great Purchaser suspect,
The Daily Own — of Love

Depreciate the Vision —
But till the Merchant buy —
Still Fable — in the Isles of Spice —
The subtle Cargoes — lie —

At least — 'tis Mutual — Risk —
Some — found it — Mutual Gain —
Sweet Debt of Life — Each Night to owe —
Insolvent — every Noon —

1. myself to Him] Him all myself —   11. Still] How — / So —

Manuscript: About 1862, in packet 26 (H 172b).
Publication: *Poems* (1891), 93, titled "The Contract." Both suggested changes are rejected. In line 9 "Depreciate," rendered "Depreciates" in the first three impressions, was corrected in the fourth.

581

I found the words to every thought
I ever had — but One —
And that — defies me —
As a Hand did try to chalk the Sun

[444]

To Races – nurtured in the Dark –
How would your own – begin?
Can Blaze be shown in Cochineal –
Or Noon – in Mazarin?

1. words] phrase   7. shown] done

MANUSCRIPT: About 1862, in packet 26 (H 173d).
PUBLICATION: *Poems* (1891), 26. Both suggested changes are adopted.
The first three words of line 4 conclude line 3.

582

Inconceivably solemn!
Things so gay
Pierce – by the very Press
Of Imagery –

Their far Parades – order on the eye
With a mute Pomp –
A pleading Pageantry –

Flags, are a brave sight –
But no true Eye
Ever went by One –
Steadily –

Music's triumphant –
But the fine Ear
Winces with delight
Are Drums too near –

2. so] too   14. Winces] aches
5. order] halt   15] The Drums to hear –
13. the] a

MANUSCRIPT: About 1862, in packet 26 (H 48a).
PUBLICATION: *London Mercury*, XIX (February 1929), 352; *FP*
(1929), 131. All suggested changes are adopted. The second stanza is
regularized as a quatrain.

A Toad, can die of Light –
Death is the Common Right
Of Toads and Men –
Of Earl and Midge
The privilege –
Why swagger, then?
The Gnat's supremacy is large as Thine –

Life – is a different Thing –
So measure Wine –
Naked of Flask – Naked of Cask –
Bare Rhine –
Which Ruby's mine?

2. Common] mutual – / equal –   8. a different] Another

MANUSCRIPT: About 1862, in packet 26 (H 47b).
PUBLICATION: *Poems* (1896), 195. The first seven lines only are printed, the last arranged as two:

> The gnat's supremacy
> Is large as thine.

In the Centenary edition (1930) and later collections the text is arranged as two quatrains, because in the previous edition, *CP* (1924), the first four lines were printed at the bottom of page 250 and the last four at the top of page 251. The entire poem is in *New England Quarterly*, XX (1947), 28, arranged as two six-line stanzas plus a final line; the text derives from a transcript of the packet copy made by Mrs. Todd. In all printings, the suggested changes are rejected.

It ceased to hurt me, though so slow
I could not see the trouble go –
But only knew by looking back –
That something – had obscured the Track –

Nor when it altered, I could say,
For I had worn it, every day,
As constant as the Childish frock –
I hung upon the Peg, at night.

But not the Grief – that nestled close
As needles – ladies softly press
To Cushions Cheeks –
To keep their place –

Nor what consoled it, I could trace –
Except, whereas 'twas Wilderness –
It's better – almost Peace –

2. see] feel –   4. obscured] *benumbed* [spelled *be-*
2. trouble] Anguish –   *mumbed*]

MANUSCRIPT: About 1862, in packet 26 (H 49a). In line 7 "frock" replaces "Gown," which is crossed out.

PUBLICATION: *Atlantic Monthly*, CXLIII (February 1929), 186; FP (1929), 189. Stanza 3 is omitted. The text is here arranged as three stanzas of 6, 4, 4 lines; in all later collections it is printed as three quatrains. In line 8 "Peg," altered to "nail," is corrected in *Poems* (current). The complete poem is in *New England Quarterly*, XX (1947), 36, derived from a transcript of the packet copy made by Mrs. Todd. The text is arranged as three quatrains and a concluding couplet. All published versions reject the suggested changes.

585

I like to see it lap the Miles –
And lick the Valleys up –
And stop to feed itself at Tanks –
And then – prodigious step

Around a Pile of Mountains –
And supercilious peer
In Shanties – by the sides of Roads –
And then a Quarry pare

To fit it's sides
And crawl between
Complaining all the while
In horrid – hooting stanza –
Then chase itself down Hill –

And neigh like Boanerges –
Then – prompter than a Star
Stop – docile and omnipotent
At it's own stable door –

1. see it] hear it –   14. And] And, or then –
9. sides] Ribs –   15. prompter than] punctual as –

MANUSCRIPT: About 1862, in packet 27 (H 144b).
PUBLICATION: *Poems* (1891), 39, titled "The Railway Train." Only
the suggested change for line 15 is adopted. Stanza 3 is arranged as a
quatrain.

586

We talked as Girls do –
Fond, and late –
We speculated fair, on every subject, but the Grave –
Of our's, none affair –

We handled Destinies, as cool –
As we – Disposers – be –
And God, a Quiet Party
To our Authority –

But fondest, dwelt upon Ourself
As we eventual – be –
When Girls to Women, softly raised
We – occupy – Degree –

We parted with a contract
To cherish, and to write
But Heaven made both, impossible
Before another night.

12. occupy – Degree] too – partake –   14. cherish, and] recollect –

MANUSCRIPT: About 1862, in packet 27 (H 148a).
PUBLICATION: *FP* (1929), 99. The text is arranged as four stanzas of
5, 4, 6, and 5 lines; in later collections the quatrains are restored, but line 2
is placed as the conclusion of line 1, and the first three words of line 3
become line 2. The suggested change for line 12 is rejected. Words in two
lines are altered:

9. Ourself] ourselves   14] To recollect – and write –

587

Empty my Heart, of Thee –
It's single Artery –
Begin, and leave Thee out –
Simply Extinction's Date –

Much Billow hath the Sea –
One Baltic – They –
Subtract Thyself, in play,
And not enough of me
Is left – to put away –
"Myself" meant Thee –

Erase the Root – no Tree –
Thee – then – no me –
The Heavens stripped –
Eternity's vast pocket, picked –

2. single] Giant –   14. vast] wide

MANUSCRIPT: About 1862, in packet 27 (H 148b).
PUBLICATION: *FP* (1929), 146. The suggested change for line 14 is
adopted. One word is altered:

3. and] to

I cried at Pity – not at Pain –
I heard a Woman say
"Poor Child" – and something in her voice
Convinced myself of me –

So long I fainted, to myself
It seemed the common way,
And Health, and Laughter, Curious things –
To look at, like a Toy –

To sometimes hear "Rich people" buy
And see the Parcel rolled –
And carried, we suppose – to Heaven,
For children, made of Gold –

But not to touch, or wish for,
Or think of, with a sigh –
And so and so – had been to us,
Had God willed differently.

I wish I knew that Woman's name –
So when she comes this way,
To hold my life, and hold my ears
For fear I hear her say

She's "sorry I am dead["] – again –
Just when the Grave and I –
Have sobbed ourselves almost to sleep,
Our only Lullaby –

4] Convicted me – of me –   15. us] me
11. we suppose] I supposed

MANUSCRIPT: Early 1862, in packet 27 (H 148c). The suggested changes are in pencil and were added probably at a later date.

PUBLICATION: Stanzas 5 and 6 were published in *Poems* (1896), 166, perhaps from a transcript prepared by Mrs. Todd and now lost. Stanzas 1–3 and the first two lines of stanza 4 are in *BM* (1945), 100–101. They derive from a transcript made by Mrs. Todd. The lines published in *BM* follow the text of a single sheet of the transcript which breaks off at line 14. Presumably the remainder was on a second sheet now lost; it may have been from the second sheet that the final two stanzas were printed in 1896. The suggested changes for lines 4 and 11 are adopted.

589

The Night was wide, and furnished scant
With but a single Star –
That often as a Cloud it met –
Blew out itself – for fear –

The Wind pursued the little Bush –
And drove away the Leaves
November left – then clambered up
And fretted in the Eaves –

No Squirrel went abroad –
A Dog's belated feet
Like intermittent Plush, be heard
Adown the empty Street –

To feel if Blinds be fast –
And closer to the fire –
Her little Rocking Chair to draw –
And shiver for the Poor –

The Housewife's gentle Task –
How pleasanter – said she
Unto the Sofa opposite –
The Sleet – than May, no Thee –

16. shiver for] recollect

MANUSCRIPT: About 1862, in packet 28 (H 151a).

PUBLICATION: *Poems* (1891), 98–99, titled "At Home." The suggested change is rejected. One word is altered:

11. be] were

[451]

Did you ever stand in a Cavern's Mouth –
Widths out of the Sun –
And look – and shudder, and block your breath –
And deem to be alone

In such a place, what horror,
How Goblin it would be –
And fly, as 'twere pursuing you?
Then Loneliness – looks so –

Did you ever look in a Cannon's face –
Between whose Yellow eye –
And your's – the Judgment intervened –
The Question of "To die" –

Extemporizing in your ear
As cool as Satyr's Drums –
If you remember, and were saved –
It's liker so – it seems –

14. As cool] distinct –

MANUSCRIPT: About 1862, in packet 28 (H 151c).
PUBLICATION: *UP* (1935), 7. The text is arranged as two eight-line
stanzas, with the suggested change adopted. "Satyr's" (line 14) reads
"satyrs'." In line 16 "so" is italicized.

591

To interrupt His Yellow Plan
The Sun does not allow
Caprices of the Atmosphere –
And even when the Snow

Heaves Balls of Specks, like Vicious Boy
Directly in His Eye –
Does not so much as turn His Head
Busy with Majesty –

'Tis His to stimulate the Earth –
And magnetize the Sea –
And bind Astronomy, in place,
Yet Any passing by

Would deem Ourselves – the busier
As the Minutest Bee
That rides – emits a Thunder –
A Bomb – to justify –

11. in place] from blame   15. emits] supports –

Manuscript: About 1862, in packet 28 (H 152b).
Publication: *FP* (1929), 64. The suggested change for line 15 is
adopted. Alterations appear in two lines:

1. interrupt] intercept   12. passing by] passer-by

592

What care the Dead, for Chanticleer –
What care the Dead for Day?
'Tis late your Sunrise vex their face –
And Purple Ribaldry – of Morning

Pour as blank on them
As on the Tier of Wall
The Mason builded, yesterday,
And equally as cool –

What care the Dead for Summer?
The Solstice had no Sun
Could waste the Snow before their Gate –
And knew One Bird a Tune –

Could thrill their Mortised Ear
Of all the Birds that be –
This One – beloved of Mankind
Henceforward cherished be –

[453]

What care the Dead for Winter?
Themselves as easy freeze –
June Noon – as January Night –
As soon the South – her Breeze

Of Sycamore – or Cinnamon –
Deposit in a Stone
And put a Stone to keep it Warm –
Give Spices – unto Men –

6. Tier] Row   13. thrill] penetrate
11. waste] melt   17. What] Nor

MANUSCRIPT: About 1862, in packet 28 (H 153a).
PUBLICATION: The first stanza only appears in the introduction to *FP*
(1929), xiii, where lines 3–4 are rendered:

'Tis late your morning vex their face
With purple ribaldry!

The entire poem is in *FF* (1932), 238–239. The text is arranged as three
eight-line stanzas. Lines 3, 4 are given as in *FP*. Other alterations are:

5. Pour] And pours   20. South – her] Southern

All suggested changes are rejected.

593

I think I was enchanted
When first a sombre Girl –
I read that Foreign Lady –
The Dark – felt beautiful –

And whether it was noon at night –
Or only Heaven – at Noon –
For very Lunacy of Light
I had not power to tell –

The Bees – became as Butterflies –
The Butterflies – as Swans –   [*no stanza break*]

[454]

Approached – and spurned the narrow Grass –
And just the meanest Tunes

That Nature murmured to herself
To keep herself in Cheer –
I took for Giants – practising
Titanic Opera –

The Days – to Mighty Metres stept –
The Homeliest – adorned
As if unto a Jubilee
'Twere suddenly confirmed –

I could not have defined the change –
Conversion of the Mind
Like Sanctifying in the Soul –
Is witnessed – not explained –

'Twas a Divine Insanity –
The Danger to be Sane
Should I again experience –
'Tis Antidote to turn –

To Tomes of solid Witchcraft –
Magicians be asleep –
But Magic – hath an Element
Like Deity – to keep –

2. sombre Girl] little Girl
10–11] [The Butterflies] – As Moons –
    lit up the low – inferior Grass –
12. meanest Tunes] Common
    Tunes – / faintest –

19. Jubilee] Sacrament
20. confirmed] ordained
26. Danger] Sorrow

MANUSCRIPT: About 1862, in packet 28 (H 154a). This is a tribute
to the memory of Elizabeth Barrett Browning whose death on 30 June 1861
had moved ED deeply. She wrote two other commemorative poems on Mrs.
Browning: "Her 'last Poems,'" and "I went to thank her."

PUBLICATION: UP (1935), 39–40. Suggested changes for lines 2, 10,
11, 12 (common), and 26 are adopted.

594

The Battle fought between the Soul
And No Man – is the One
Of all the Battles prevalent –
By far the Greater One –

No News of it is had abroad –
It's Bodiless Campaign
Establishes, and terminates –
Invisible – Unknown –

Nor History – record it –
As Legions of a Night
The Sunrise scatters – These endure –
Enact – and terminate –

12. terminate] dissipate –

MANUSCRIPT: About 1862, in packet 28 (H 154c). In line 12 ED wrote
"Eanact."
PUBLICATION: *FP* (1929) 125. The suggested change is rejected. Stanza
3, arranged in five lines, in later collections is restored to a quatrain.

595

Like Mighty Foot Lights – burned the Red
At Bases of the Trees –
The far Theatricals of Day
Exhibiting – to These –

'Twas Universe – that did applaud –
While Chiefest – of the Crowd –
Enabled by his Royal Dress –
Myself distinguished God –

5. applaud] attend   6. of] in –

MANUSCRIPT: About 1862, in packet 29 (H 155d).
PUBLICATION: *Poems* (1891), 163. Neither suggested change is adopted.

When I was small, a Woman died –
Today – her Only Boy
Went up from the Potomac –
His face all Victory

To look at her – How slowly
The Seasons must have turned
Till Bullets clipt an Angle
And He passed quickly round –

If pride shall be in Paradise –
Ourself cannot decide –
Of their imperial Conduct –
No person testified –

But, proud in Apparition –
That Woman and her Boy
Pass back and forth, before my Brain
As even in the sky –

I'm confident that Bravoes –
Perpetual break abroad
For Braveries, remote as this
In Yonder Maryland –

8. passed] went
8. quickly] softly –
18. break] be – / go –

19. remote as this] just sealed in /
    proved –
19. this] His
20. Yonder] Scarlet

MANUSCRIPT: Early 1862, in packet 29 (H 70a). Francis H. Dickinson
of Belchertown, serving with the 15th regiment, Company F, was killed in
action at the battle of Ball's Bluff, 21 October 1861. He is said to be "the
first man on Amherst's quota to give up his life for his country." (Carpen-
ter and Morehouse, *The History of the Town of Amherst, Massachusetts*,
Amherst, 1896, page 478.) Ball's Bluff, Virginia, is on the Potomac about
forty-four miles northwest of Washington on the Maryland border.
PUBLICATION: *Poems* (1890), 145, titled "Along the Potomac." All sug-

gested changes are rejected. The final stanza is omitted. Words in two lines are altered:

10. Ourself cannot] I never can   16. even] ever

597

It always felt to me – a wrong
To that Old Moses – done –
To let him see – the Canaan –
Without the entering –

And tho' in soberer moments –
No Moses there can be
I'm satisfied – the Romance
In point of injury –

Surpasses sharper stated –
Of Stephen – or of Paul –
For these – were only put to death –
While God's adroiter will

On Moses – seemed to fasten
With tantalizing Play
As Boy – should deal with lesser Boy –
To prove ability.

The fault – was doubtless Israel's –
Myself – had banned the Tribes –
And ushered Grand Old Moses
In Pentateuchal Robes

Upon the Broad Possession
'Twas little – He should see –
Old Man on Nebo! Late as this –
My justice bleeds – for Thee!

14. With] in   22] But titled Him – to see –
16. prove ability] show supremacy   24. My] One –
21. Broad Possession] Lawful Manor –

[458]

MANUSCRIPT: About 1862, in packet 29 (H 19b).

PUBLICATION: *Atlantic Monthly*, CXLIII (February 1929), 182; *FP* (1929), 46. The text of stanzas 4 and 5, arranged as five lines, is restored in later collections to quatrains. The suggested changes for lines 14, 16, 22, and 24 are adopted.

598

Three times – we parted – Breath – and I –
Three times – He would not go –
But strove to stir the lifeless Fan
The Waters – strove to stay.

Three Times – the Billows threw me up –
Then caught me – like a Ball –
Then made Blue faces in my face –
And pushed away a sail

That crawled Leagues off – I liked to see –
For thinking – while I die –
How pleasant to behold a Thing
Where Human faces – be –

The Waves grew sleepy – Breath – did not –
The Winds – like Children – lulled –
Then Sunrise kissed my Chrysalis –
And I stood up – and lived –

3. lifeless Fan] flickering fan   13. The Waves grew sleepy] The
5. threw] tossed   Ocean – tired – / wearied –

MANUSCRIPT: Early 1862, in packet 29 (H 156a).

PUBLICATION: *FP* (1929), 98. The text is arranged as four six-line stanzas. In the Centenary edition (1930) and later collections the text is without stanza division. The suggested changes for lines 3 and 5 are adopted. Two words are altered:

3. strove] stood   15. Then] The

In line 7 "my" is italicized.

There is a pain – so utter –
It swallows substance up –
Then covers the Abyss with Trance –
So Memory can step
Around – across – upon it –
As one within a Swoon –
Goes safely – where an open eye –
Would drop Him – Bone by Bone.

2. substance] Being   8. drop] spill Him –
7. safely] steady –

MANUSCRIPT: Early 1862, in packet 29 (H 156b).
PUBLICATION: *Nation*, CXXVIII (13 March 1929), 315; *FP* (1929),
177. The suggested changes for lines 2 and 7 are adopted. One word is
altered:

7. where] when

It troubled me as once I was –
For I was once a Child –
Concluding how an Atom – fell –
And yet the Heavens – held –

The Heavens weighed the most – by far –
Yet Blue – and solid – stood –
Without a Bolt – that I could prove –
Would Giants – understand?

Life set me larger – problems –
Some I shall keep – to solve
Till Algebra is easier –
Or simpler proved – above –

Then – too – be comprehended –
What sorer – puzzled me –
Why Heaven did not break away –
And tumble – Blue – on me –

3. Concluding] Deciding
5. weighed the most – by far] were the
   weightiest – far –
6. solid] easy

8. Would] did – / might
10. keep] save
11. Till] Where

MANUSCRIPT: About 1862, in packet 29 (H 156c). In line 10 ED first wrote "prove," then crossed it out and substituted "solve."

PUBLICATION: *BM* (1945), 83. The text derives from a transcript made by Mrs. Todd. The suggested change for line 3 is adopted.

601

A still – Volcano – Life –
That flickered in the night –
When it was dark enough to do
Without erasing sight –

A quiet – Earthquake Style –
Too subtle to suspect
By natures this side Naples –
The North cannot detect

The Solemn – Torrid – Symbol –
The lips that never lie –
Whose hissing Corals part – and shut –
And Cities – ooze away –

3. do] show
4. erasing] endangering

6. subtle] smouldering
12. ooze] slip – / slide – / melt –

MANUSCRIPT: About 1862, in packet 29 (H 156d). ED had first written "Volcanic" (line 1), but crossed it out and wrote "Volcano" among the suggested changes.

PUBLICATION: *FP* (1929) 36. All suggested changes are adopted (with choice of "slip" for "ooze"). The published version attaches as a fourth and final stanza one beginning "Therefore we do Life's Labor", lines which are in fact the conclusion of "I tie my hat, I crease my shawl," (*q.v.*).

Of Brussels – it was not –
Of Kidderminster? Nay –
The Winds did buy it of the Woods –
They – sold it unto me

It was a gentle price –
The poorest – could afford –
It was within the frugal purse
Of Beggar – or of Bird –

Of small and spicy Yards –
In hue – a mellow Dun –
Of Sunshine – and of Sere – Composed –
But, principally – of Sun –

The Wind – unrolled it fast –
And spread it on the Ground –
Upholsterer of the Pines – is He –
Upholsterer – of the Pond –

4. They – sold it] Then – sell it   15. of the Pines] Of the Sea / of the
9. Yards] Breadths –   land – / [of the] Hills –

MANUSCRIPT: About 1862, in packet 29 (H 383a).
PUBLICATION: *BM* (1945), 331. A notation at the end reads: "With a
pine needle". The text derives from a transcript made by Mrs. Todd. All
suggested changes are rejected. There are two changes:

12. principally] princip'ly   15, 16. Upholsterer] Upholst'rer

603

He found my Being – set it up –
Adjusted it to place –
Then carved his name – upon it –
And bade it to the East

Be faithful – in his absence –
And he would come again –   [*no stanza break*]

With Equipage of Amber –
That time – to take it Home –

3. Then carved] He wrote   4. And] then –

MANUSCRIPT: About 1862, in packet 29 (H 383b).
PUBLICATION: *BM* (1945), 152. The text derives from a transcript of
the packet copy made by Mrs. Todd. Both suggested changes are rejected.

604

Unto my Books – so good to turn –
Far ends of tired Days –
It half endears the Abstinence –
And Pain – is missed – in Praise –

As Flavors – cheer Retarded Guests
With Banquettings to be –
So Spices – stimulate the time
Till my small Library –

It may be Wilderness – without –
Far feet of failing Men –
But Holiday – excludes the night –
And it is Bells – within –

I thank these Kinsmen of the Shelf –
Their Countenances Kid
Enamor – in Prospective –
And satisfy – obtained –

2. tired] Homely –   4. is missed in] Forgets – for –

MANUSCRIPT: About 1862, in packet 29 (H 383c). A facsimile of this
copy is reproduced in *The Book Scorpion*, The Hampshire Bookshop,
Northampton, Mass., June 1924.
PUBLICATION: *Poems* (1891), 74. Both suggested changes are rejected.
One word is altered:

14. Kid] bland

The Spider holds a Silver Ball
In unperceived Hands –
And dancing softly to Himself
His Yarn of Pearl – unwinds –

He plies from Nought to Nought –
In unsubstantial Trade –
Supplants our Tapestries with His –
In half the period –

An Hour to rear supreme
His Continents of Light –
Then dangle from the Housewife's Broom –
His Boundaries – forgot –

3. to Himself] as He knits   10. Continents] Theories
4. Yarn] Coil –   11. dangle from] perish by
4. unwinds] expends –   12. Boundaries] Sophistries –
4] Pursues his pearly strands –

MANUSCRIPT: About 1862, in packet 29 (H 283d).
PUBLICATION: *BM* (1945), 74–75. The suggested changes for lines 10 and 12 are adopted. The text derives from a transcript made by Mrs. Todd.

606
The Trees like Tassels – hit – and swung –
There seemed to rise a Tune
From Miniature Creatures
Accompanying the Sun –

Far Psalteries of Summer –
Enamoring the Ear
They never yet did satisfy –
Remotest – when most fair

The Sun shone whole at intervals –
Then Half – then utter hid –   *[no stanza break]*

As if Himself were optional
And had Estates of Cloud

Sufficient to enfold Him
Eternally from view –
Except it were a whim of His
To let the Orchards grow –

A Bird sat careless on the fence –
One gossipped in the Lane
On silver matters charmed a Snake
Just winding round a Stone –

Bright Flowers slit a Calyx
And soared upon a Stem
Like Hindered Flags – Sweet hoisted –
With Spices – in the Hem –

'Twas more – I cannot mention –
How mean – to those that see –
Vandykes Delineation
Of Nature's – Summer Day!

8. fair] near –   22. And] Or
12. had] owned

MANUSCRIPT: Early 1862, in packet 29 (H 158a). Stanzas 1–4 are on the recto of the sheet, stanzas 5–7 on the verso. The seven stanzas depict, in the words of the last line, a "Summer Day," and appear to constitute a single poem. Mrs. Bingham (AB, 394) says that the poem "is in reality two poems. The first four stanzas describe a summer storm; to the last three, beginning 'A bird sat careless on the fence,' Emily herself gave the title 'Summer's Day.'" However, no other autograph copy is known. A copyist who sometimes assisted Mrs. Todd made a transcript of the seven stanzas from the packet copy. The first four stanzas Mrs. Todd placed in her class C group; the last three among her transcripts in class B. The title "Summer's Day" appears to be Mrs. Todd's.

PUBLICATION: UP (1935), 51–52. The suggested changes for lines 8 and 22 are adopted. The misprint "The" for "Far" (line 5) is corrected in Poems (current). One word is altered:

12. Cloud] clouds

Of nearness to her sundered Things
The Soul has special times –
When Dimness – looks the Oddity –
Distinctness – easy – seems –

The Shapes we buried, dwell about,
Familiar, in the Rooms –
Untarnished by the Sepulchre,
The Mouldering Playmate comes –

In just the Jacket that he wore –
Long buttoned in the Mold
Since we – old mornings, Children – played –
Divided – by a world –

The Grave yields back her Robberies –
The Years, our pilfered Things –
Bright Knots of Apparitions
Salute us, with their wings –

As we – it were – that perished –
Themself – had just remained till we rejoin them –
And 'twas they, and not ourself
That mourned.

8. The] Our

MANUSCRIPT: About 1862, in packet 32 (H 171b).
PUBLICATION: *Atlantic Monthly*, CXLIII (February 1929), 185; *FP* (1929), 104. In line 14 "our," printed "are," is corrected in *Poems* (current). The last stanza, arranged in five lines, is restored in later collections as a quatrain. The suggested change is adopted. Two words are altered:

18. Themself] Themselves   20. ourself] Ourselves

[466]

Afraid! Of whom am I afraid?
Not Death – for who is He?
The Porter of my Father's Lodge
As much abasheth me!

Of Life? 'Twere odd I fear [a] thing
That comprehendeth me
In one or two existences –
Just as the case may be –

Of Resurrection? Is the East
Afraid to trust the Morn
With her fastidious forehead?
As soon impeach my Crown!

7. two] more –   8] As Deity decree –

MANUSCRIPT: About 1862, in packet 32 (H 61b).
PUBLICATION: *Poems* (1890), 135. Both suggested changes are adopted, but the second is altered to read:

At Deity's decree

609

I Years had been from Home
And now before the Door
I dared not enter, lest a Face
I never saw before

Stare stolid into mine
And ask my Business there –
"My Business but a Life I left
Was such remaining there?"

I leaned upon the Awe –
I lingered with Before –
The Second like an Ocean rolled
And broke against my ear –

[467]

I laughed a crumbling Laugh
That I could fear a Door
Who Consternation compassed
And never winced before.

I fitted to the Latch
My Hand, with trembling care
Lest back the awful Door should spring
And leave me in the Floor –

Then moved my Fingers off
As cautiously as Glass
And held my ears, and like a Thief
Fled gasping from the House –

MANUSCRIPTS: There are two, both copied into packets. The copy re-
produced above, in packet 36 (H 194), was written in late 1872. It is a
redaction of an earlier version in packet 34 (H 181a), written about 1862:

I – Years had been – from Home –
And now – before the Door –
I dared not open – lest a face
I never saw before

Stare vacant into mine –
And ask my Business there –
My Business – just a Life I left –
Was such – still dwelling there?

I fumbled at my nerve –
I scanned the Windows o'er –
The Silence – like an Ocean rolled –
And broke against my Ear –

I laughed a Wooden laugh –
That I – could fear a Door –
Who Danger – and the Dead – had faced –
But never shook – before –

I fitted to the Latch – my Hand –
With trembling care –
Lest back the Awful Door should spring –
And leave me – in the Floor –

I moved my fingers off, as cautiously as Glass –
And held my Ears – and like a Thief
Stole – gasping – from the House.

8. still dwelling there] Remaining   16. shook] quaked –
    there   23. Stole] fled
12. broke] smote –

The later version creates new images in and entirely alters stanza 3; it
adopts two of the suggested changes from the earlier version (lines 8 and
23), and it introduces several variant readings in stanzas 2 and 4. The
later version cannot be termed a fair copy, however. In pencil ED has
written marginally beside "stolid" (line 5) "or – horrid."

PUBLICATION: *Poems* (1891) 80–81, titled "Returning." It follows the
text of the 1862 version. The suggested changes for lines 16 and 23 are
adopted. The last two words of line 17 are arranged as the first two of line
18. Line 21 is divided in two and the stanza printed as a quatrain. Altera-
tions are made in two lines:

10. o'er] near   20. in the Floor] standing there

610

You'll find – it when you try to die –
The Easier to let go –
For recollecting such as went –
You could not spare – you know.

And though their places somewhat filled –
As did their Marble names
With Moss – they never grew so full –
You chose the newer names –

And when this World – sets further back –
As Dying – say it does –
The former love – distincter grows –
And supersedes the fresh –

And Thought of them – so fair invites –
It looks too tawdry Grace   *[no stanza break]*

[469]

To stay behind – with just the Toys
We bought – to ease their place –

8. names] times –

MANUSCRIPT: About 1862, in packet 34 (H 181b).
PUBLICATION: *London Mercury, XIX* (1929), 351–352; *FP* (1929)
105. The suggested change is adopted. One word is altered:

1. try] come

611

I see thee better – in the Dark –
I do not need a Light –
The Love of Thee – a Prism be –
Excelling Violet –

I see thee better for the Years
That hunch themselves between –
The Miner's Lamp – sufficient be –
To nullify the Mine –

And in the Grave – I see Thee best –
It's little Panels be
Aglow – All ruddy – with the Light
I held so high, for Thee –

What need of Day –
To Those whose Dark – hath so – surpassing Sun –
It deem it be – Continually –
At the Meridian?

6. hunch themselves] pile themselves –

MANUSCRIPT: About 1862, in packet 34 (H 182a). For a poem which
may be a variant of this, see "I see thee clearer for the Grave."
PUBLICATION: *SH* (1914), 85. The suggested change is rejected. Lines
13 and 14 are regularized.

[470]

It would have starved a Gnat –
To live so small as I –
And yet I was a living Child –
With Food's nescessity

Upon me – like a Claw –
I could no more remove
Than I could coax a Leech away –
Or make a Dragon – move –

Nor like the Gnat – had I –
The privilege to fly
And seek a Dinner for myself –
How mightier He – than I –

Nor like Himself – the Art
Upon the Window Pane
To gad my little Being out –
And not begin – again –

2. live] dine   11. seek] gain
7. coax a Leech away] modify a Leech

MANUSCRIPT: About 1862, in packet 34 (H 182c).
PUBLICATION: *BM* (1945), 100. The text derives from a transcript made
by Mrs. Todd. The suggested change for line 2 is adopted.

613

They shut me up in Prose –
As when a little Girl
They put me in the Closet –
Because they liked me "still" –

Still! Could themself have peeped –
And seen my Brain – go round –
They might as wise have lodged a Bird
For Treason – in the Pound –

Himself has but to will
And easy as a Star
Look down upon Captivity –
And laugh – No more have I –

11. Look down upon] Abolish his –

MANUSCRIPT: About 1862, in packet 34 (H 182d).
PUBLICATION: *UP* (1935), 34. The suggested change is rejected. Two words are altered:

5. themself] themselves   12. no] Nor

614

In falling Timbers buried –
There breathed a Man –
Outside – the spades – were plying –
The Lungs – within –

Could He – know – they sought Him –
Could They – know – He breathed –
Horrid Sand Partition –
Neither – could be heard –

Never slacked the Diggers –
But when Spades had done –
Oh, Reward of Anguish,
It was dying – Then –

Many Things – are fruitless –
'Tis a Baffling Earth –
But there is no Gratitude
Like the Grace – of Death –

1. falling] crashing   6. breathed] lived
3. Outside] Without   11. Oh! Reward of] Recompense of –

MANUSCRIPT: About 1862, in packet 34 (H 183b).
PUBLICATION: *BM* (1945), 187. The suggested changes for lines 1 and

11 are adopted. Line 11 reads: "Oh, recompense of anguish", but ED has marked the line at "Oh,", implying that all three words would be changed if the substitute words were adopted. The text derives from a transcript of the packet copy made by Mrs. Todd. One word is altered:

12. It] He

615

Our journey had advanced –
Our feet were almost come
To that odd Fork in Being's Road –
Eternity – by Term –

Our pace took sudden awe –
Our feet – reluctant – led –
Before – were Cities – but Between –
The Forest of the Dead –

Retreat – was out of Hope –
Behind – a Sealed Route –
Eternity's White Flag – Before –
And God – at every Gate –

11. White] Cool   11. Before] in front –

MANUSCRIPT: About 1862, in packet 34 (H 186a).
PUBLICATION: *Poems* (1891), 206, titled "The Journey." Both suggested changes are rejected.

616

I rose – because He sank –
I thought it would be opposite –
But when his power dropped –
My Soul grew straight.

I cheered my fainting Prince –
I sang firm – even – Chants –
I helped his Film – with Hymn –

And when the Dews drew off
That held his Forehead stiff –
I met him –
Balm to Balm –

I told him Best – must pass
Through this low Arch of Flesh –
No Casque so brave
It spurn the Grave –

I told him Worlds I knew
Where Emperors grew –
Who recollected us
If we were true –

And so with Thews of Hymn –
And Sinew from within –
And ways I knew not that I knew – till then –
I lifted Him –

3. dropped] bent
4. grew] felt – / bent – / stood
6. firm – even – Chants] straight –
   steady chants –
7. helped] stayed

10. met him] gave him –
11. Balm to Balm] Balm – for Balm
16. him Worlds] a world
17. Emperors] Monarchs –

MANUSCRIPT: About 1862, in packet 34 (H 186b).
PUBLICATION: *Atlantic Monthly*, CXLIII (March 1929), 327; *FP* (1929), 93; and *AB* (1945), 386–387. The text in *AM* and *FP* derives from the packet copy, but stanzas 2 and 3 are omitted, and the stanza division is not retained; three suggested changes are adopted:

3. bent   17. monarchs
4. stood

The text in *AB* derives from a transcript of the packet copy made by Mrs. Todd. Stanzas 2 and 3, as well as the stanza division, are restored. The suggested changes for lines 3, 7, 10, 11, and 17 are adopted. Line 6 reads:

I sang firm steady chants

Dont put up my Thread & Needle –
I'll begin to Sow
When the Birds begin to whistle –
Better Stitches – so –

These were bent – my sight got crooked –
When my mind – is plain
I'll do seams – a Queen's endeavor
Would not blush to own –

Hems – too fine for Lady's tracing
To the sightless Knot –
Tucks – of dainty interspersion –
Like a dotted Dot –

Leave my Needle in the furrow –
Where I put it down –
I can make the zigzag stitches
Straight – when I am strong –

Till then – dreaming I am sowing
Fetch the seam I missed –
Closer – so I – at my sleeping –
Still surmise I stitch –

17. dreaming] deeming   19. sleeping] sighing –

MANUSCRIPT: About 1862, in packet 40 (H 214b). The spelling of "Sow" and "sowing" (lines 2 and 17) is undoubtedly a mistake for "sewing." In line 1 "up" replaces "down" which is crossed out.

PUBLICATION: FP (1929), 103. Neither suggested change is adopted. One word is altered:

14. Where] When

At leisure is the Soul
That gets a Staggering Blow –
The Width of Life – before it spreads
Without a thing to do –

It begs you give it Work –
But just the placing Pins –
Or humblest Patchwork – Children do –
To still it's noisy Hands –

3. spreads] runs   8] [To] Help it's Vacant Hands –
7. do] may –

MANUSCRIPT: About 1862, in packet 40 (H 214d).
PUBLICATION: *London Mercury*, XIX (February 1929), 357–358; *New York Herald Tribune Book Review*, 10 March 1929, page 4; *FP* (1929), 185. The text is arranged as two five-line stanzas. In later collections the quatrains are restored. The suggested change for line 8 is adopted.

Glee – The great storm is over –
Four – have recovered the Land –
Forty – gone down together –
Into the boiling Sand –

Ring – for the Scant Salvation –
Toll – for the bonnie Souls –
Neighbor – and friend – and Bridegroom –
Spinning upon the Shoals –

How they will tell the Story –
When Winter shake the Door –
Till the Children urge –
But the Forty –
Did they – come back no more?

Then a softness – suffuse the Story –
And a silence – the Teller's eye –
And the Children – no further question –
And only the Sea – reply –

11. urge] ask –

MANUSCRIPT: About 1862, in packet 40 (H 215b). In the last stanza
ED wrote 2 over "softness" and 1 over "silence," indicating they should
be interchanged.

PUBLICATION: This was one of fourteen poems selected for publication
in an article contributed by T. W. Higginson to the *Christian Union*,
XLII (25 September 1890), 392–393, titled "By the Sea." The text is
identical with that in *Poems* (1890), 17, which is without title. Stanza 3
is arranged as a quatrain. The alternate and the suggested interchange are
adopted. Four words are altered:

 9. Story] shipwreck   13. suffuse] suffuses
10. shake] shakes   16. Sea] waves

620

It makes no difference abroad –
The Seasons – fit – the same –
The Mornings blossom into Noons –
And split their Pods of Flame –

Wild flowers – kindle in the Woods –
The Brooks slam – all the Day –
No Black bird bates his Banjo –
For passing Calvary –

Auto da Fe – and Judgment –
Are nothing to the Bee –
His separation from His Rose –
To Him – sums Misery –

6. slam] brag –

MANUSCRIPT: About 1862, in packet 40 (H 215c).

[477]

PUBLICATION: *Poems* (1890), 92, titled "Two Worlds." The suggested change is adopted. Two words are altered:

7. Banjo] jargoning   12. sums] seems

The first word of line 9 is regularized:

Auto-da-fé

621

I asked no other thing –
No other – was denied –
I offered Being – for it –
The Mighty Merchant sneered –

Brazil? He twirled a Button –
Without a glance my way –
"But – Madam – is there nothing else –
That We can show – Today?"

4. sneered] smiled –

MANUSCRIPT: About 1862, in packet 40 (H 215d).
PUBLICATION: *Poems* (1890), 25. The suggested change is adopted.

622

To know just how He suffered – would be dear –
To know if any Human eyes were near
To whom He could entrust His wavering gaze –
Until it settled broad – on Paradise –

To know if He was patient – part content –
Was Dying as He thought – or different –
Was it a pleasant Day to die –
And did the Sunshine face His way –

[478]

What was His furthest mind – Of Home – or God –
Or what the Distant say –
At news that He ceased Human Nature
Such a Day –

And Wishes – Had He Any –
Just His Sigh – Accented –
Had been legible – to Me –
And was He Confident until
Ill fluttered out – in Everlasting Well –

And if He spoke – What name was Best –
What last
What One broke off with
At the Drowsiest –

Was He afraid – or tranquil –
Might He know
How Conscious Consciousness – could grow –
Till Love that was – and Love too best to be –
Meet – and the Junction be Eternity

4. broad] full – / firm –   26. be] mean –
19. last] first

MANUSCRIPT: About 1862, in packet 40 (H 216a).

PUBLICATION: *Poems* (1890), 128–129. The suggested changes for lines 4 ("firm") and 19 are adopted. Two words are altered:

3. entrust] intrust   25. best] blest

One word is added:

12. On such a day

623

It was too late for Man –
But early, yet, for God –
Creation – impotent to help –
But Prayer – remained – Our Side –

[479]

How excellent the Heaven –
When Earth – cannot be had –
How hospitable – then – the face
Of Our Old Neighbor – God –

8. Old] New

MANUSCRIPT: About 1862, in packet 40 (H 216b).
PUBLICATION: *Poems* (1890), 144. The suggested change is rejected.

624

Forever – is composed of Nows –
'Tis not a different time –
Except for Infiniteness –
And Latitude of Home –

From this – experienced Here –
Remove the Dates – to These –
Let Months dissolve in further Months –
And Years – exhale in Years –

Without Debate – or Pause –
Or Celebrated Days –
No different Our Years would be
From Anno Dominies –

7. further] other –   11. No different] As infinite –
9. Debate] Certificate –

MANUSCRIPT: About 1862, in packet 40 (H 216c).
PUBLICATION: *FP* (1929), 25. The suggested changes for lines 9 and
11 are adopted. "Dominies" (last line) is regularized to "Domini's".

625

'Twas a long Parting – but the time
For Interview – had Come –
Before the Judgment Seat of God –
The last – and second time

These Fleshless Lovers met –
A Heaven in a Gaze –
A Heaven of Heavens – the Privilege
Of one another's Eyes –

No Lifetime set – on Them –
Appareled as the new
Unborn – except They had beheld –
Born infiniter – now –

Was Bridal – e'er like This?
A Paradise – the Host –
And Cherubim – and Seraphim –
The unobtrusive Guest –

12. infiniter] everlasting   16. unobtrusive] most familiar –

MANUSCRIPT: About 1862, in packet 40 (H 217a).
PUBLICATION: *Poems* (1890), 62, titled "Resurrection." The suggested changes are adopted.

626

Only God – detect the Sorrow –
Only God –
The Jehovahs – are no Babblers –
Unto God –

God the Son – confide it –
Still secure –
God the Spirit's Honor –
Just as sure –

1. detect the Sorrow] Possess the   5. confide it] disclose it
    Secret –   8] Equal sure –

MANUSCRIPT: About 1862, in packet 40 (H 217b).
PUBLICATION: *UP* (1935), 149. All suggested changes are adopted. The poem is printed without stanza division. There is a period at the end of line 3, and no punctuation at the end of line 4.

[481]

The Tint I cannot take – is best –
The Color too remote
That I could show it in Bazaar –
A Guinea at a sight –

The fine – impalpable Array –
That swaggers on the eye
Like Cleopatra's Company –
Repeated – in the sky –

The Moments of Dominion
That happen on the Soul
And leave it with a Discontent
Too exquisite – to tell –

The eager look – on Landscapes –
As if they just repressed
Some Secret – that was pushing
Like Chariots – in the Vest –

The Pleading of the Summer –
That other Prank – of Snow –
That Cushions Mystery with Tulle,
For fear the Squirrels – know.

Their Graspless manners – mock us –
Until the Cheated Eye
Shuts arrogantly – in the Grave –
Another way – to see –

16] [Like] Columns – in the Breast –   19] [That] covers mystery with
                                              Blonde –

MANUSCRIPT: About 1862, in packet 40 (H 218b).
PUBLICATION: *Saturday Review of Literature*, V (9 March 1929), 751;
FP (1929), 54. The suggested changes are in part adopted:

16] Like chariots, in the breast –   19] That covers mystery with tulle

They called me to the Window, for
" 'Twas Sunset" – Some one said –
I only saw a Sapphire Farm –
And just a Single Herd –

Of Opal Cattle – feeding far
Upon so vain a Hill –
As even while I looked – dissolved –
Nor Cattle were – nor Soil –

But in their Room – a Sea – displayed –
And Ships – of such a size
As Crew of Mountains – could afford –
And Decks – to seat the skies –

This – too – the Showman rubbed away –
And when I looked again –
Nor Farm – nor Opal Herd – was there –
Nor Mediterranean –

3. a Sapphire] an Amber –   9. Room] stead –

MANUSCRIPT: About 1862, in packet 84 (Bingham 20a).
PUBLICATION: *BM* (1945), 20. Both suggested changes are adopted.

I watched the Moon around the House
Until upon a Pane –
She stopped – a Traveller's privilege – for Rest –
And there upon

I gazed – as at a stranger –
The Lady in the Town
Doth think no incivility
To lift her Glass – upon –

But never Stranger justified
The Curiosity
Like Mine – for not a Foot – nor Hand –
Nor Formula – had she –

But like a Head – a Guillotine
Slid carelessly away –
Did independent, Amber –
Sustain her in the sky –

Or like a Stemless Flower –
Upheld in rolling Air
By finer Gravitations –
Than bind Philosopher –

No Hunger – had she – nor an Inn –
Her Toilette – to suffice –
Nor Avocation – nor Concern
For little Mysteries

As harass us – like Life – and Death –
And Afterward – or Nay –
But seemed engrossed to Absolute –
With shining – and the Sky –

The privilege to scrutinize
Was scarce upon my Eyes
When, with a Silver practise –
She vaulted out of Gaze –

And next – I met her on a Cloud –
Myself too far below
To follow her superior Road –
Or it's advantage – Blue –

5. gazed] turned   35. Road] pace

MANUSCRIPT: About 1862, in packet 84 (Bingham 21a).
PUBLICATION: *BM* (1945), 27–28. Both suggested changes are rejected. The last two words in line 3 begin line 4.

[484]

The Lightning playeth – all the while –
But when He singeth – then –
Ourselves are conscious He exist –
And we approach Him – stern –

With Insulators – and a Glove –
Whose short – sepulchral Bass
Alarms us – tho' His Yellow feet
May pass – and counterpass –

Upon the Ropes – above our Head –
Continual – with the News –
Nor We so much as check our speech –
Nor stop to cross Ourselves –

4. approach] accost

MANUSCRIPT: About 1862, in packet 84 (Bingham 21c).
PUBLICATION: *BM* (1945), 18. The suggested change is rejected.

631

Ourselves were wed one summer – dear –
Your Vision – was in June –
And when Your little Lifetime failed,
I wearied – too – of mine –

And overtaken in the Dark –
Where You had put me down –
By Some one carrying a Light –
I – too – received the Sign.

'Tis true – Our Futures different lay –
Your Cottage – faced the sun –
While Oceans – and the North must be –
On every side of mine

'Tis true, Your Garden led the Bloom,
For mine – in Frosts – was sown –   [*no stanza break*]

And yet, one Summer, we were Queens –
But You – were crowned in June –

11. must be] did play   16] but Your's was first – in June –
15. Queens] wed –

MANUSCRIPT: About 1862, in packet 84 (Bingham 24a).
PUBLICATION: *BM* (1945), 108–109. The suggested change for line
11 is adopted.

632

The Brain – is wider than the Sky –
For – put them side by side –
The one the other will contain
With ease – and You – beside –

The Brain is deeper than the sea –
For – hold them – Blue to Blue –
The one the other will absorb –
As Sponges – Buckets – do –

The Brain is just the weight of God –
For – Heft them – Pound for Pound –
And they will differ – if they do –
As Syllable from Sound –

3. contain] include

MANUSCRIPT: About 1862, in packet 84 (Bingham 24c).
PUBLICATION: *Poems* (1896), 58, titled "The Brain." The suggested
change is adopted. One word is altered:

10. Heft] lift

633

When Bells stop ringing – Church – begins –
The Positive – of Bells –
When Cogs – stop – that's Circumference –
The Ultimate – of Wheels.

MANUSCRIPT: About 1862, in packet 84 (Bingham 25b).
PUBLICATION: *BM* (1945), 279. The suggested change is rejected.

634

You'll know Her – by Her Foot –
The smallest Gamboge Hand
With Fingers – where the Toes should be –
Would more affront the Sand –

Than this Quaint Creature's Boot –
Adjusted by a Stem –
Without a Button – I c'd vouch –
Unto a Velvet Limb –

You'll know Her – by Her Vest –
Tight fitting – Orange – Brown –
Inside a Jacket duller –
She wore when she was born –

Her Cap is small – and snug –
Constructed for the Winds –
She'd pass for Barehead – short way off –
But as She Closer stands –

So finer 'tis than Wool –
You cannot feel the Seam –
Nor is it Clasped unto of Band –
Nor held upon – of Brim –

You'll know Her – by Her Voice –
At first – a doubtful Tone –
A sweet endeavor – but as March
To April – hurries on –

She squanders on your Head
Such Threnodies of Pearl –   [*no stanza break*]

[487]

You beg the Robin in your Brain
To keep the other – still –

2. smallest] finest
20. held upon – of] has it any
25. Head] Ear

26. Threnodies] Extacies – / Reve-
nues -/ *Arguments*
27–28] Deny she is a Robin – now –
And you're an Infidel –

MANUSCRIPT: About 1862, in packet 84 (Bingham 26a).
PUBLICATION: *BM* (1945), 64–65. Three suggested changes are adopted:

20. has it any
25. ear

26. arguments

635

I think the longest Hour of all
Is when the Cars have come –
And we are waiting for the Coach –
It seems as though the Time

Indignant – that the Joy was come –
Did block the Gilded Hands –
And would not let the Seconds by –
But slowest instant – ends –

The Pendulum begins to count –
Like little Scholars – loud –
The steps grow thicker – in the Hall –
The Heart begins to crowd –

Then I – my timid service done –
Tho' service 'twas, of Love –
Take up my little Violin –
And further North – remove.

5. Indignant] Affronted

MANUSCRIPT: About 1862, in packet 84 (Bingham 27b).
PUBLICATION: *BM* (1945), 103. The suggested change is adopted.

[488]

636

The Way I read a Letter's – this –
'Tis first – I lock the Door –
And push it with my fingers – next –
For transport it be sure –

And then I go the furthest off
To counteract a knock –
Then draw my little Letter forth
And slowly pick the lock –

Then – glancing narrow, at the Wall –
And narrow at the floor
For firm Conviction of a Mouse
Not exorcised before –

Peruse how infinite I am
To no one that You – know –
And sigh for lack of Heaven – but not
The Heaven God bestow –

1. this] so   10. floor] door
8. slowly] slily / softly

MANUSCRIPT: About 1862, in packet 9 (H 39a).
PUBLICATION: *Poems* (1891), 96. The suggested change "softly" is
adopted. Words are altered in two lines:

8. the] its   16. God] the creeds

637

The Child's faith is new –
Whole – like His Principle –
Wide – like the Sunrise
On fresh Eyes –
Never had a Doubt –
Laughs – at a Scruple –
Believes all sham
But Paradise –

[489]

Credits the World –
Deems His Dominion
Broadest of Sovreignties –
And Caesar – mean –
In the Comparison –
Baseless Emperor –
Ruler of Nought,
Yet swaying all –

Grown bye and bye
To hold mistaken
His pretty estimates
Of Prickly Things
He gains the skill
Sorrowful – as certain –
Men – to anticipate
Instead of Kings –

23. anticipate] propitiate –

MANUSCRIPT: About 1862, in packet 9 (H 39b).
PUBLICATION: *FP* (1929), 24. The suggested change is adopted. In the last two lines, "Men" and "kings" are italicized. Four words are altered:

9. Credits] Audits   19. estimates] estimate
13. In the] By

638

To my small Hearth His fire came –
And all my House aglow
Did fan and rock, with sudden light –
'Twas Sunrise – 'twas the Sky –

Impanelled from no Summer brief –
With limit of Decay –
'Twas Noon – without the News of Night –
Nay, Nature, it was Day –

6. limit] license
7. the News of Night] Report of Night

8. Nay, Nature] 'Twas further –

MANUSCRIPT: About 1862, in packet 9 (H 39d).
PUBLICATION: FF (1932), 223. The suggested changes for lines 6 and 7 are adopted. Line 8 reads:

Nay further, it was Day.

It is printed as one of a group of three poems sent to Sue. If so, it presumably derives from a fair copy in which the alternative readings represent choices made by ED. Such a fair copy is not known.

639

My Portion is Defeat – today –
A paler luck than Victory –
Less Paeans – fewer Bells –
The Drums dont follow Me – with tunes –
Defeat – a somewhat slower – means –
More Arduous than Balls –

Tis populous with Bone and stain –
And Men too straight to stoop again,
And Piles of solid Moan –
And Chips of Blank – in Boyish Eyes –
And scraps of Prayer –
And Death's surprise,
Stamped visible – in Stone –

There's somewhat prouder, over there –
The Trumpets tell it to the Air –
How different Victory
To Him who has it – and the One
Who to have had it, would have been
Contenteder – to die –

5. somewhat slower] something dumber
6. Arduous] difficult –

8. stoop] bend
11. scraps] shreds
14. somewhat] something

MANUSCRIPT: About 1862, in packet 9 (H 40a).

PUBLICATION: *Saturday Review of Literature*, V (9 March 1929), 751; *FP* (1929), 126. The text is arranged as a single twenty-two-line stanza. In later collections the line arrangement is restored but not the stanza division. All suggested changes are adopted. One word is altered:

6. Balls] bells

640

I cannot live with You –
It would be Life –
And Life is over there –
Behind the Shelf

The Sexton keeps the Key to –
Putting up
Our Life – His Porcelain –
Like a Cup –

Discarded of the Housewife –
Quaint – or Broke –
A newer Sevres pleases –
Old Ones crack –

I could not die – with You –
For One must wait
To shut the Other's Gaze down –
You – could not –

And I – Could I stand by
And see You – freeze –
Without my Right of Frost –
Death's privilege?

Nor could I rise – with You –
Because Your Face
Would put out Jesus' –
That New Grace

Glow plain – and foreign
On my homesick Eye –
Except that You than He
Shone closer by –

They'd judge Us – How –
For You – served Heaven – You know,
Or sought to –
I could not –

Because You saturated Sight –
And I had no more Eyes
For sordid excellence
As Paradise

And were You lost, I would be –
Though My Name
Rang loudest
On the Heavenly fame –

And were You – saved –
And I – condemned to be
Where You were not –
That self – were Hell to Me –

So We must meet apart –
You there – I – here –
With just the Door ajar
That Oceans are – and Prayer –
And that White Sustenance –
Despair –

35. excellence] consequence   49. Sustenance] exercise – /privilege –

MANUSCRIPT: About 1862, in packet 9 (H 41a).
PUBLICATION: *Poems* (1890), 55–57, titled "In Vain." The suggested changes are rejected. Three words are altered:

10. Broke] broken
45. meet] keep   49. White] pale

[493]

Size circumscribes – it has no room
For petty furniture –
The Giant tolerates no Gnat
For Ease of Gianture –

Repudiates it, all the more –
Because intrinsic size
Ignores the possibility
Of Calumnies – or Flies.

3. tolerates] entertains   7. Ignores] Excludes
4. Ease of Gianture] Simple Gianture –   8. Calumnies] Jealousies –
4] Because of Gianture

MANUSCRIPT: About 1862, in packet 9 (H 41b).
PUBLICATION: *UP* (1935), 70. All suggested changes are rejected.

Me from Myself – to banish –
Had I Art –
Invincible my Fortress
Unto All Heart –

But since Myself – assault Me –
How have I peace
Except by subjugating
Consciousness?

And since We're mutual Monarch
How this be
Except by Abdication –
Me – of Me?

3. Invincible] impregnable   4] To foreign Heart –

MANUSCRIPT: About 1862, in packet 9 (H 42b).

PUBLICATION: *FP* (1929), 123. The first suggested change is adopted. Two words are altered:

4. All] foreign   12. of] or

643

I could suffice for Him, I knew –
He – could suffice for Me –
Yet Hesitating Fractions – Both
Surveyed Infinity –

"Would I be Whole" He sudden broached –
My syllable rebelled –
'Twas face to face with Nature – forced –
'Twas face to face with God –

Withdrew the Sun – to Other Wests –
Withdrew the furthest Star
Before Decision – stooped to speech –
And then – be audibler

The Answer of the Sea unto
The Motion of the Moon –
Herself adjust Her Tides – unto –
Could I – do else – with Mine?

4. Surveyed] delayed – / deferred –

MANUSCRIPT: About 1862, in packet 9 (H 44b).
PUBLICATION: *UP* (1935), 95. The suggested changes are rejected.

644

You left me – Sire – two Legacies –
A Legacy of Love
A Heavenly Father would suffice
Had He the offer of –

[495]

You left me Boundaries of Pain –
Capacious as the Sea –
Between Eternity and Time –
Your Consciousness – and Me –

1. Sire] Sweet   3. suffice] content –

MANUSCRIPT: About 1862, in packet 9 (H 44c).
PUBLICATION: *Poems* (1890), 44, titled "Bequest." Both suggested changes are adopted.

645

Bereavement in their death to feel
Whom We have never seen –
A Vital Kinsmanship import
Our Soul and their's – between –

For Stranger – Strangers do not mourn –
There be Immortal friends
Whom Death see first – 'tis news of this
That paralyze Ourselves –

Who, vital only to Our Thought –
Such Presence bear away
In dying – 'tis as if Our Souls
Absconded – suddenly –

11. Souls] World – / Selves – / Sun –

MANUSCRIPT: About 1862, in packet 11 (H 50a).
PUBLICATION: *UP* (1935), 118. The suggested changes are rejected. Two words, correctly rendered in *UP*, were altered in later collections:

4. Soul] souls   5. Stranger] strangers

One word is altered in all printings:

3. import] impart

646

I think To Live – may be a Bliss
To those who dare to try –
Beyond my limit to conceive –
My lip – to testify –

I think the Heart I former wore
Could widen – till to me
The Other, like the little Bank
Appear – unto the Sea –

I think the Days – could every one
In Ordination stand –
And Majesty – be easier –
Than an inferior kind –

No numb alarm – lest Difference come –
No Goblin – on the Bloom –
No start in Apprehension's Ear,
No Bankruptcy – no Doom –

But Certainties of Sun –
Midsummer – in the Mind –
A steadfast South – upon the Soul –
Her Polar time – behind –

The Vision – pondered long –
So plausible becomes
That I esteem the fiction – real –
The Real – fictitious seems –

How bountiful the Dream –
What Plenty – it would be –
Had all my Life but been Mistake
Just rectified – in Thee

1. Bliss] Life
2. who dare] allowed
15. start] click

16. Bankruptcy] Sepulchre – / Wilderness
17. Sun] Noon

[497]

18. Midsummer] Meridian
20. night] Night
22. plausible] tangible – / positive
23. real] true

24. Real] Truth
27. but been] been one / bleak
28. rectified] qualified –

MANUSCRIPT: About 1862, in packet 11 (H 50b). In line 22 "appears" is crossed out, and "becomes" substituted.
PUBLICATION: *UP* (1935), 85–86. All suggested changes are rejected. Three words are altered:

4. lip] lips
25. bountiful] beautiful

28. in] by

647

A little Road – not made of Man –
Enabled of the Eye –
Accessible to Thill of Bee –
Or Cart of Butterfly –

If Town it have – beyond itself –
'Tis that – I cannot say –
I only know – no Curricle that rumble there
Bear Me –

5. beyond] besides
7. know] sigh –

7. Curricle] Vehicle
8. Bear] hold –

MANUSCRIPT: About 1862, in packet 11 (H 50c).
PUBLICATION: *Poems* (1890), 80. The second and third suggested changes are adopted. Lines 7 and 8 read:

I only sigh, – no vehicle
Bears me along that way.

648

Promise This – When You be Dying –
Some shall summon Me –
Mine belong Your latest Sighing –
Mine – to Belt Your Eye –

Not with Coins – though they be Minted
From an Emperor's Hand –
Be my lips – the only Buckle
Your low Eyes – demand –

Mine to stay – when all have wandered –
To devise once more
If the Life be too surrendered –
Life of Mine – restore –

Poured like this – My Whole Libation –
Just that You should see
Bliss of Death – Life's Bliss extol thro
Imitating You –

Mine – to guard Your Narrow Precinct –
To seduce the Sun
Longest on Your South, to linger,
Largest Dews of Morn

To demand, in Your low favor
Lest the Jealous Grass
Greener lean – Or fonder cluster
Round some other face –

Mine to supplicate Madonna –
If Madonna be
Could behold so far a Creature –
Christ – omitted – Me –

Just to follow Your dear feature –
Ne'er so far behind –
For My Heaven –
Had I not been
Most enough – denied?

2. Some shall] Some One   16] More resembling You
8. low] meek –   15-16] Bliss of Death – Life's Bliss
13. Whole] best   excel in
15. extol thro] surpass in   More resembling You –

[499]

18. seduce] entice – / persuade
19. Longest] latest
20. Largest] newest – / freshest
23. fonder cluster] later linger
27. behold] regard
27. far] small – / dim

27] Could regard so scarce a Creature –
29. Just] Still
32] Of All Her Glories –
33. Most enough] Amplest –
33] Worthiest – to have gained –

MANUSCRIPT: About 1862, in packet 11 (H 51a). Since this manuscript is included in a packet, it cannot in a strict sense be called a worksheet. Yet unless the suggested changes be entirely ignored the poem remains so unfinished that ED's final intent is beyond editorial construction. All suggested changes are written at the end of the poem and occupy two-thirds of a page. They are not in sequence and it may be questioned whether the choices here editorially sorted out have been given their correct association in every instance.

PUBLICATION: *UP* (1935), 90–91. The last stanza is arranged as a quatrain. The following suggested changes are adopted:

15–16] Bliss of Death – Life's Bliss
                                    pass
In more resembling you.
18. entice

27] Could regard so scarce a crea-
                                    ture, —
32–33] For my Heaven, of all Her
                                    glories
Worthiest to have gained.

Two words are altered:

20. Largest] Regal   29. feature] features

649

Her Sweet turn to leave the Homestead
Came the Darker Way –
Carriages – Be sure – and Guests – True –
But for Holiday

'Twas more pitiful Endeavor
Than did Loaded Sea
O'er the Curls attempt to caper
It had cast away –

Never Bride had such Assembling –
Never kinsmen kneeled
To salute so fair a Forehead –
Garland be indeed –

[500]

Fitter Feet – of Her before us –
Than whatever Brow
Art of Snow – or Trick of Lily
Possibly bestow

Of Her Father – Whoso ask Her –
He shall seek as high
As the Palm – that serve the Desert –
To obtain the Sky –

Distance – be Her only Motion –
If 'tis Nay – or Yes –
Acquiescence – or Demurral –
Whosoever guess –

He – must pass the Crystal Angle
That obscure Her face –
He – must have achieved in person
Equal Paradise –

3. True] too	17. ask] claim
6. Loaded] Swelling	21. Motion] Signal
13. Fitter feet – of Her] fitter for the feet	25. He] first
	25. Angle] limit
16] Ever could endow –	26. obscure] divide –

MANUSCRIPT: About 1862, in packet 11 (H 52a).

PUBLICATION: *UP* (1935), 127–128. The suggested changes for lines 3, 6, 16, and 17 are adopted. The last two stanzas are reversed. Three words are altered:

10. kinsmen] kinsman	23. Demurral] demurrer
12. Garland be] Garlanded	

650

Pain – has an Element of Blank –
It cannot recollect
When it begun – or if there were
A time when it was not –

[501]

It has no Future – but itself –
It's Infinite contain
It's Past – enlightened to perceive
New Periods – of Pain.

4. time] Day –

MANUSCRIPT: About 1862, in packet 11 (H 52b).
PUBLICATION: *Poems* (1890), 33, titled "The Mystery of Pain." The
suggested change is adopted. There are two alterations:

3. begun] began   6. Infinite contain] infinite realms
contain

651

So much Summer
Me for showing
Illegitimate –
Would a Smile's minute bestowing
Too exorbitant

To the Lady
With the Guinea
Look – if She should know
Crumb of Mine
A Robin's Larder
Would suffice to stow –

5. exorbitant] extravagant –/ impor-　　　7. Guinea] [Guinea]s
tunate –　　　　　　　　　　　　　　　　11. Would] Could –

MANUSCRIPT: About 1862, in packet 11 (H 52c).
PUBLICATION: *BM* (1945), 109. The text derives from a transcript
made by Mrs. Todd. The lines are printed as two quatrains. The second
of the suggested changes for line 5 is adopted; so also is the suggested
change for line 11.

A Prison gets to be a friend –
Between it's Ponderous face
And Our's – a Kinsmanship express –
And in it's narrow Eyes –

We come to look with gratitude
For the appointed Beam
It deal us – stated as our food –
And hungered for – the same –

We learn to know the Planks –
That answer to Our feet –
So miserable a sound – at first –
Nor even now – so sweet –

As plashing in the Pools –
When Memory was a Boy –
But a Demurer Circuit –
A Geometric Joy –

The Posture of the Key
That interrupt the Day
To Our Endeavor – Not so real
The Cheek of Liberty –

As this Phantasm Steel –
Whose features – Day and Night –
Are present to us – as Our Own –
And as escapeless – quite –

The narrow Round – the Stint –
The slow exchange of Hope –
For something passiver – Content
Too steep for looking up –

The Liberty we knew
Avoided – like a Dream –
Too wide for any Night but Heaven –
If That – indeed – redeem –

3. express] exist – / subsist – / arise –
5. gratitude] fondness – / pleasure
7. deal us] furnish
15. Circuit] Measure –
19. real] true – / close – / near

21. Phantasm] Companion
30. like] As
32. That – indeed – redeem –] Even
    That – redeem –

MANUSCRIPT: About 1862, in packet 19 (H 103a).
PUBLICATION: *FP* (1929), 21–22. Two suggested changes are adopted:

3. exist   21. Companion

The text is arranged as four eight-line stanzas. Three words are altered:

3. exist] exists   18. interrupt] interrupts
7. deal] deals

653

Of Being is a Bird
The likest to the Down
An Easy Breeze do put afloat
The General Heavens – upon –

It soars – and shifts – and whirls –
And measures with the Clouds
In easy – even – dazzling pace –
No different the Birds –

Except a Wake of Music
Accompany their feet –
As did the Down emit a Tune –
For Extasy – of it

11. did] should

MANUSCRIPT: About 1862, in packet 19 (H 105a).
PUBLICATION: *FP* (1929), 20. The suggested change is adopted. The
following alterations are made:

1] A bird is of all beings   7. even] ever
2. Down] dawn   11. Down] Dawn
3. do] does

[504]

The text is correctly published in *AB* (1945), 386, from a transcript of the
packet copy made by Mrs. Todd. The suggested change is adopted.

654

A long – long Sleep – A famous – Sleep –
That makes no show for Morn –
By Stretch of Limb – or stir of Lid –
An independant One –

Was ever idleness like This?
Upon a Bank of Stone
To bask the Centuries away –
Nor once look up – for Noon?

1. long – long] vast – vast – / Brave –   5. idleness] Arrogance
   Brave –   6] Within a Hut of Stone –

MANUSCRIPT: About 1862, in packet 19 (H 105b).
PUBLICATION: *Poems* (1896), 197, titled "Sleeping." The suggested
change for line 6 is adopted. One word is altered:

2. Morn] dawn

655

Without this – there is nought –
All other Riches be
As is the Twitter of a Bird –
Heard opposite the Sea –

I could not care – to gain
A lesser than the Whole –
For did not this include themself –
As Seams – include the Ball?

I wished a way might be
My Heart to subdivide –
'Twould magnify – the Gratitude –
And not reduce – the Gold –

4. Heard] Held   9. way] sort

MANUSCRIPT: About 1862, in packet 19 (H 105c).
PUBLICATION: *UP* (1935), 97. The suggested changes are rejected.
Three words are altered:

3. a] the   9. I] Or
7. themself] themselves

656

The name – of it – is "Autumn" –
The hue – of it – is Blood –
An Artery – upon the Hill –
A Vein – along the Road –

Great Globules – in the Alleys –
And Oh, the Shower of Stain –
When Winds – upset the Basin –
And spill the Scarlet Rain –

It sprinkles Bonnets – far below –
It gathers ruddy Pools –
Then – eddies like a Rose – away –
Upon Vermillion Wheels –

8. spill] tip –   10. gathers ruddy] makes Vermillion –
10. gathers] stands in –   12] And leaves me with the Hills.

MANUSCRIPT: About 1862, in packet 19 (H 105d).
PUBLICATION: It first appeared in *Youth's Companion*, LXV (8 September 1892), 448, titled "Autumn." The text there used presumably was supplied by Mrs. Todd, and the suggested change for line 12 is adopted. It is also in *BM* (1945), 38, derived from a transcript made by Mrs. Todd. The transcript, though it does not note the suggested changes for lines 8 and 10, records that for line 12. In *BM* the suggested change is rejected.

657

I dwell in Possibility –
A fairer House than Prose –
More numerous of Windows –
Superior – for Doors –

Of Chambers as the Cedars –
Impregnable of Eye –
And for an Everlasting Roof
The Gambrels of the Sky –

Of Visiters – the fairest –
For Occupation – This –
The spreading wide my narrow Hands
To gather Paradise –

8. Gambrels] Gables –

MANUSCRIPT: About 1862, in packet 19 (H 106a).
PUBLICATION: *FP* (1929), 30. The suggested change is adopted. One word is altered:

4. for] of

658

Whole Gulfs – of Red, and Fleets – of Red –
And Crews – of solid Blood –
Did place about the West – Tonight –
As 'twere specific Ground –

And They – appointed Creatures –
In Authorized Arrays –
Due – promptly – as a Drama –
That bows – and disappears –

4. specific] a signal Ground –

MANUSCRIPT: About 1862, in packet 19 (H 106c).
PUBLICATION: *BM* (1945), 23–24. The text derives from a transcript made by Mrs. Todd; the suggested change is adopted.

659

That first Day, when you praised Me, Sweet,
And said that I was strong –
And could be mighty, if I liked –
That Day – the Days among –

[507]

Glows Central – like a Jewel
Between Diverging Golds –
The Minor One – that gleamed behind –
And Vaster – of the World's.

7. gleamed] shone   8. Vaster] this One – / different –

MANUSCRIPT: About 1862, in packet 19 (H 106e).
PUBLICATION: *UP* (1935), 92. The suggested changes are rejected.
One word is altered:

8. Vaster] Master

660

'Tis good – the looking back on Grief –
To re-endure a Day –
We thought the Mighty Funeral –
Of All Conceived Joy –

To recollect how Busy Grass
Did meddle – one by one –
Till all the Grief with Summer – waved
And none could see the stone.

And though the Wo you have Today
Be larger – As the Sea
Exceeds it's Unremembered Drop –
They're Water – equally –

1. good] well   7. waved] blew –
3. Mighty] monstrous   11. Unremembered] Undeveloped
6. meddle] tamper   12] They prove One Chemistry –

MANUSCRIPT: About 1862, in packet 19 (H 107b).
PUBLICATION: *UP* (1935), 116. The suggested changes for lines 1 and
12 are adopted. One line is altered:

4. Conceived] conceived by

[508]

Could I but ride indefinite
As doth the Meadow Bee
And visit only where I liked
And No one visit me

And flirt all Day with Buttercups
And marry whom I may
And dwell a little everywhere
Or better, run away

With no Police to follow
Or chase Him if He do
Till He should jump Peninsulas
To get away from me –

I said "But just to be a Bee"
Upon a Raft of Air
And row in Nowhere all Day long
And anchor "off the Bar"

What Liberty! So Captives deem
Who tight in Dungeons are.

7. everywhere] generally

MANUSCRIPT: About 1862, in packet 88 (Bingham 49a).
PUBLICATION: *Poems* (1896), 124. The suggested change is rejected.
The following words are altered:

4. one] man 11. He] I
10. Him if He do] me if I do 12. me] you

The final couplet is attached to the preceding quatrain.

662

Embarrassment of one another
And God
Is Revelation's limit,
Aloud   [*no stanza break*]

Is nothing that is chief,
But still,
Divinity dwells under seal.

3. limit] caution

MANUSCRIPT: About 1862, in packet 88 (Bingham 49b).
PUBLICATION: *BM* (1945), 249. The suggested change is adopted.

663

Again – his voice is at the door –
I feel the old *Degree* –
I hear him ask the servant
For such an one – as me –

I take a *flower* – as I go –
My face to *justify* –
He never *saw* me – *in this life* –
I might *surprise* his eye!

I cross the Hall with *mingled* steps –
I – silent – pass the door –
I look on all this world *contains* –
Just his face – nothing more!

We talk in *careless* – and in *toss* –
A kind of *plummet* strain –
Each – sounding – shily –
Just – how – deep –
The *other's* one – had been –

We *walk* – I leave my Dog – at home –
A *tender* – *thoughtful* Moon
Goes with us – just a little way –
And – then – we are *alone* –

Alone – if *Angels* are "alone" –
First time they *try* the *sky!*   [*no stanza break*]

[510]

Alone – if those "vailed faces" – be –
We cannot *count* – on High!

I'd give – to live that hour – *again* –
The *purple* – *in my Vein* –
But *He* must *count the drops* – *himself* –
My price for *every stain*!

8. *surprise*] not please
10. silent] speechless
13. *careless*] venture
17. one] foot

18. at home] behind
25] That murmur so – chant so – far –
28. must] should

MANUSCRIPT: About 1862, in packet 89 (Bingham 59d).
PUBLICATION: *BM* (1945), 142–143. The italics are not reproduced. Stanza 4 is regularized into a quatrain. The suggested changes for lines 13, 17, 18 are adopted.

<h2 style="text-align:center">664</h2>

Of all the Souls that stand create –
I have elected – One –
When Sense from Spirit – files away –
And Subterfuge – is done –
When that which is – and that which was –
Apart – intrinsic – stand –
And this brief Tragedy of Flesh –
Is shifted – like a Sand –
When Figures show their royal Front –
And Mists – are carved away,
Behold the Atom – I preferred –
To all the lists of Clay!

7. Tragedy of Flesh] *Drama in the flesh*

MANUSCRIPT: About 1862 (Bingham 98–3–21).
PUBLICATION: *Poems* (1891), 89, titled "Choice." The suggested change is rejected. The text is arranged as three quatrains.

665

Dropped into the Ether Acre –
Wearing the Sod Gown –
Bonnet of Everlasting Laces –
Brooch – frozen on –

Horses of Blonde – and Coach of Silver –
Baggage a strapped Pearl –
Journey of Down – and Whip of Diamond –
Riding to meet the Earl –

MANUSCRIPTS: There are two, identical in text, and both written about 1863. The copy reproduced above is in packet 18 (H 101c). In line 6 ED substituted "a" in pencil for "of," which she crossed out. The second copy (H 247) is addressed "Sue" and signed "Emily."

> Dropped into the Ether Acre!
> Wearing the Sod Gown –
> Bonnet of Everlasting laces –
> Brooch – frozen on!
> Horses of Blonde –
> And Coach – of Silver –
> Baggage – a Strapped Pearl!
> Journey of Down –
> And Whip of Diamond –
> Riding to meet the Earl!

PUBLICATION: *SH* (1914), 79. The text derives from the copy to Sue. The first line is arranged as two lines.

666

Ah, Teneriffe!
Retreating Mountain!
Purples of Ages – pause for *you* –

Sunset – reviews her Sapphire Regiment –
Day – drops you her Red Adieu!

Still – Clad in your Mail of ices –
Thigh of Granite – and thew – of Steel –
Heedless – alike – of pomp – or parting

[512]

Ah, Teneriffe!
I'm kneeling – still –

MANUSCRIPTS: There are two, both written about 1863. The copy reproduced above (H 226) is addressed "Sue" and signed "Emily –." It is a variant of the copy in packet 18 (H 101d):

> Ah, Teneriffe – Receding Mountain –
> Purples of Ages halt for You –
> Sunset reviews Her Sapphire Regiments –
> Day – drops You His Red Adieu –
> Still clad in Your Mail of Ices –
> Eye of Granite – and Ear of Steel –
> Passive alike – to Pomp – and Parting –
> Ah, Teneriffe – We're pleading still –

The great peak of the chain of volcanic mountains that traverse the largest of the Canary Islands rises to a height of 12,200 feet. The view from the highest point takes in the whole archipelago, with the horizon some 140 miles distant.

PUBLICATION: *SH* (1914), 37. The text is a composite of the two versions and a new line arrangement has been created. One word is altered:

2. Purples] Purple

667

Bloom upon the Mountain – stated –
Blameless of a Name –
Efflorescence of a Sunset –
Reproduced – the same –

Seed, had I, my Purple Sowing
Should endow the Day –
Not a Tropic of a Twilight –
Show itself away –

Who for tilling – to the Mountain
Come, and disappear –
Whose be Her Renown, or fading,
Witness, is not here –

[513]

While I state – the Solemn Petals,
Far as North – and East,
Far as South and West – expanding –
Culminate – in Rest –

And the Mountain to the Evening
Fit His Countenance –
Indicating, by no Muscle –
The Experience –

MANUSCRIPTS: There are two, both written about 1863. The copy reproduced above (H 240) was sent to Sue. The copy in packet 12 (H 59a) proposes several alternative readings of which ED selected only two (for lines 6 and 20) when she prepared the fair copy for Sue:

Bloom upon the Mountain stated –
Blameless of a name –
Efflorescence of a Sunset –
Reproduced – the same –

Seed had I, my Purple Sowing
Should address the Day –
Not – a Tropic of a Twilight –
Show itself away –

Who for tilling – to the Mountain
Come – and disappear –
Whose be her Renown – or fading –
Witness is not here –

While I state – the Solemn Petals –
Far as North – and East –
Far as South – and West Expanding –
Culminate – in Rest –

And the Mountain to the Evening
Fit His Countenance –
Indicating by no Muscle
His Experience –

3] Flower of a Single Sunset –
6. address] endow – / reward
7. Tropic] Manner
8. Show] shift
11. her] this

15. Expanding] disclosing
18. Fit] Strain
19. Muscle] feature
20. His] the –

PUBLICATION: *SH* (1914), 51–52. It follows the copy to Sue. One word is altered:

7. a twilight] the twilight

668

"Nature" is what we see –
The Hill – the Afternoon –
Squirrel – Eclipse – the Bumble bee –
Nay – Nature is Heaven –
Nature is what we hear –
The Bobolink – the Sea –
Thunder – the Cricket –
Nay – Nature is Harmony –
Nature is what we know –
Yet have no art to say –
So impotent Our Wisdom is
To her Simplicity

MANUSCRIPTS: There are two, both written about 1863. The fair copy reproduced above (H 293), signed "Emily," was probably sent to Sue. It is a redaction of the semifinal copy in packet 22 (H 119c):

"Nature" is what We see –
The Hill – the Afternoon –
Squirrel – Eclipse – the Bumblebee –
Nay – Nature is Heaven –

"Nature" is what We hear –
The Bobolink – the Sea –
Thunder – the Cricket –
Nay – Nature is Harmony –

"Nature" is what We know –
But have no Art to say –
So impotent Our Wisdom is
To Her Sincerity –

8. Harmony] Melody   11. is] be –

ED adopted neither of the suggested changes in her fair copy; she introduced variants in lines 10 and 12.

PUBLICATION: *SH* (1914), 36. It follows the packet copy in stanza division and the use of "But" in line 10, but adopts "simplicity" (line 12) from the fair copy. Neither suggested change is adopted.

669

No Romance sold unto
Could so enthrall a Man
As the perusal of
His Individual One –
'Tis Fiction's – to dilute to Plausibility
Our Novel – When 'tis small enough
To Credit – 'Tis'nt true!

MANUSCRIPTS: The copy reproduced above (H 296) was written about 1863, addressed "Sue –" and signed "Emily –." The copy in packet 84 (Bingham 20b) was written early in 1862. It is arranged as two stanzas, the second of which suggests four alternative readings none of which is adopted in the fair copy to Sue:

No Romance sold unto
Could so enthrall a Man –
As the perusal of
His individual One –

'Tis Fiction's – to dilute to plausibility
Our – Novel – When 'tis small eno'
To credit – 'Tis'nt true –

5. dilute] contract	6. Novel] Romance	
5. plausibility] credibility	7. credit] compass	

PUBLICATION: *SH* (1914), 14. The text derives from the copy to Sue and is printed as an eight-line stanza.

670

One need not be a Chamber – to be Haunted –
One need not be a House –
The Brain has Corridors – surpassing
Material Place –

Far safer, of a Midnight Meeting
External Ghost
Than it's interior Confronting –
That Cooler Host.

Far safer, through an Abbey gallop,
The Stones a'chase –
Than Unarmed, one's a'self encounter –
In lonesome Place –

Ourself behind ourself, concealed –
Should startle most –
Assassin hid in our Apartment
Be Horror's least.

The Body – borrows a Revolver –
He bolts the Door –
O'erlooking a superior spectre –
Or More –

Manuscripts: There are two. The fair copy reproduced above (H 304), written about 1863, and signed "Emily –," was sent to Sue. An earlier semifinal draft, in packet 13 (H 65a), was written about 1862:

One need not be a Chamber – to be Haunted –
One need not be a House –
The Brain – has Corridors surpassing
Material Place –

Far safer of a Midnight – meeting
External Ghost –
Than an Interior – Confronting –
That cooler – Host.

Far safer, through an Abbey – gallop –
The Stones a'chase –
Than Moonless – One's A'self encounter –
In lonesome place –

Ourself – behind Ourself – Concealed –
Should startle – most –
Assassin – hid in our Apartment –
Be Horror's least –

[517]

The Prudent – carries a Revolver –
He bolts the Door –
O'erlooking a Superior Spectre –
More near –

4. Material] Corporeal
8] That Whiter Host.
17. The Prudent] The Body
17. a] the

19–20] A Spectre – infinite – accom-
    panying –
    He fails to fear –
19–20] Maintaining a Superior
    Spectre –
    None saw –

Of the many suggested changes in the packet copy, ED adopted only
"Body" (line 17) in the fair copy. But she made four other changes not
previously indicated:

7. an] it's
11. Moonless] Unarmed

17. carries] borrows
20] Or More

PUBLICATION: *Poems* (1891), 214–215, titled "Ghosts." The text de-
rives from the packet copy and adopts the suggested change for line 8.
In line 11 "A'self" is regularized to "own self." Both autographs are repro-
duced in facsimile in *Harvard Library Bulletin*, VII (1953), between pages
260 and 261.

671

She dwelleth in the Ground –
Where Daffodils – abide –
Her Maker – Her Metropolis –
The Universe – Her Maid –

To fetch Her Grace – and Hue –
And Fairness – and Renown –
The Firmament's – To Pluck Her –
And fetch Her Thee – be mine –

MANUSCRIPTS: There are two, both written about 1863. The copy re-
produced above (H 99b) is in packet 18. The other copy (H 311) is
addressed "Sue –" and signed "Emily." It is identical in text with the
packet copy; it lacks internal punctuation in lines 2 and 5, and "Fairness"
(line 6) is not capitalized.

PUBLICATION: *BM* (1945), 332. The text derives from a transcript made by Mrs. Todd. One word is altered:

5. Hue] awe

The comment accompanying it reads: "With a crocus."

672

The Future – never spoke –
Nor will He – like the Dumb –
Reveal by sign – a syllable
Of His Profound To Come –

But when the News be ripe –
Presents it – in the Act –
Forestalling Preparation –
Escape – or Substitute –

Indifferent to Him –
The Dower – as the Doom –
His Office – but to execute
Fate's – Telegram – to Him –

MANUSCRIPTS: There are two. The copy reproduced above (H 336) is addressed "Sue –" and signed "Emily –"; it is a redaction, evidently written sometime during 1863, of the copy below in packet 5 (H 20a), written about 1862.

The Future never spoke –
Nor will he like the Dumb
Report by Sign a Circumstance
Of his profound To Come –

But when the News be ripe
Presents it in the Act –
Forestalling Preparation –
Escape – or Substitute –

Indifferent to him
The Dower – as the Doom –
His Office but to execute
Fate's Telegram – to Him –

[519]

3] Reveal by sign a Syllable –   4. profound] Opaque –

In her fair copy ED adopted her suggested change for line 3 but not the one for line 4.

PUBLICATION: *SH* (1914), 33. The text, lacking stanza division, derives from the copy to Sue. One word is altered:

3. a] or

673

The Love a Life can show Below
Is but a filament, I know,
Of that diviner thing
That faints upon the face of Noon –
And smites the Tinder in the Sun –
And hinders Gabriel's Wing –

'Tis this – in Music – hints and sways –
And far abroad on Summer days –
Distils uncertain pain –
'Tis this enamors in the East –
And tints the Transit in the West
With harrowing Iodine –

'Tis this – invites – appalls – endows –
Flits – glimmers – proves – dissolves –
Returns – suggests – convicts – enchants –
Then – flings in Paradise –

MANUSCRIPTS: There are two, both written early in 1863. The copy reproduced above is in packet 22 (H 123a). The copy below (Bingham 98–4A–15), evidently sent to Sue, is headed "*Excuse* me – Dollie –" and is signed "Emily."

The Love a Child can show – below –
Is but a Filament – I know –
Of that Diviner – Thing –
That faints upon the face of Noon –
And smites the Tinder in the Sun –
And hinders – Gabriel's – Wing!

[520]

'Tis This – in Music – hints – and sways –
And far abroad – on Summer Days –
Distils – uncertain – pain –
'Tis This – afflicts us in the East –
And tints the Transit in the West –
With Harrowing – Iodine!

'Tis This – invites – appalls – endows –
Flits – glimmers – proves – dissolves –
Returns – suggests – convicts – enchants –
Then – flings in Paradise!

Two lines are variant:

1. Life] Child   10. enamors] afflicts us

PUBLICATION: *FP* (1929), 147. The text derives from the packet copy. The text, arranged as two stanzas of 9 and 18 lines, is correctly rendered in later collections.

674

The Soul that hath a Guest
Doth seldom go abroad –
Diviner Crowd at Home –
Obliterate the need –

And Courtesy forbid
A Host's departure when
Upon Himself be visiting
The Emperor of Men –

MANUSCRIPTS: There are two. The fair copy reproduced above (Yale), addressed "Sue" and signed "Emily –," was written about 1863. It is a redaction of an earlier semifinal copy in packet 84 (Bingham 20d), written in 1862:

The Soul that hath a Guest,
Doth seldom go abroad –
Diviner Crowd at Home,
Obliterate the need –

[521]

And Courtesy forbids
The Host's departure – when
Upon Himself – be visiting
The Mightiest – of Men –

3. at Home] within   8] The Emperor of Men –

ED adopted in the fair copy her alternative reading in line 8, and changed
two other words:

5. forbids] forbid   6. The] A

PUBLICATION: *SH* (1914), 4. The text derives from the fair copy to
Sue, printed without stanza division. The same text is reproduced in *LL*
(1924), 194, among the poems sent to Sue. In *CP* (1924) and later collec-
tions, one word is altered:

1. hath] has

675

Essential Oils – are wrung –
The Attar from the Rose
Be not expressed by Suns – alone –
It is the gift of Screws –

The General Rose – decay –
But this – in Lady's Drawer
Make Summer – When the Lady lie
In Ceaseless Rosemary –

MANUSCRIPTS: There are two, both written about 1863. The copy re-
produced above (H 133d) is in packet 24. A second copy signed "Emily –"
(H 249) was sent to Sue:

Essential Oils are wrung –
The Attar from the Rose
Is not expressed by Suns – alone –
It is the gift of Screws –
The General Rose decay –
While this – in Lady's Drawer
Make Summer, when the Lady lie
In Spiceless Sepulchre.

It is variant in lines 3, 6, and 8.

PUBLICATION: *Poems* (1891), 210. The text derives from the packet copy. Four words are altered:

3. Be] Is   7. Make] Makes
5. decay] decays   7. lie] lies

676

Least Bee that brew –
A Honey's Weight
The Summer multiply –
Content Her smallest fraction help
The Amber Quantity –

MANUSCRIPTS: The version above is reproduced from packet 81 (Bingham 8b), written about 1863. Another copy (H B 180), written at the same time, was evidently sent to Sue. The bottom third of the sheet, containing the last line, is missing. One word is a variant:

2. Weight] Worth

In other ways the texts are identical, except that "brew" is capitalized.

PUBLICATION: *BM* (1945), 70. It follows the text of the packet copy. Lines 1 and 2 are arranged as one line.

677

To be alive – is Power –
Existence – in itself –
Without a further function –
Omnipotence – Enough –

To be alive – and Will!
'Tis able as a God –
The Maker – of Ourselves – be what –
Such being Finitude!

MANUSCRIPTS: The copy reproduced above is in packet 81 (Bingham 7e), written about 1863. The copy to Sue (H 362), written about the same time, is signed "Emily –":

To be alive, is power –
Existence – in itself –
Without a further function –
Omnipotence – Enough –
To be alive and Will –
'Tis able as a God –
The Further of Ourselves, be what –
Such being Finitude?

One word is a variant:

7. Maker] Further

PUBLICATION: *SH* (1914), 11. It derives from the copy to Sue with the text arranged as two quatrains.

678

Wolfe demanded during dying
"Which obtain the Day"?
"General, the British" – "Easy"
Answered Wolfe "to die"

Montcalm, his opposing Spirit
Rendered with a smile
"Sweet" said he "my own Surrender
Liberty's beguile"

MANUSCRIPTS: There are three. The fair copy reproduced above (Bingham 98–4A–23) was written about 1866. It is a variant of the earliest copy (H 166a), in packet 31, written about 1863:

Wolfe demanded during Dying
"Which controlled the Day?"
"General – the British" – "Easy"
Answered He – "to die" –

Montcalm – His opposing Spirit –
Rendered with a smile –
"Sweet" said He, "my own Surrender
Liberty's – forestall – "

The third copy (H 379), signed "Emily – ," was written about the same time as the packet copy and probably was sent to Sue. It too is a variant:

"Wolfe" demanded during Dying
"Which Control the Day"?
"General, the British" – "Easy"
Answered Wolfe, "to die" –

"Montcalm," his opposing Spirit
Rendered with a smile –
"Sweet," said he – My own Surrender
Liberty's forestall" –

PUBLICATION: *BM* (1945), 130. Mrs. Bingham had at hand Mrs. Todd's transcript of the packet copy version as well as the 1866 autograph. Her text supplies "controlled" (line 2) and "forestall" (line 8) from Mrs. Todd's transcript, and "Wolfe" (line 4) from the version of 1866.

679

Conscious am I in my Chamber,
Of a shapeless friend –
He doth not attest by Posture –
Nor Confirm – by Word –

Neither Place – need I present Him –
Fitter Courtesy
Hospitable intuition
Of His Company –

Presence – is His furthest license –
Neither He to Me
Nor Myself to Him – by Accent –
Forfeit Probity –

Weariness of Him, were quainter
Than Monotony
Knew a Particle – of Space's
Vast Society –

Neither if He visit Other –
Do He dwell – or Nay – know I –
But Instinct esteem Him
Immortality –

19. esteem Him] Report Him

[525]

MANUSCRIPTS: The copy reproduced above, in packet 12 (H 55a), is supplemented in part by a penciled copy (H 297) sent to Sue, signed "Emily." Both were written about 1863. Evidently the first page of the copy to Sue is missing, for the existing page begins at line 11:

> Nor myself to Him, by accent
> Forfeit probity.
> Weariness of Him, were quainter
> Than Monotony
> Knew a particle, of Space's
> Vast society –
> Neither if He visit other –
> Do He dwell or nay
> Know I – just instinct esteem Him
> Immortality –

ED rejects her suggested change. One word is variant:

> 19. But] just

PUBLICATION: FP (1929), 117. The suggested change is adopted but altered. The last stanza reads:

> Neither if he visit Other –
> Does he dwell — or nay —
> Know I,
> But instinct reports Him
> Immortality.

In later collections the final stanza is arranged as a quatrain.

680

Each Life Converges to some Centre –
Expressed – or still –
Exists in every Human Nature
A Goal –

Embodied scarcely to itself – it may be –
Too fair
For Credibility's presumption
To mar –

Adored with caution – as a Brittle Heaven –
To reach
Were hopeless, as the Rainbow's Raiment
To touch –

Yet persevered toward – surer – for the Distance –
How high –
Unto the Saints' slow diligence –
The Sky –

Ungained – it may be – by a Life's low Venture –
But then –
Eternity enable the endeavoring
Again.

5. Embodied] Admitted
7. presumption / To mar] temerity to
   dare –
9. Adored] Beheld

11. the] a
13. surer] stricter –
15. diligence] industry
17. by] in –

MANUSCRIPTS: The copy reproduced above, written about 1863, is in packet 22 (H 120b). ED sent a fair copy (H 368) of the final stanza to Sue, written at the same time in pencil:

> Ungained – it may be
> By a Life's low Venture –
> But then
> Eternity enable the endeavoring
> Again.
> Springfield

The selection of the stanza, placed as it is over the signature "Springfield," suggests that ED is commiserating with Sue that she has been unexpectedly prevented from going to Springfield, perhaps to visit the Bowleses.

PUBLICATION: *Poems* (1891), 58–59, titled "The Goal." The suggested changes for lines 5 and 7 are adopted. One word is altered:

19. enable] enables

The copy to Sue is not published.

Soil of Flint, if steady tilled –
Will refund the Hand –
Seed of Palm, by Lybian Sun
Fructified in Sand –

MANUSCRIPTS: There are two, both written about 1863. The copy re-
produced above (H 316) was sent to Sue and is signed "Emily." The copy
in packet 30 (H 164a) is a semifinal draft and consists of two stanzas:

On the Bleakness of my Lot
Bloom I strove to raise –
Late – My Garden of a Rock –
Yielded Grape – and Maise –

Soil of Flint, if steady tilled
Will refund the Hand –
Seed of Palm, by Lybian Sun
Fructified in Sand –

3. Garden of] Acre of   6. refund] reward – / repay –
5. steady tilled] steadfast tilled

All suggested changes are rejected in the stanza of the fair copy sent to Sue.
PUBLICATION: *Poems* (1896), 41. It follows the text of the packet copy
and adopts the suggested changes, selecting "reward" for line 6.

'Twould ease – a Butterfly –
Elate – a Bee –
Thou'rt neither –
Neither – thy capacity –

But, Blossom, were I,
I would rather be
Thy moment
Than a Bee's Eternity –

Content of fading
Is enough for me –
Fade I unto Divinity –

And Dying – Lifetime –
Ample as the Eye –
Her least attention raise on me –

MANUSCRIPTS: The copy reproduced above, in packet 81 (Bingham
11b), was written late in 1863 or early in 1864. The final six lines, arranged
as a quatrain, are in a penciled draft (H 242) written at the same time.
They may have been sent to Sue:

> Content of fading is enough for me
> Fade I unto Divinity –
> And Dying – Lifetime – ample as the eye
> Her least attention raise on me.

PUBLICATION: *BM* (1945), 169. The commas before and after "Blos-
som" (line 5), which indicate direct address, are omitted.

683

The Soul unto itself
Is an imperial friend –
Or the most agonizing Spy –
An Enemy – could send –

Secure against it's own –
No treason it can fear –
Itself – it's Sovreign – of itself
The Soul should stand in Awe –

MANUSCRIPTS: There are three fair copies. The copy reproduced above,
in packet 16 (H 88b), was written about 1862. A second copy (Bingham),
signed "Emily –," was sent to an unidentified recipient about 1862. It is
without stanza division but is identical in text. It differs in form only in that
line 3 lacks punctuation and the last word of the poem is not capitalized. A
third copy (BPL Higg 16) was enclosed in a letter to T. W. Higginson
(BPL Higg 56) written in April 1863. One variant is introduced:

8. stand] be

It is otherwise identical with the packet copy except that it entirely lacks
punctuation.

PUBLICATION: *Poems* (1891), 37. It derives from the text of the packet copy.

684

Best Gains—must have the Losses' Test—
To constitute them—Gains—

MANUSCRIPT: About April 1863, in a letter to T. W. Higginson (BPL Higg 56).
PUBLICATION: The letter was first published in *Atlantic Monthly*, LXVIII (October 1891), 449, in an article which Higginson wrote dealing with the letters and poems he had received from ED. It is included in *Letters* (ed. 1894), 309; (ed. 1931), 279; also *LL* (1924), 248.

685

Not "Revelation"—'tis—that waits,
But our unfurnished eyes—

MANUSCRIPT: About April 1863, in a letter to T. W. Higginson (BPL Higg 56). A copy, now lost, was sent to Sue, who made a transcript (H ST 22a).
PUBLICATION: The letter was first published in *Atlantic Monthly*, LXVIII (October 1891), 449, in an article which Higginson wrote dealing with the letters and poems he had received from ED. It is included in *Letters* (ed. 1894), 309; (ed. 1931), 279; also *LL* (1924), 248.

686

They say that "Time assuages"—
Time never did assuage—
An actual suffering strengthens
As Sinews do, with age—

Time is a Test of Trouble—
But not a Remedy—
If such it prove, it prove too
There was no Malady—

MANUSCRIPTS: The copy reproduced above was written late in 1863 in packet 30 (H 163c). A second copy of the second stanza only is incorporated in a letter (BPL Higg 60) to T. W. Higginson, postmarked 9 June 1866. It is identical in text with packet copy; in form it differs only in that capitals are retained only for the initial words of lines, and that the quatrain concludes with a period.

PUBLICATION: The two quatrains were first published in the *Independent*, XLVIII (21 May 1896), 1, titled "Time's Healing." They were sent to the magazine by Mrs. Todd and derived from a transcript she had previously made of the packet copy. They were also included in *Poems* (1896), 141, without title. The stanza to Higginson is in *Letters* (ed. 1931 only), 283.

687

I'll send the feather from my Hat!
Who knows – but at the sight of *that*
My Sovreign will relent?
As trinket – worn by faded Child –
Confronting eyes long – comforted –
Blisters the Adamant!

MANUSCRIPT: About 1861 (Bingham). It is signed "Emily –" and addressed "Mr Bowles –."

PUBLICATION: *Letters* (ed. 1894), 214; (ed. 1931), 202; also *LL* (1924), 248.

688

"*Speech*" – is a prank of *Parliament* –
"*Tears*" – a trick of the *nerve* –
But the Heart with the heaviest freight on –
Does'nt – always – move –

MANUSCRIPT: About 1862 (Bingham). The lines are incorporated in a letter to Samuel Bowles. A second copy identical in text, now lost, was sent to the Norcross cousins. Frances Norcross supplied a transcript of it to Lavinia Dickinson in 1891.

PUBLICATION: The letter to Bowles is in *Letters* (ed. 1894), 210–211; (ed. 1931), 200; also *LL* (1924), 244. One word is altered:

4. move] swerve.

The Norcross transcript is in *AB* (1945), 147.

689

The Zeroes – taught us – Phosphorus –
We learned to like the Fire
By playing Glaciers – when a Boy –
And Tinder – guessed – by power
Of Opposite – to balance Odd –
If White – a Red – must be!
Paralysis – our Primer – dumb –
Unto Vitality!

MANUSCRIPTS: There are two, both written early in 1863. That reproduced above (Bingham) was sent to Samuel Bowles with ED's notation on the rear:

"I couldn't let Austin's note go – without a word – Emily."

It is a redaction of the semifinal draft in packet 22 (H 122c):

The Zeros taught Us – Phosphorus –
We learned to like the Fire
By handling Glaciers – when a Boy –
And Tinder – guessed – by power

Of Opposite – to equal Ought –
Eclipses – Suns – imply –
Paralysis – our Primer dumb
Unto Vitality –

7. dumb] numb –

In her fair copy she rejected the suggested change of the packet copy, and introduced new readings in lines 3, 5, and 6.

PUBLICATION: *Letters* (ed. 1894), 200; and *LL* (1924), 227, follow the text of the note to Bowles, arranged as two quatrains. A footnote gives the reading of line 6 in the packet copy. The footnote, slightly altered, is retained in *Letters* (ed. 1931), 191, but the stanza division is not retained. The packet copy furnishes the text in *FP* (1929), 201. It is without stanza division and the suggested change is adopted. The misreading "sums" (line 6) was later corrected to "suns."

690

Victory comes late –
And is held low to freezing lips –
Too rapt with frost
To take it –
How sweet it would have tasted –
Just a Drop –
Was God so economical?
His Table's spread too high for Us –
Unless We dine on tiptoe –
Crumbs – fit such little mouths –
Cherries – suit Robins –
The Eagle's Golden Breakfast strangles – Them –
God keep His Oath to Sparrows –
Who of little Love – know how to starve –

MANUSCRIPTS: The copy reproduced above, in packet 24 (H 132b), was written about 1863. It is a redaction perhaps, written some two years later, of the version which constitutes a letter (Hooker) written to Samuel Bowles in 1861. The letter has a salutation: "Dear Mr. Bowles." and is signed "Emily." The poem reads:

Victory comes late,
And is held low to freezing lips
Too rapt with frost
To mind it!
How sweet it would have tasted!
Just a drop!
Was God so economical?
His table's spread too high
Except we dine on tiptoe!
Crumbs fit such little mouths –
Cherries – suit *Robins* –   [*no stanza break*]

The Eagle's golden breakfast – *dazzles them!*
God keep his vow to "*Sparrows*",
Who of little love – know how to starve!

The letter is unpublished.

PUBLICATION: *Poems* (1891), 49. Lines 12 and 14 are printed as two lines each.

691

Would you like summer? Taste of ours.
Spices? Buy here!
Ill! We have berries, for the parching!
Weary! Furloughs of down!
Perplexed! Estates of violet trouble ne'er looked on!
Captive! We bring reprieve of roses!
Fainting! Flasks of air!
Even for Death, a fairy medicine.
But, which is it, sir?

No autograph copy of this poem is known. It is here reproduced from the published text where it concludes a letter to Samuel Bowles said to have been written in 1863.

PUBLICATION: *Letters* (ed. 1894), 214; (ed. 1931), 202; also *LL* (1924), 247.

692

The Sun kept setting – setting – still
No Hue of Afternoon –
Upon the Village I perceived –
From House to House 'twas Noon –

The Dusk kept dropping – dropping – still
No Dew upon the Grass –
But only on my Forehead stopped –
And wandered in my Face –

My Feet kept drowsing – drowsing – still
My fingers were awake –   [*no stanza break*]

Yet why so little sound – Myself
Unto my Seeming – make?

How well I knew the Light before –
I could not see it now –
'Tis Dying – I am doing – but
I'm not afraid to know –

MANUSCRIPT: About 1863, in packet 22 (H 118a).
PUBLICATION: *Poems* (1890), 136, titled "Dying."

693

Shells from the Coast mistaking –
I cherished them for All –
Happening in After Ages
To entertain a Pearl –

Wherefore so late – I murmured –
My need of Thee – be done –
Therefore – the Pearl responded –
My Period begin

MANUSCRIPT: About 1863, in packet 22 (H 118b).
PUBLICATION: *BM* (1945), 119. The text derives from a transcript
made by Mrs. Todd. The second stanza reads:

"Wherefore so late?" I murmured,
"My need of thee be done."
"Therefore," the pearl responded,
"My period begin."

694

The Heaven vests for Each
In that small Deity
It craved the grace to worship
Some bashful Summer's Day –

[535]

Half shrinking from the Glory
It importuned to see
Till these faint Tabernacles drop
In full Eternity —

How imminent the Venture —
As one should sue a Star —
For His mean sake to leave the Row
And entertain Despair —

A Clemency so common —
We almost cease to fear —
Enabling the minutest —
And furthest — to adore —

MANUSCRIPT: About 1863, in packet 22 (H 118c).
PUBLICATION: *UP* (1935), 420–421. A misprint, "vest" for "vests"
(line 1), is corrected in *Poems* (current).

695

As if the Sea should part
And show a further Sea —
And that — a further — and the Three
But a presumption be —

Of Periods of Seas —
Unvisited of Shores —
Themselves the Verge of Seas to be —
Eternity — is Those —

MANUSCRIPT: About 1863, in packet 22 (H 119b).
PUBLICATION: *London Mercury*, XIX (February 1929), 359; *FP* (1929),
192. The text is arranged as a single eight-line stanza. One word is altered:

8. Those] these

Their Hight in Heaven comforts not –
Their Glory – nought to me –
'Twas best imperfect – as it was –
I'm finite – I cant see –

The House of Supposition –
The Glimmering Frontier that
skirts the Acres of Perhaps –
To Me – shows insecure –

The Wealth I had – contented me –
If 'twas a meaner size –
Then I had counted it until
It pleased my narrow Eyes –

Better than larger values –
That show however true –
This timid life of Evidence
Keeps pleading – "I dont know."

MANUSCRIPT: Early 1863, in packet 22 (H 121a).
PUBLICATION: *Poems* (1891), 197. The last word of line 6 is printed
as the first of line 7. One line is altered:

14] However true their show

I could bring You Jewels – had I a mind to –
But You have enough – of those –
I could bring You Odors from St Domingo –
Colors – from Vera Cruz –

Berries of the Bahamas – have I –
But this little Blaze
Flickering to itself – in the Meadow –
Suits Me – more than those –

Never a Fellow matched this Topaz –
And his Emerald Swing –
Dower itself – for Bobadilo –
Better – Could I bring?

MANUSCRIPT: About 1863, in packet 22 (H 121b).
PUBLICATION: *BM* (1945), 328. The first stanza is divided into two.
The text derives from a transcript made by Mrs. Todd, and is followed by
the notation: "With jewelweed."

698

Life – is what we make it –
Death – We do not know –
Christ's acquaintance with Him
Justify Him – though –

He – would trust no stranger –
Other – could betray –
Just His own endorsement –
That – sufficeth Me –

All the other Distance
He hath traversed first –
No New Mile remaineth –
Far as Paradise –

His sure foot preceding –
Tender Pioneer –
Base must be the Coward
Dare not venture – now –

MANUSCRIPT: About 1863, in packet 22 (H 121c).
PUBLICATION: *FP* (1929), 106. Three words are altered:

4. Justify] Justifies   15. Coward] cowards
13. foot] feet

The Judge is like the Owl –
I've heard my Father tell –
And Owls do build in Oaks –
So here's an Amber Sill –

That slanted in my Path –
When going to the Barn –
And if it serve You for a House –
Itself is not in vain –

About the price – 'tis small –
I only ask a Tune
At Midnight – Let the Owl select
His favorite Refrain.

MANUSCRIPT: About 1863, in packet 22 (H 121d).
PUBLICATION: *BM* (1945), 74. The text derives from a transcript of
the packet copy made by Mrs. Todd.

You've seen Balloons set – Hav'nt You?
So stately they ascend –
It is as Swans – discarded You,
For Duties Diamond –

Their Liquid Feet go softly out
Upon a Sea of Blonde –
They spurn the Air, as 'twere too mean
For Creatures so renowned –

Their Ribbons just beyond the eye –
They struggle – some – for Breath –
And yet the Crowd applaud, below –
They would not encore – Death –

The Gilded Creature strains – and spins –
Trips frantic in a Tree –   [*no stanza break*]

Tears open her imperial Veins –
And tumbles in the Sea –

The Crowd – retire with an Oath –
The Dust in Streets – go down –
And Clerks in Counting Rooms
Observe – " 'Twas only a Balloon" –

MANUSCRIPT: About 1863, in packet 22 (H 122b).
PUBLICATION: *Poems* (1896), 128–129, titled "The Balloon." The first
word of line 20 is arranged as the last of line 19. Two words are altered:

    11. applaud] applauds   18. go] goes

701

A Thought went up my mind today –
That I have had before –
But did not finish – some way back –
I could not fix the Year –

Nor where it went – nor why it came
The second time to me –
Nor definitely, what it was –
Have I the Art to say –

But somewhere – in my Soul – I know –
I've met the Thing before –
It just reminded me – 'twas all –
And came my way no more –

MANUSCRIPT: About 1863, in packet 22 (H 122d).
PUBLICATION: *Poems* (1891), 42.

702

A first Mute Coming –
In the Stranger's House –
A first fair Going –
When the Bells rejoice –

A first Exchange – of
What hath mingled – been –
For Lot – exhibited to
Faith – alone –

MANUSCRIPT: About 1863, in packet 22 (H 123b). The story of Lot's entertaining strangers, who proved to be angels, is told in Genesis 19.

PUBLICATION: *UP* (1935), 139. The second stanza is altered to read:

> A first exchange
> Of what hath mingled firm
> For lot – exhibited
> To Faith alone.

703

Out of sight? What of that?
See the Bird – reach it!
Curve by Curve – Sweep by Sweep –
Round the Steep Air –
Danger! What is that to Her?
Better 'tis to fail – there –
Than debate – here –

Blue is Blue – the World through –
Amber – Amber – Dew – Dew –
Seek – Friend – and see –
Heaven is shy of Earth – that's all –
Bashful Heaven – thy Lovers small –
Hide – too – from thee –

MANUSCRIPT: About 1863, in packet 22 (H 123c).

PUBLICATION: *Saturday Review of Literature*, V (9 March 1929), 751; *FP* (1929), 66. Stanza 2 is arranged in seven lines. Three words are altered:

3. by . . . by] on . . . on   11. shy] sky

No matter – now – Sweet –
But when I'm Earl –
Wont you wish you'd spoken
To that dull Girl?

Trivial a Word – just –
Trivial – a Smile –
But wont you wish you'd spared one
When I'm Earl?

I shant need it – then –
Crests – will do –
Eagles on my Buckles –
On my Belt – too –

Ermine – my familiar Gown –
Say – Sweet – then
Wont you wish you'd smiled – just –
Me upon?

MANUSCRIPT: About 1863, in packet 22 (H 123d–124).

PUBLICATION: *BM* (1945), 161. The last word of line 15 is printed as
the first of line 16. The text derives from a transcript of the packet copy
made by Mrs. Todd.

Suspense – is Hostiler than Death –
Death – thosoever Broad,
Is just Death, and cannot increase –
Suspense – does not conclude –

But perishes – to live anew –
But just anew to die –
Annihilation – plated fresh
With Immortality –

MANUSCRIPT: About 1863, in packet 12 (H 55c).

PUBLICATION: *FP* (1929), 127. The text arranged without stanza division.

706

Life, and Death, and Giants –
Such as These – are still –
Minor – Apparatus – Hopper of the Mill –
Beetle at the Candle –
Or a Fife's Fame –
Maintain – by Accident that they proclaim –

MANUSCRIPT: About 1863, in packet 12 (H 56b).
PUBLICATION: *Poems* (1896), 54. It is printed as a seven-line stanza. Line 5 is altered to read:

> Or a fife's small fame.

707

The Grace – Myself – might not obtain –
Confer upon My flower –
Refracted but a Countenance –
For I – inhabit Her –

MANUSCRIPT: About 1863, in packet 12 (H 56d).
PUBLICATION: *UP* (1935), 61.

708

I sometimes drop it, for a Quick –
The Thought to be alive –
Anonymous Delight to know –
And Madder – to concieve –

Consoles a Wo so monstrous
That did it tear all Day,
Without an instant's Respite –
'Twould look too far – to Die –

[543]

Delirium – diverts the Wretch
For Whom the Scaffold neighs –
The Hammock's Motion lulls the Heads
So close on Paradise –

A Reef – crawled easy from the Sea
Eats off the Brittle Line –
The Sailor does'nt know the Stroke –
Until He's past the Pain –

MANUSCRIPT: About 1863, in packet 12 (H 58b).
PUBLICATION: *UP* (1935), 79. The spelling of "concieve" (line 4) is corrected. A misreading, "calls" for "lulls" (line 11), was corrected in *Poems* (current).

709

Publication – is the Auction
Of the Mind of Man –
Poverty – be justifying
For so foul a thing

Possibly – but We – would rather
From Our Garret go
White – Unto the White Creator –
Than invest – Our Snow –

Thought belong to Him who gave it –
Then – to Him Who bear
It's Corporeal illustration – Sell
The Royal Air –

In the Parcel – Be the Merchant
Of the Heavenly Grace –
But reduce no Human Spirit
To Disgrace of Price –

MANUSCRIPT: About 1863, in packet 12 (H 59b).
PUBLICATION: *FP* (1929), 4. There is no line spacing between stanzas

3 and 4. In later editions "Sell" (line 11) is placed as the first word of line 12. One word is altered:

9. belong] belongs

710

The Sunrise runs for Both –
The East – Her Purple Troth
Keeps with the Hill –
The Noon unwinds Her Blue
Till One Breadth cover Two –
Remotest – still –

Nor does the Night forget
A Lamp for Each – to set –
Wicks wide away –
The North – Her blazing Sign
Erects in Iodine –
Till Both – can see –

The Midnight's Dusky Arms
Clasp Hemispheres, and Homes
And so
Upon Her Bosom – One –
And One upon Her Hem –
Both lie –

MANUSCRIPT: About 1863, in packet 24 (H 131b).

PUBLICATION: *FP* (1929), 152. In the Centenary edition (1930) and later collections line 15 is printed as the conclusion of line 14. One word is altered:

11. Erects] Enacts

711

Strong Draughts of Their Refreshing Minds
To drink – enables Mine
Through Desert or the Wilderness
As bore it Sealed Wine –

[545]

To go elastic – Or as One
The Camel's trait – attained –
How powerful the Stimulus
Of an Hermetic Mind –

MANUSCRIPT: About 1863, in packet 24 (H 133b).
PUBLICATION: *FP* (1929), 13. The text is arranged as a nine-line stanza; in later collections, as a single eight-line stanza.

712

Because I could not stop for Death –
He kindly stopped for me –
The Carriage held but just Ourselves –
And Immortality.

We slowly drove – He knew no haste
And I had put away
My labor and my leisure too,
For His Civility –

We passed the School, where Children strove
At Recess – in the Ring –
We passed the Fields of Gazing Grain –
We passed the Setting Sun –

Or rather – He passed Us –
The Dews drew quivering and chill –
For only Gossamer, my Gown –
My Tippet – only Tulle –

We paused before a House that seemed
A Swelling of the Ground –
The Roof was scarcely visible –
The Cornice – in the Ground –

Since then – 'tis Centuries – and yet
Feels shorter than the Day
I first surmised the Horses Heads
Were toward Eternity –

MANUSCRIPT: About 1863, in packet 31 (H 165a).

PUBLICATION: *Poems* (1890), 138–139, titled "The Chariot." Stanza 4 is omitted. There are alterations in four lines:

9. strove] played	20. in the Ground] but a mound
10] Their lessons scarcely done	21. and yet] but each

When the poem was included in *CP* (1924) and later collections, the fourth stanza was still omitted. There are the same alterations in lines 9, 20, and 21, but line 10 is altered in a different way:

> At wrestling in a ring

713

Fame of Myself, to justify,
All other Plaudit be
Superfluous – An Incense
Beyond Nescessity –

Fame of Myself to lack – Although
My Name be else Supreme –
This were an Honor honorless –
A futile Diadem –

MANUSCRIPT: About 1863, in packet 31 (H 165c).

PUBLICATION: *BM* (1945), 237. The text derives from a transcript made by Mrs. Todd.

714

Rests at Night
The Sun from shining,
Nature – and some Men –
Rest at Noon – some Men –
While Nature
And the Sun – go on –

MANUSCRIPT: About 1863, in packet 31 (H 168b).

PUBLICATION: *BM* (1945), 15. The text, derived from a transcript made by Mrs. Todd, is printed as two three-line stanzas. There is some alteration in line spacing.

[547]

The World – feels Dusty
When We stop to Die –
We want the Dew – then –
Honors – taste dry –

Flags – vex a Dying face –
But the least Fan
Stirred by a friend's Hand –
Cools – like the Rain –

Mine be the Ministry
When thy Thirst comes –
Dews of Thessaly, to fetch –
And Hybla Balms –

MANUSCRIPT: About 1863, in packet 31 (H 168c).
PUBLICATION: *Atlantic Monthly*, CXLIII (February 1929), 186; *FP* (1929), 109. Two words are altered:

11. Thessaly] thyself   12. Hybla] holy

716

The Day undressed – Herself –
Her Garter – was of Gold –
Her Petticoat – of Purple plain –
Her Dimities – as old

Exactly – as the World –
And yet the newest Star –
Enrolled upon the Hemisphere
Be wrinkled – much as Her –

Too near to God – to pray –
Too near to Heaven – to fear –
The Lady of the Occident
Retired without a care –

Her Candle so expire
The flickering be seen
On Ball of Mast in Bosporus –
And Dome – and Window Pane –

MANUSCRIPTS: There are three, all written about 1863. That repro-
duced above (Bingham 106–10), signed "Emily.," has been folded as if
enclosed in an envelope. It is a redaction of the semifinal copy in packet
31 (H 170a):

The Day undressed – Herself –
Her Garter – was of Gold –
Her Petticoat of Purple – just –
Her Dimities as old

Exactly – as the World
And yet the newest Star
Enrolled upon the Hemisphere –
Be wrinkled – much as Her –

Too near to God – to pray –
Too near to Heaven – to fear –
The Lady of the Occident
Retired without a Care –

Her Candle so expire
The Flickering be seen
On Ball of Mast – in Foreign Port –
And Spire – and Window Pane.

3. just] plain –
5. Exactly] precisely
7. Hemisphere] Firmament
12. Retired] laid down –

15. Foreign Port] Bosporus –
16. And Spire] And Dome – /
Church –

In her redaction ED adopted these suggested alternatives:

3. plain   16. Dome
15. Bosporus

A third copy (Bingham) was sent to the Hollands. It is identical in text
and form with the fair copy reproduced above.

PUBLICATION: *UP* (1935), 45. The text derives from the packet copy;
the alternatives for lines 5 and 7 are adopted. The last word of line 3 is

[549]

omitted and the alternative is not adopted. The suggested change for line 15 has been incorporated into line 16, which reads:

> On Bosphorus and dome

Two other words are altered:

> 7. Enrolled] Unrolled   13. Candle] candles

717

The Beggar Lad – dies early –
It's Somewhat in the Cold –
And Somewhat in the Trudging feet –
And haply, in the World –

The Cruel – smiling – bowing World –
That took it's Cambric Way –
Nor heard the timid cry for "Bread" –
"Sweet Lady – Charity" –

Among Redeemed Children
If Trudging feet may stand –
The Barefoot time forgotten – so –
The Sleet – the bitter Wind –

The Childish Hands that teazed for Pence
Lifted adoring – then –
To Him whom never Ragged – Coat
Did supplicate in vain –

MANUSCRIPT: About 1863, in packet 31 (H 170b).
PUBLICATION: *BM* (1945), 93–94. The text derives from a transcript of the packet copy made by Mrs. Todd.

718

I meant to find Her when I came –
Death – had the same design –
But the Success – was His – it seems –
And the Surrender – Mine –

I meant to tell Her how I longed
For just this single time –
But Death had told Her so the first –
And she had past, with Him –

To wander – now – is my Repose –
To rest – To rest would be
A privilege of Hurricane
To Memory – and Me.

MANUSCRIPT: About 1863, in packet 81 (Bingham 9a). The text re-
produced above is that originally set down in ink in the packet. A great
many years later – about 1878 one might judge from the handwriting –
ED turned the presumably finished poem into a worksheet. With a pencil
she suggested revisions in several lines but left no indication of a final
choice. In line 4 "Surrender" is crossed out and "*Discomfit*" replaces it.
Suggested changes for other lines are these:

6] For this peculiar time
    just this only
7] But Death *specific* told her first
    enamored
8. had past, with] had *fled* with
    had trusted
    had *hearkened*

9. Repose] *Abode*
10] To pause – To pause would be
    stay
    dwell
11. Hurricane] misery

PUBLICATION: *Poems* (1896), 169. It follows the 1863 text with the
following selection from the alternatives:

4. Surrender] discomfit
8. past, with] hearkened

9. Repose] abode

719

A South Wind – has a pathos
Of individual Voice –
As One detect on Landings
An Emigrant's address.

A Hint of Ports and Peoples –
And much not understood –   [*no stanza break*]

The fairer –for the farness –
And for the foreignhood.

MANUSCRIPT: About 1863, in packet 81 (Bingham 9c).
PUBLICATION: *BM* (1945), 16.

720

No Prisoner be –
Where Liberty –
Himself –abide with Thee –

MANUSCRIPT: About 1863, in packet 18 (H 98c).
PUBLICATION: *FF* (1932), 239. One word is altered:

2. Where] When

721

Behind Me – dips Eternity –
Before Me – Immortality –
Myself – the Term between –
Death but the Drift of Eastern Gray,
Dissolving into Dawn away,
Before the West begin –

'Tis Kingdoms – afterward – they say –
In perfect – pauseless Monarchy –
Whose Prince – is Son of None –
Himself – His Dateless Dynasty –
Himself – Himself diversify –
In Duplicate divine –

'Tis Miracle before Me – then –
'Tis Miracle behind – between –
A Crescent in the Sea –
With Midnight to the North of Her –
And Midnight to the South of Her –
And Maelstrom – in the Sky –

[552]

MANUSCRIPT: About 1863, in packet 18 (H 99a).
PUBLICATION: *London Mercury*, XIX (February 1929), 358–359; *FP* (1929), 191. Five words are altered:

6. begin] begins   14. 'Tis] Then
7. Kingdoms] Kingdom   15. in] is
7. afterward] afterwards

722

Sweet Mountains – Ye tell Me no lie –
Never deny Me – Never fly –
Those same unvarying Eyes
Turn on Me – when I fail – or feign,
Or take the Royal names in vain –
Their far – slow – Violet Gaze –

My Strong Madonnas – Cherish still –
The Wayward Nun – beneath the Hill –
Whose service – is to You –
Her latest Worship – When the Day
Fades from the Firmament away –
To lift Her Brows on You –

MANUSCRIPT: About 1863, in packet 18 (H 99c).
PUBLICATION: *BM* (1945), 24. The text derives from a transcript made by Mrs. Todd.

723

It tossed – and tossed –
A little Brig I knew – o'ertook by Blast –
It spun – and spun –
And groped delirious, for Morn –

It slipped – and slipped –
As One that drunken – stept –
It's white foot tripped –
Then dropped from sight –

Ah, Brig – Good Night
To Crew and You –
The Ocean's Heart too smooth – too Blue –
To break for You –

MANUSCRIPT: About 1863, in packet 18 (H 99d).
PUBLICATION: *Poems* (1891), 48, titled "Shipwreck." Line 2 is arranged
as two lines.

724

It's easy to invent a Life –
God does it – every Day –
Creation – but the Gambol
Of His Authority –

It's easy to efface it –
The thrifty Deity
Could scarce afford Eternity
To Spontaneity –

The Perished Patterns murmur –
But His Perturbless Plan
Proceed – inserting Here – a Sun –
There – leaving out a Man –

MANUSCRIPT: About 1863, in packet 18 (H 100a).
PUBLICATION: *Atlantic Monthly*, CXLIII (March 1929), 328; *FP*
(1929), 41. The text of stanza 3, arranged in five lines, in later collections
is restored as a quatrain. One word is altered:

3. the] a

725

Where Thou art – that – is Home –
Cashmere – or Calvary – the same –
Degree – or Shame –
I scarce esteem Location's Name –
So I may Come –

[554]

What Thou dost – is Delight –
Bondage as Play – be sweet –
Imprisonment – Content–
And Sentence – Sacrament –
Just We two – meet –

Where Thou art not – is Wo –
Tho' Bands of Spices – row –
What Thou dost not – Despair –
Tho' Gabriel – praise me – Sir –

MANUSCRIPT: About 1863, in packet 18 (H 100c).
PUBLICATION: *Atlantic Monthly*, CXLIII (March 1929), 328; *FP*
(1929), 154. One word is altered:

12. row] blow

726

We thirst at first – 'tis Nature's Act –
And later – when we die –
A little Water supplicate –
Of fingers going by –

It intimates the finer want –
Whose adequate supply
Is that Great Water in the West –
Termed Immortality –

MANUSCRIPT: About 1863, in packet 18 (H 100d).
PUBLICATION: *Poems* (1896), 191, titled "Thirst."

727

Precious to Me – She still shall be –
Though She forget the name I bear –
The fashion of the Gown I wear –
The very Color of My Hair –

So like the Meadows – now –
I dared to show a Tress of Their's
If haply – She might not despise
A Buttercup's Array –

I know the Whole – obscures the Part –
The fraction – that appeased the Heart
Till Number's Empery –
Remembered – as the Milliner's flower
When Summer's Everlasting Dower –
Confronts the dazzled Bee.

MANUSCRIPT: About 1863, in packet 18 (H 101b).
PUBLICATION: *BM* (1945), 109–110. "I dared" (line 6) concludes line
5. The text derives from a transcript made by Mrs. Todd. One word is
altered:

11. Number's] numbers'

728

Let Us play Yesterday –
I – the Girl at school –
You – and Eternity – the
Untold Tale –

Easing my famine
At my Lexicon –
Logarithm – had I – for Drink –
'Twas a dry Wine –

Somewhat different – must be –
Dreams tint the Sleep –
Cunning Reds of Morning
Make the Blind – leap –

Still at the Egg-life –
Chafing the Shell –
When you troubled the Ellipse –
And the Bird fell –

[556]

Manacles be dim – they say –
To the new Free –
Liberty – Commoner –
Never could – to me –

'Twas my last gratitude
When I slept – at night –
'Twas the first Miracle
Let in – with Light –

Can the Lark resume the Shell –
Easier – for the Sky –
Would'nt Bonds hurt more
Than Yesterday?

Would'nt Dungeons sorer grate
On the Man – free –
Just long enough to taste –
Then – doomed new –

God of the Manacle
As of the Free –
Take not my Liberty
Away from Me –

MANUSCRIPT: About 1863, in packet 18 (H 102b).

PUBLICATION: *UP* (1935), 105–106. The last word in line 3 is arranged as the first in line 4. One misreading, "your" for "my" (line 6), is corrected in *Poems* (current). One line is altered:

24] Let in with the light

729

Alter! When the Hills do –
Falter! When the Sun
Question if His Glory
Be the Perfect One –

Surfeit! When the Daffodil
Doth of the Dew –   [*no stanza break*]

[557]

Even as Herself – Sir –
I will – of You –

MANUSCRIPT: About 1863, in packet 18 (H 102c).
PUBLICATION: *Poems* (1890), 45. In line 7, "Sir" is rendered "O friend."

730

Defrauded I a Butterfly –
The lawful Heir – for Thee –

MANUSCRIPT: About 1863, in packet 30 (H 160b).
PUBLICATION: *FP* (1929), 72. It is arranged as a four-line stanza with the notation: "Sent with a Flower."

731

"I want" – it pleaded – All it's life –
I want – was chief it said
When Skill entreated it – the last –
And when so newly dead –

I could not deem it late – to hear
That single – steadfast sigh –
The lips had placed as with a "Please"
Toward Eternity –

MANUSCRIPT: About 1863, in packet 30 (H 160c).
PUBLICATION: *BM* (1945), 210. The text derives from a transcript of the packet copy made by Mrs. Todd.

732

She rose to His Requirement – dropt
The Playthings of Her Life
To take the honorable Work
Of Woman, and of Wife –

If ought She missed in Her new Day,
Of Amplitude, or Awe –   [*no stanza break*]

[558]

Or first Prospective – Or the Gold
In using, wear away,

It lay unmentioned – as the Sea
Develope Pearl, and Weed,
But only to Himself – be known
The Fathoms they abide –

MANUSCRIPT: About 1863, in packet 30 (H 162b).
PUBLICATION: *Poems* (1890), 64, titled "The Wife." Four words are
altered:

5. ought] aught	10. Develope] Develops
8. wear] wore	11. be] is

733

The Spirit is the Conscious Ear.
We actually Hear
When We inspect – that's audible –
That is admitted – Here –

For other Services – as Sound –
There hangs a smaller Ear
Outside the Castle – that Contain –
The other – only – Hear –

5. Services] purposes	7. Castle] Centre – / City
6. smaller] minor	7. Contain] present –

MANUSCRIPT: Early 1863, in packet 22 (H 118d).
PUBLICATION: *BM* (1945), 229. The suggested changes for lines 5 and
6 are adopted. The text derives from a transcript made by Mrs. Todd.

734

If He were living – dare I ask –
And how if He be dead –
And so around the Words I went –
Of meeting them – afraid –

I hinted Changes – Lapse of Time –
The Surfaces of Years –
I touched with Caution – lest they crack –
And show me to my fears –

Reverted to adjoining Lives –
Adroitly turning out
Wherever I suspected Graves –
'Twas prudenter – I thought –

And He – I pushed – with sudden force –
In face of the Suspense –
"Was buried" – "Buried"! "He!"
My Life just holds the Trench –

7. crack] slit –

MANUSCRIPT: About 1863, in packet 22 (H 119a).
PUBLICATION: *Atlantic Monthly*, CXLIII (March 1929), 329; *FP*
(1929), 173. The suggested change is adopted. Stanza 4 is arranged in 3
lines; in later collections it is restored to a quatrain. Two words are altered:

2. be] were   13. pushed] rushed

735

Upon Concluded Lives
There's nothing cooler falls –
Than Life's sweet Calculations –
The mixing Bells and Palls –

Makes Lacerating Tune –
To Ears the Dying Side –
'Tis Coronal – and Funeral –
Saluting – in the Road –

3. sweet] new   8. Saluting] Confronting / Contrasting

MANUSCRIPT: Early 1863, in packet 22 (H 119d).
PUBLICATION: *BM* (1945), 209. The text derives from a transcript
made by Mrs. Todd. The suggested changes are rejected.

Have any like Myself
Investigating March,
New Houses on the Hill descried –
And possibly a Church –

That were not, We are sure –
As lately as the Snow –
And are Today – if We exist –
Though how may this be so?

Have any like Myself
Conjectured Who may be
The Occupants of these Abodes –
So easy to the Sky –

Twould seem that God should be
The nearest Neighbor to –
And Heaven – a convenient Grace
For Show, or Company –

Have any like Myself
Preserved the Charm secure
By shunning carefully the Place
All Seasons of the Year,

Excepting March – 'Tis then
My Villages be seen –
And possibly a Steeple –
Not afterward – by Men –

18. Charm secure] Vision sure – /   19. Place] spot / site
      clear   22. My] the

MANUSCRIPT: About 1863, in packet 22 (H 120a).
PUBLICATION: *UP* (1935), 48. All suggested changes are rejected. Two
words are italicized:

5. not   7. are

The Moon was but a Chin of Gold
A Night or two ago –
And now she turns Her perfect Face
Upon the World below –

Her Forehead is of Amplest Blonde –
Her Cheek – a Beryl hewn –
Her Eye unto the Summer Dew
The likest I have known –

Her Lips of Amber never part –
But what must be the smile
Upon Her Friend she could confer
Were such Her Silver Will –

And what a privilege to be
But the remotest Star –
For Certainty She take Her Way
Beside Your Palace Door –

Her Bonnet is the Firmament –
The Universe – Her Shoe –
The Stars – the Trinkets at Her Belt –
Her Dimities – of Blue –

11. confer] bestow – 18] The Valleys – are Her Shoe –
16. Palace] twinkling – / glimmering –

MANUSCRIPT: Early 1863, in packet 22 (H 125a).
PUBLICATION: *Poems* (1896), 125–126, titled "The Moon." The suggested changes "bestow" and "twinkling" are adopted. Two lines are altered:

6] Her cheek like beryl stone 15] For certainly her way might pass

You said that I "was Great" – one Day –
Then "Great" it be – if that please Thee –
Or Small – or any size at all –
Nay – I'm the size suit Thee –

Tall – like the Stag – would that?
Or lower – like the Wren –
Or other hights of Other Ones
I've seen?

Tell which – it's dull to guess –
And I must be Rhinoceros
Or Mouse
At once – for Thee –

So say – if Queen it be –
Or Page – please Thee –
I'm that – or nought –
Or other thing – if other thing there be –
With just this Stipulus –
I suit Thee –

17. Stipulus] Reservation –

MANUSCRIPT: About 1863, in packet 22 (H 125b).
PUBLICATION: *BM* (1945), 172–173. The text, which derives from a
transcript made by Mrs. Todd, is arranged as five quatrains. One word is
altered:

6. lower] cower

In line 17 Mrs. Todd did not set down either "Stipulus" or "Reservation,"
so the line reads:

With just this –

739

I many times thought Peace had come
When Peace was far away –
As Wrecked Men – deem they sight the Land –
At Centre of the Sea –

And struggle slacker – but to prove
As hopelessly as I –
How many the fictitious Shores –
Or any Harbor be –

8] Before the Harbor be –

MANUSCRIPT: About 1863, in packet 22 (H 125c).
PUBLICATION: *Poems* (1891), 73. The suggested change is adopted.
One word is altered:

8. be] lie

740

You taught me Waiting with Myself –
Appointment strictly kept –
You taught me fortitude of Fate –
This – also – I have learnt –

An Altitude of Death, that could
No bitterer debar
Than Life – had done – before it –
Yet – there is a Science more –

The Heaven you know – to understand
That you be not ashamed
Of Me – in Christ's bright Audience
Upon the further Hand –

11. Audience] Latitude

MANUSCRIPT: About 1863, in packet 12 (H 55b).
PUBLICATION: *London Mercury*, XIX (1929), 356; FP (1929), 170.
The suggested change is rejected. In line 9 "you" is italicized. The text
is arranged as two stanzas of 4 and 8 lines.

741

Drama's Vitallest Expression is the Common Day
That arise and set about Us –
Other Tragedy

Perish in the Recitation –
This – the best enact
When the Audience is scattered
And the Boxes shut –

[564]

"Hamlet" to Himself were Hamlet –
Had not Shakespeare wrote –
Though the "Romeo" left no Record
Of his Juliet,

It were infinite enacted
In the Human Heart –
Only Theatre recorded
Owner cannot shut –

5. best enact] more exert   12. infinite] tenderer –
10. left] leave   15] Never yet was shut –

MANUSCRIPT: About 1863, in packet 12 (H 56a).
PUBLICATION: FP (1929), 28. The text is arranged as two eight-line
stanzas. The first three suggested changes are adopted. The misreading
"second" for "record" (line 10) is corrected in Poems (current).
    Line 2 is altered to read:

That arises, sets, about us:

742

Four Trees – upon a solitary Acre –
Without Design
Or Order, or Apparent Action –
Maintain –

The Sun – upon a Morning meets them –
The Wind –
No nearer Neighbor – have they –
But God –

The Acre gives them – Place –
They – Him – Attention of Passer by –
Of Shadow, or of Squirrel, haply –
Or Boy –

What Deed is Their's unto the General Nature –
What Plan
They severally – retard – or further –
Unknown –

[565]

3. Action] signal – /notice   15. retard – or further] promote – or
4. Maintain] Do reign –   hinder –
13. is Their's] they bear

MANUSCRIPT: About 1863, in packet 12 (H 56c).
PUBLICATION: *BM* (1945), 76. The suggested change for line 15 is
adopted. The text derives from a transcript made by Mrs. Todd.

743

The Birds reported from the South –
A News express to Me –
A spicy Charge, My little Posts –
But I am deaf – Today –

The Flowers – appealed – a timid Throng –
I reinforced the Door –
Go blossom to the Bees – I said –
And trouble Me – no More –

The Summer Grace, for Notice strove –
Remote – Her best Array –
The Heart – to stimulate the Eye
Refused too utterly –

At length, a Mourner, like Myself,
She drew away austere –
Her frosts to ponder – then it was
I recollected Her –

She suffered Me, for I had mourned –
I offered Her no word –
My Witness – was the Crape I bore –
Her – Witness – was Her Dead –

Thenceforward – We – together dwelt –
I never questioned Her –
Our Contract
A Wiser Sympathy

3. Posts] friends –
4. I am deaf – Today] you must go
   away
6. reinforced] only sealed
8. trouble] harass
16. recollected] rose to comfort –

19. Crape] Black –
21. dwelt] walked
22–23] She – never questioned Me –
   Nor I – Herself – Our Compact –
24. Wiser] wordless – / silent – /
   speechless –

MANUSCRIPT: About 1863, in packet 12 (H 57a). The suggested changes for the final stanza are complicated: ED may have intended only part of them to be adopted, but by what combination is not discoverable. Though the poem is transcribed into a packet, it is hardly more than a worksheet.

PUBLICATION: *UP* (1935), 49. In the first five stanzas, only the suggested change in line 19 is adopted. The final stanza reads:

> Thence forward we together dwelt;
> She never questioned me,
> Nor I herself, – our compact
> A wordless sympathy.

In *UP* "mourner" (line 13) is correctly rendered; in *Poems* (current) it is misprinted as "mourned." One word is altered:

20. Her Dead] the Dead

744

Remorse – is Memory – awake –
Her Parties all astir –
A Presence of Departed Acts –
At window – and at Door –

It's Past – set down before the Soul
And lighted with a Match –
Perusal – to facilitate –
And help Belief to stretch –

Remorse is cureless – the Disease
Not even God – can heal –
For 'tis His institution – and
The Adequate of Hell –

2. Parties all] Companies   8] Of it's Condensed Despatch
8. stretch] reach   12. Adequate] Complement –

MANUSCRIPT: About 1863, in packet 12 (H 57b).
PUBLICATION: *Poems* (1891), 68, titled "Remorse." The line adoptions
are 2, 8 *entire*, and 12. In line 11 "and" is omitted.

745

Renunciation – is a piercing Virtue –
The letting go
A Presence – for an Expectation –
Not now –
The putting out of Eyes –
Just Sunrise –
Lest Day –
Day's Great Progenitor –
Outvie
Renunciation – is the Choosing
Against itself –
Itself to justify
Unto itself –
When larger function –
Make that appear –
Smaller – that Covered Vision – Here –

9. Outvie] Outshow – / Outglow –   16. Covered] flooded – / sated –

MANUSCRIPT: About 1863, in packet 12 (H 57c).
PUBLICATION: *FP* (1929), 167. From among suggested changes, "Out-
show" and "sated" are selected. The text is given a three-stanza division
and some alteration of line spacing.

Never for Society
He shall seek in vain –
Who His own acquaintance
Cultivate – Of Men
Wiser Men may weary –
But the Man within

Never knew Satiety –
Better entertain
Than could Border Ballad –
Or Biscayan Hymn –
Neither introduction
Need You – unto Him –

5. Men] One – / Ear   8. Better] braver –

MANUSCRIPT: About 1863, in packet 12 (H 58a).
PUBLICATION: The poem was first published in an editorial section of
Letters (1894), 369; (ed. 1931), 360. It is without stanza division and
neither suggested change is adopted; in line 4 "Cultivate" is altered to
"Cultivates." It also appears in *UP* (1935), 37, where the suggested change
"ear" is adopted (line 5); and "He" is altered to "One" (line 2).

747

It dropped so low – in my Regard –
I heard it hit the Ground –
And go to pieces on the Stones
At bottom of my Mind –

Yet blamed the Fate that fractured – *less*
Than I reviled Myself,
For entertaining Plated Wares
Upon my Silver Shelf –

3. on the Stones] in the Ditch –   6. reviled] *denounced*
5. fractured] *flung it*

MANUSCRIPT: About 1863, in packet 12 (H 58c). All suggested changes — including the underlining of "less" — are in pencil, and on the evidence of handwriting were almost certainly entered some fifteen or sixteen years after the poem was written.

PUBLICATION: *Independent*, XLVIII (2 July 1896), 1; *Poems* (1896), 50, titled "Disenchantment." All suggested changes are rejected.

748

Autumn – overlooked my Knitting –
Dyes – said He – have I –
Could disparage a Flamingo –
Show Me them – said I –

Cochineal – I chose – for deeming
It resemble Thee –
And the little Border – Dusker –
For resembling Me –

3. disparage] dishonor
4. Show Me them] Give them Me –

6. It] That
8] That – resemble me –

MANUSCRIPT: About 1863, in packet 12 (H 58d).

PUBLICATION: FP (1929), 83. The suggested changes for lines 3, 4, and 8 are adopted, though "resemble" is altered to "resembles." The second stanza is arranged in five lines. In later collections it is restored as a quatrain.

749

All but Death, can be Adjusted –
Dynasties repaired –
Systems – settled in their Sockets –
Citadels – dissolved –

Wastes of Lives – resown with Colors
By Succeeding Springs –
Death – unto itself – Exception –
Is exempt from Change –

4] Centuries removed
6. Succeeding Springs] supremer springs –

MANUSCRIPT: About 1863, in packet 12 (H 59c).

PUBLICATION: *New York Herald Tribune Book Review*, 10 March 1929, page 4; *FP* (1929), 89. Both suggested changes are adopted. The misreading "superior" for "supremer" (line 6) is corrected in *Poems* (current). The text is arranged as two stanzas of 6 and 5 lines; in later collections the quatrains are restored.

750

Growth of Man – like Growth of Nature –
Gravitates within –
Atmosphere, and Sun endorse it –
But it stir – alone –

Each – it's difficult Ideal
Must achieve – Itself –
Through the solitary prowess
Of a Silent Life –

Effort – is the sole condition –
Patience of Itself –
Patience of opposing forces –
And intact Belief –

Looking on – is the Department
Of it's Audience –
But Transaction – is assisted
By no Countenance –

3. endorse] Confirm –   12. intact] direct – / distinct
5. difficult] absolute

MANUSCRIPT: About 1863, in packet 12 (H 60a).

PUBLICATION: *FP* (1929), 16. The text of stanza 1, arranged in five lines, in later collections is restored as a quatrain. Two suggested changes are adopted:

3. confirm   12. distinct

One word is altered:

4. stir] stirs

[571]

My Worthiness is all my Doubt –
His Merit – all my fear –
Contrasting which, my quality
Do lowlier – appear –

Lest I should insufficient prove
For His beloved Need –
The Chiefest Apprehension
Upon my thronging Mind –

'Tis true – that Deity to stoop
Inherently incline –
For nothing higher than Itself
Itself can rest upon –

So I – the undivine abode
Of His Elect Content –
Conform my Soul – as twere a Church,
Unto Her Sacrament –

5. prove] be   12. rest] lift – / base –
8. thronging] crowded – / happy

MANUSCRIPT: About 1863, in packet 12 (H 60b).

PUBLICATION: *Poems* (1896), 74, titled "Love's Humility." Only stanzas 1, 2, and 4 are here published and the suggested changes are rejected. In line 3 "quality" is altered to "qualities," and line 8 is altered entirely to read: "Within my loving creed." Mrs. Bingham edited the poem correctly, with the missing third stanza restored, in *New England Quarterly*, XX (1947), 21. It here derives from the transcript prepared by Mrs. Todd as printer's copy for the 1896 edition of *Poems*. The suggested changes are rejected.

752

So the Eyes accost – and sunder
In an Audience –
Stamped – occasionally – forever –
So may Countenance

Entertain – without addressing
Countenance of One
In a Neighboring Horizon –
Gone – as soon as known –

3. occasionally] in instances   4. may] can –

MANUSCRIPT: About 1863, in packet 12 (H 60c).
PUBLICATION: *FP* (1929), 136. The suggested change for line 3 is
adopted. There is no stanza division.

753

My Soul – accused me – And I quailed –
As Tongues of Diamond had reviled
All else accused me – and I smiled –
My Soul – that Morning – was My friend –

Her favor – is the best Disdain
Toward Artifice of Time – or Men –
But Her Disdain – 'twere lighter bear
A finger of Enamelled Fire –

2. Tongues] Throngs – / Eyes –   7. lighter] cooler
3. All else] The World

MANUSCRIPT: About 1863, in packet 12 (H 60d).
PUBLICATION: *FP* (1929), 122. The text is arranged as three stanzas
of 4, 4, 7 lines. The suggested change for line 7 is adopted. When the
poem was issued in *CP* (1924) and later collections, the text was arranged
as three quatrains, and the misprint "tongue" (line 2) was corrected.

My Life had stood – a Loaded Gun –
In Corners – till a Day
The Owner passed – identified –
And carried Me away –

And now We roam in Sovreign Woods –
And now We hunt the Doe –
And every time I speak for Him –
The Mountains straight reply –

And do I smile, such cordial light
Upon the Valley glow –
It is as a Vesuvian face
Had let it's pleasure through –

And when at Night – Our good Day done –
I guard My Master's Head –
'Tis better than the Eider-Duck's
Deep Pillow – to have shared –

To foe of His – I'm deadly foe –
None stir the second time –
On whom I lay a Yellow Eye –
Or an emphatic Thumb –

Though I than He – may longer live
He longer must – than I –
For I have but the power to kill,
Without – the power to die –

5. in] the –	18. stir] harm
16. Deep] low	23. power] art

MANUSCRIPT: About 1863, in packet 24 (H 131a).

PUBLICATION: *London Mercury*, XIX (February 1929), 354–355; *FP* (1929), 143. The suggested changes for lines 5 and 23 are adopted.

No Bobolink – reverse His Singing
When the only Tree
Ever He minded occupying
By the Farmer be –

Clove to the Root –
His Spacious Future –
Best Horizon – gone –
Whose Music be His
Only Anodyne –
Brave Bobolink –

5. Root] Core   7. gone] known ⌐
7. Best] All

MANUSCRIPT: About 1863, in packet 24 (H 131c). ED placed numerals 2 and 1 before lines 8 and 10 respectively, evidently to indicate she meant the last three lines to read:

Brave Bobolink –
Whose music be His
Only Anodyne –

PUBLICATION: *BM* (1945), 62. The suggested change for line 5 is adopted, as is the line-order arrangement at the end. The text, arranged as two quatrains, derives from a transcript made by Mrs. Todd. One word is altered:

5. Clove] Close

756

One Blessing had I than the rest
So larger to my Eyes
That I stopped guaging – satisfied –
For this enchanted size –

It was the limit of my Dream –
The focus of my Prayer –
A perfect – paralyzing Bliss –
Contented as Despair –

I knew no more of Want – or Cold –
Phantasms both become
For this new Value in the Soul –
Supremest Earthly Sum –

The Heaven below the Heaven above –
Obscured with ruddier Blue –
Life's Latitudes leant over – full –
The Judgment perished – too –

Why Bliss so scantily disburse –
Why Paradise defer –
Why Floods be served to Us – in Bowls –
I speculate no more –

10. Phantasms] fictitious   17. scantily] cautiously –
11. Value] fortune – / portion –   17. disburse] express – / afford
14. ruddier] nearer / comelier   18. defer] demur –

MANUSCRIPT: About 1863, in packet 24 (H 132a).
PUBLICATION: *Poems* (1896), 76–77, titled "Satisfied." All suggested
changes are rejected. The spelling of "guaging" (line 3) is regularized.
The following alterations are made:

14. Blue] hue   17. Bliss] joys
15] Life's latitude leant over-full 19. be] are

757

The Mountains – grow unnoticed –
Their Purple figures rise
Without attempt – Exhaustion –
Assistance – or Applause –

In Their Eternal Faces
The Sun – with just delight
Looks long – and last – and golden –
For fellowship – at night –

6. just] broad   8. fellowship] sympathy –

[576]

MANUSCRIPT: About 1863, in packet 24 (H 132c).
PUBLICATION: *FP* (1929), 78. The suggested change for line 6 is adopted. The second stanza, arranged as five lines, was restored to a quatrain in later collections.

758

These – saw Visions –
Latch them softly –
These – held Dimples –
Smooth them slow –
This – addressed departing accents –
Quick – Sweet Mouth – to miss thee so –

This – We stroked –
Unnumbered Satin –
These – we held among our own –
Fingers of the Slim Aurora –
Not so arrogant – this Noon –

These – adjust – that ran to meet us –
Pearl – for Stocking – Pearl for Shoe –
Paradise – the only Palace
Fit for Her reception – now –

2. Latch] Bar / bind   9. held among] fondled in
6. Quick] soon   13. for] the –

MANUSCRIPT: About 1863, in packet 24 (H 133a).
PUBLICATION: *UP* (1935), 125. The text is arranged as three quatrains. All suggested changes are rejected. Three words are altered:

1. Visions] vision   9. These] Those
6. thee] them

759

He fought like those Who've nought to lose –
Bestowed Himself to Balls
As One who for a further Life
Had not a further Use –

Invited Death – with bold attempt –
But Death was Coy of Him
As Other Men, were Coy of Death –
To Him – to live – was Doom –

His Comrades, shifted like the Flakes
When Gusts reverse the Snow –
But He – was left alive Because
Of Greediness to die –

2. Bestowed Himself] He gave him-
self
6. Coy] shy

11. was left] remained
12. Greediness] Urgency – / Vehemence

MANUSCRIPT: About 1863, in packet 31 (H 165b).
PUBLICATION: *UP* (1935), 6. Two suggested changes are adopted:

11. remained   12. vehemence

760

Most she touched me by her muteness –
Most she won me by the way
She presented her small figure –
Plea itself – for Charity –

Were a Crumb my whole possession –
Were there famine in the land –
Were it my resource from starving –
Could I such a plea withstand –

Not upon her knee to thank me
Sank this Beggar from the Sky –
But the Crumb partook – departed –
And returned On High –

I supposed – when sudden
Such a Praise began
'Twas as Space sat singing
To herself – and men –

[578]

'Twas the Winged Beggar –
Afterward I learned
To her Benefactor
Making Gratitude

8. plea] face   20. Making] paying
10. this] the

MANUSCRIPT: About 1863, in packet 31 (H 166d). The letters "an" are lightly written in pencil beneath the "en" of "men" (line 16), perhaps by ED.

PUBLICATION: *Atlantic Monthly*, CXLIII (March 1929), 330; *FP* (1929), 81. The text is arranged without division as a thirty-line stanza; in later collections the lines are correctly restored but still arranged without stanza division. The suggested changes for lines 8 and 20 are adopted. Line 16 adopts the reading "man"; "itself" (line 4) is omitted.

761

From Blank to Blank –
A Threadless Way
I pushed Mechanic feet –
To stop – or perish – or advance –
Alike indifferent –

If end I gained
It ends beyond
Indefinite disclosed –
I shut my eyes – and groped as well
'Twas lighter – to be Blind –

2. Way] Course   10. lighter] firmer
6. gained] reached

MANUSCRIPT: About 1863, in packet 31 (H 166c).
PUBLICATION: *FP* (1929), 182. All suggested changes are rejected. The text is arranged as two six-line stanzas. One word is altered:

7. It] If

[579]

The Whole of it came not at once –
'Twas Murder by degrees –
A Thrust – and then for Life a chance –
The Bliss to cauterize –

The Cat reprieves the Mouse
She eases from her teeth
Just long enough for Hope to teaze –
Then mashes it to death –

'Tis Life's award – to die –
Contenteder if once –
Than dying half – then rallying
For consciouser Eclipse –

4] The certain prey to teaze –   11. half] part
7. teaze] stir   12. consciouser] totaller –
8. mashes] crunches

MANUSCRIPT: About 1863, in packet 31 (H 167a).
PUBLICATION: *BM* (1945), 257. The text derives from a transcript made by Mrs. Todd. All suggested changes are rejected.

763

He told a homely tale
And spotted it with tears –
Upon his infant face was set
The Cicatrice of years –

All crumpled was the cheek
No other kiss had known
Than flake of snow, divided with
The Redbreast of the Barn –

If Mother – in the Grave –
Or Father – on the Sea –
Or Father in the Firmament –
Or Bretheren, had he –

If Commonwealth below,
Or Commonwealth above
Have missed a Barefoot Citizen –
I've ransomed it – alive –

7. divided with] imprinted swift –
8] When hurrying to the town

15. missed] lost
16] I've found it – 'tis alive –

MANUSCRIPT: About 1863, in packet 31 (H 167b).
PUBLICATION: *BM* (1945), 90. The text derives from a transcript of
the packet copy made by Mrs. Todd. All suggested changes are rejected.

764

Presentiment – is that long Shadow – on the Lawn–
Indicative that Suns go down –

The Notice to the startled Grass
That Darkness – is about to pass –

3. The Notice] Monition –

MANUSCRIPT: About 1863, in packet 31 (H 167c).
PUBLICATION: *Poems* (1890), 88. The suggested change is rejected.
There is no stanza division.

765

You constituted Time –
I deemed Eternity
A Revelation of Yourself –
'Twas therefore Deity

The Absolute – removed
The Relative away –
That I unto Himself adjust
My slow idolatry –

5. removed] withdrew –

MANUSCRIPT: About 1863, in packet 31 (H 167d).

[581]

PUBLICATION: *BM* (1945), 176. The text derives from a transcript made by Mrs. Todd. The suggested change is rejected.

766

My Faith is larger than the Hills –
So when the Hills decay –
My Faith must take the Purple Wheel
To show the Sun the way –

'Tis first He steps upon the Vane –
And then – upon the Hill –
And then abroad the World He go
To do His Golden Will –

And if His Yellow feet should miss –
The Bird would not arise –
The Flowers would slumber on their Stems –
No Bells have Paradise –

How dare I, therefore, stint a faith
On which so vast depends –
Lest Firmament should fail for me –
The Rivet in the Bands

5. 'Tis first] You see	11. slumber on] sleep upon –
10. Bird] Day	15. Firmament] Universe – / Deity –

MANUSCRIPT: About 1863, in packet 31 (H 168a).
PUBLICATION: *FP* (1929), 58. All suggested changes are rejected. Two words are altered:

7. go] goes   10. bird] birds

767

To offer brave assistance
To Lives that stand alone –
When One has failed to stop them –
Is Human – but Divine

To lend an Ample Sinew
Unto a Nameless Man –
Whose Homely Benediction
No other – stopped to earn –

3. One] You   8. stopped] cared –

MANUSCRIPT: About 1863, in packet 31 (H 168d).
PUBLICATION: *FP* (1929), 27. The suggested change for line 8 is adopted. The text is without stanza division. In line 6 "nameless" is italicized.

768

When I hoped, I recollect
Just the place I stood –
At a Window facing West –
Roughest Air – was good –

Not a Sleet could bite me –
Not a frost could cool –
Hope it was that kept me warm –
Not Merino shawl –

When I feared – I recollect
Just the Day it was –
Worlds were lying out to Sun –
Yet how Nature froze –

Icicles upon my soul
Prickled Blue and Cool –
Bird went praising everywhere –
Only Me – was still –

And the Day that I despaired –
This – if I forget
Nature will – that it be Night
After Sun has set –
Darkness intersect her face –
And put out her eye –
Nature hesitate – before
Memory and I –

3. At a Window] In a Chamber
6] No November cool
11] Worlds were swimming in the
Sun – / [Worlds were] lying [in
the Sun –]

14. Blue] Raw and Cool
16. Only Me] Still Myself – / Me alone
20] When the Sun is set
21–22] Dark shall overtake the Hill – /
Overtake the Sky –

MANUSCRIPT: About 1863, in packet 31 (H 169a).
PUBLICATION: *FP* (1929), 181. The text is arranged as six quatrains.
The suggested changes for lines 3, 11 ("swimming"), 14, 20, 21, 22 are
adopted. There are alterations in three lines:

15. Bird] Birds   24. I] me
16. Only Me] Mine alone

769

One and One – are One –
Two – be finished using –
Well enough for Schools –
But for Minor Choosing –

Life – just – Or Death –
Or the Everlasting –
More – would be too vast
For the Soul's Comprising –

4. Minor] inner   7. More] Two –

MANUSCRIPT: About 1863, in packet 31 (H 170c).
PUBLICATION: *FP* (1929), 156. Both suggested changes are adopted.
The text is printed as a single eight-line stanza.

770

I lived on Dread –
To Those who know
The Stimulus there is
In Danger – Other impetus
Is numb – and Vitalless –

As 'twere a Spur – upon the Soul –
A Fear will urge it where
To go without the Spectre's aid
Were Challenging Despair.

8. aid] help –

MANUSCRIPT: About 1863, in packet 31 (H 170d).
PUBLICATION: *Poems* (1891), 211. The suggested change is rejected.
Line 2 is incorporated into line 1.

771

None can experience stint
Who Bounty – have not known –
The fact of Famine – could not be
Except for Fact of Corn –

Want – is a meagre Art
Acquired by Reverse –
The Poverty that was not Wealth –
Cannot be Indigence

3] Nor fact of Famine could exist –   7–8] It is that Poverty was Wealth
                                                Enables Indigence –

MANUSCRIPT: About 1863, in packet 81 (Bingham 6a).
PUBLICATION: *BM* (1945), 291. The suggested changes are rejected.

772

The hallowing of Pain
Like hallowing of Heaven,
Obtains at a corporeal cost –
The Summit is not given

To Him who strives severe
At middle of the Hill –
But He who has achieved the Top –
All – is the price of All –

[585]

6. middle] Bottom – / Centre   7. Top] Crest –

MANUSCRIPT: About 1863, in packet 81 (Bingham 6b).
PUBLICATION: *BM* (1945), 216–217. The suggested change "Bottom"
is adopted.

773

Deprived of other Banquet,
I entertained Myself –
At first – a scant nutrition –
An insufficient Loaf –

But grown by slender addings
To so esteemed a size
'Tis sumptuous enough for me –
And almost to suffice

A Robin's famine able –
Red Pilgrim, He and I –
A Berry from our table
Reserve – for charity –

3. scant nutrition] plain Regaling   9. famine] palate – / hunger –
4] An innutritious Loaf

MANUSCRIPT: About 1863, in packet 81 (Bingham 7a).
PUBLICATION: *BM* (1945), 122. One suggested change is adopted:

9. hunger

774

It is a lonesome Glee –
Yet sanctifies the Mind –
With fair association –
Afar upon the Wind

A Bird to overhear
Delight without a Cause –

[586]   [*no stanza break*]

Arrestless as invisible –
A matter of the Skies.

4. Afar] remote – / astray –

MANUSCRIPT: About 1863, in packet 81 (Bingham 7b).
PUBLICATION: *BM* (1945), 60. In line 4 "remote" is adopted.

775

If Blame be my side – forfeit Me –
But doom me not to forfeit Thee –
To forfeit Thee? The very name
Is sentence from Belief – and Home –

4. sentence] exile –

MANUSCRIPT: About 1863, in packet 81 (Bingham 7c).
PUBLICATION: *BM* (1945), 163. The suggested change is adopted.

776

Purple –

The Color of a Queen, is this –
The Color of A Sun
At setting – this and Amber –
Beryl – and this, at Noon –

And when at night – Auroran widths
Fling suddenly on men –
'Tis this – and Witchcraft – nature keeps
A Rank – for Iodine –

7. 'Tis] that's   7–8 Nature keeps/ A Rank – for]
                      Nature knows the rank of /
                      Nature has an awe of –

MANUSCRIPT: About 1863, in packet 81 (Bingham 7d). This is one of
the three poems in packets for which ED herself supplied a title.
PUBLICATION: *BM* (1945), 24. The second of the changes suggested
for lines 7 and 8 is adopted.

The Loneliness One dare not sound –
And would as soon surmise
As in it's Grave go plumbing
To ascertain the size –

The Loneliness whose worst alarm
Is lest itself should see –
And perish from before itself
For just a scrutiny –

The Horror not to be surveyed –
But skirted in the Dark –
With Consciousness suspended –
And Being under Lock –

I fear me this – is Loneliness –
The Maker of the soul
It's Caverns and it's Corridors
Illuminate – or seal –

3. plumbing] measuring
4. To ascertain] to register
8] [For] simple scrutiny

9. Horror] chasm –
16. Illuminate] Make populate – /
    [Make] manifest

MANUSCRIPT: About 1863, in packet 81 (Bingham 8a).
PUBLICATION: *BM* (1945), 250. The suggested change for line 9 is adopted.

778

This that would greet – an hour ago –
Is quaintest Distance – now –
Had it a Guest from Paradise –
Nor glow, would it, nor bow –

Had it a notice from the Noon
Nor beam would it nor warm –
Match me the Silver Reticence –
Match me the Solid Calm –

[588]

2. Distance] stiffness –   7. Silver] crystal
5. notice] summons

MANUSCRIPT: About 1863, in packet 81 (Bingham 8c).
PUBLICATION: *BM* (1945), 192. Of the suggested changes, "summons"
is adopted.

779

The Service without Hope –
Is tenderest, I think –
Because 'tis unsustained
By stint – Rewarded Work –

Has impetus of Gain –
And impetus of Goal –
There is no Diligence like that
That knows not an Until –

4. stint] end

MANUSCRIPT: About 1863, in packet 81 (Bingham 8d).
PUBLICATION: *BM* (1945), 243. The suggested change is adopted, but
the meaning is altered by the reading "end-rewarded."

780

The Truth – is stirless –
Other force – may be presumed to move –
This – then – is best for confidence –
When oldest Cedars swerve –

And Oaks untwist their fists –
And Mountains – feeble – lean –
How excellent a Body, that
Stands without a Bone –

How vigorous a Force
That holds without a Prop –
Truth stays Herself – and every man
That trusts Her – boldly up –

5. untwist] unknot – / [un]knit – /   7. Body] Giant
   [un]clinch

MANUSCRIPT: About 1863, in packet 81 (Bingham 9b).
PUBLICATION: *BM* (1945), 232. In line 5 "unclinch" is adopted. The
first two words of line 2 conclude line 1. The last word of line 7 becomes
the first of line 8.

781

To wait an Hour – is long –
If Love be just beyond –
To wait Eternity – is short –
If Love reward the end –

4 [If Love] Be at the end –

MANUSCRIPT: About 1863, in packet 81 (Bingham 9d).
PUBLICATION: *BM* (1945), 157. The suggested change is adopted.

782

There is an arid Pleasure –
As different from Joy –
As Frost is different from Dew –
Like element – are they –

Yet one – rejoices Flowers –
And one – the Flowers abhor –
The finest Honey – curdled –
Is worthless – to the Bee –

8] Repels the healthy Bee –

MANUSCRIPT: About 1863, in packet 81 (Bingham 9e).
PUBLICATION: *BM* (1945), 256. The suggested change is rejected.

The Birds begun at Four o'clock –
Their period for Dawn –
A Music numerous as space –
But neighboring as Noon –

I could not count their Force –
Their Voices did expend
As Brook by Brook bestows itself
To multiply the Pond.

Their Witnesses were not –
Except occasional man –
In homely industry arrayed –
To overtake the Morn –

Nor was it for applause –
That I could ascertain –
But independant Extasy
Of Deity and Men –

By Six, the Flood had done –
No Tumult there had been
Of Dressing, or Departure –
And yet the Band was gone –

The Sun engrossed the East –
The Day controlled the World –
The Miracle that introduced
Forgotten, as fulfilled.

3. numerous as space] measureless as
   Noon –
6. Voices] numbers
8. multiply] magnify
9. Witnesses were not] Listener was
   none

11. arrayed] attired
13. applause] Parade – / Result
16. Deity] Universe
17. Flood] Gush
20. And yet] Yet all
22. controlled] Resumed –

MANUSCRIPT: About 1863, in packet 81 (Bingham 10a).
PUBLICATION: *BM* (1945), 11–12. Suggested changes are adopted for lines 8, 9, 16, 20. Line 4 reads:

And measureless as noon.

Bereaved of all, I went abroad –
No less bereaved was I
Upon a New Peninsula –
The Grave preceded me –

Obtained my Lodgings, ere myself –
And when I sought my Bed –
The Grave it was reposed upon
The Pillow for my Head –

I waked, to find it first awake –
I rose – It followed me –
I tried to drop it in the Crowd –
To lose it in the Sea –

In Cups of artificial Drowse
To steep it's shape away –
The Grave – was finished – but the Spade
Remained in Memory –

     5. Obtained] Engrossed   11. drop] shift

MANUSCRIPT: About 1863, in packet 81 (Bingham 10b).
PUBLICATION: *Poems* (1896), 167, titled "Trying to Forget." The suggested changes are rejected. Three words are altered:

     2. was I] to be   14. steep] sleep

They have a little Odor – that to me
Is metre – nay – 'tis melody –
And spiciest at fading – indicate –
A Habit – of a Laureate –

     2. melody] Poesy –   3. indicate] celebrate –

MANUSCRIPT: About 1863, in packet 81 (Bingham 10c).

PUBLICATION: In *Ancestors' Brocades* (1945), 36, where the lines serve as a motto to introduce the chapter called "Creative Editing," "Poesy" is adopted in line 2; in *BM* (1945), 50, both suggested changes are rejected.

786

Severer Service of myself
I – hastened to demand
To fill the awful Vacuum
Your life had left behind –

I worried Nature with my Wheels
When Her's had ceased to run –
When she had put away Her Work
My own had just begun.

I strove to weary Brain and Bone –
To harass to fatigue
The glittering Retinue of nerves –
Vitality to clog

To some dull comfort Those obtain
Who put a Head away
They knew the Hair to –
And forget the color of the Day –

Affliction would not be appeased –
The Darkness braced as firm
As all my strategem had been
The Midnight to confirm –

No Drug for Consciousness – can be –
Alternative to die
Is Nature's only Pharmacy
For Being's Malady –

3. Vacuum] Longitude –   18. Darkness] trouble –
16. color] figure –

MANUSCRIPT: About 1863, in packet 81 (Bingham 11a).

PUBLICATION: *BM* (1945), 155–156. A comma is placed after "harass" (line 10). The first two words of line 16 conclude line 15. All suggested changes are rejected.

787

Such is the Force of Happiness –
The Least – can lift a Ton
Assisted by it's stimulus –

Who Misery – sustain –
No Sinew can afford –
The Cargo of Themselves –
Too infinite for Consciousness'
Slow capabilities.

1. Force] strength   8] benumbed abilities –

MANUSCRIPT: About 1863, in packet 81 (Bingham 11c).
PUBLICATION: *BM* (1945), 256. Both suggested changes are adopted. The text is arranged as two quatrains.

788

Joy to have merited the Pain –
To merit the Release –
Joy to have perished every step –
To Compass Paradise –

Pardon – to look upon thy face –
With these old fashioned Eyes –
Better than new – could be – for that –
Though bought in Paradise –

Because they looked on thee before –
And thou hast looked on them –
Prove Me – My Hazel Witnesses
The features are the same –

So fleet thou wert, when present –
So infinite – when gone –
An Orient's Apparition –
Remanded of the Morn –

The Hight I recollect –
'Twas even with the Hills –
The Depth upon my Soul was notched –
As Floods – on Whites of Wheels –

To Haunt – till Time have dropped
His last Decade away,
And Haunting actualize – to last
At least – Eternity –

11. Hazel Witnesses] Swimming Witnesses –   22. last Decade away] slow Decades away –

MANUSCRIPT: About 1863, in packet 18 (H 97b).
PUBLICATION: *FP* (1929), 178. The text of stanzas 5 and 6, arranged in 5 and 6 lines respectively, is restored as quatrains in later collections. The suggested change for line 22 is adopted. Five words are altered:

4. Paradise] thee at last   21. have] has
10. hast] hadst   22. Decades] decade
18. even] ever

789

On a Columnar Self –
How ample to rely
In Tumult – or Extremity –
How good the Certainty

That Lever cannot pry –
And Wedge cannot divide
Conviction – That Granitic Base –
Though None be on our Side –

Suffice Us – for a Crowd –
Ourself – and Rectitude –   [*no stanza break*]

And that Assembly – not far off
From furthest Spirit – God –

12. Spirit] Faithful

11–12] [And that] Companion – not far off
from furthest Good Man – God –

MANUSCRIPT: About 1863, in packet 18 (H 98a).
PUBLICATION: *FP* (1929), 128. The suggested change for lines 11, 12 entire is adopted. The text is arranged as three stanzas of 4, 5, 6 lines. In later editions it is arranged as 4, 4, 5 lines. One word is altered:

10. Ourself] Ourselves

790

Nature – the Gentlest Mother is,
Impatient of no Child –
The feeblest – or the waywardest –
Her Admonition mild –

In Forest – and the Hill –
By Traveller – be heard –
Restraining Rampant Squirrel –
Or too impetuous Bird –

How fair Her Conversation –
A Summer Afternoon –
Her Household – Her Assembly –
And when the Sun go down –

Her Voice among the Aisles
Incite the timid prayer
Of the minutest Cricket –
The most unworthy Flower –

When all the Children sleep –
She turns as long away
As will suffice to light Her lamps –
Then bending from the Sky –

[596]

With infinite Affection –
And infiniter Care –
Her Golden finger on Her lip –
Wills Silence – Everywhere –

   3. feeblest] dullest   20. bending] stooping –

MANUSCRIPT: About 1863, in packet 18 (H 98b).

PUBLICATION: *Poems* (1891), 111–112, titled "Mother Nature." Both suggested changes are rejected. The final word in line 1 is omitted. Three words are altered:

    6. be] is   14. Incite] Incites
   12. go] goes

791

God gave a Loaf to every Bird –
But just a Crumb – to Me –
I dare not eat it – tho' I starve –
My poignant luxury –

To own it – touch it –
Prove the feat – that made the Pellet mine –
Too happy – for my Sparrow's chance –
For Ampler Coveting –

It might be Famine – all around –
I could not miss an Ear –
Such Plenty smiles upon my Board –
My Garner shows so fair –

I wonder how the Rich – may feel –
An Indiaman – An Earl –
I deem that I – with but a Crumb –
Am Sovreign of them all –

    7. for] in

MANUSCRIPT: About 1863, in packet 18 (H 100b). There is an extra stroke after "a" in "eat" (line 3).

[597]

PUBLICATION: *Poems* (1891), 50, titled "Enough." The suggested change is adopted. The text is arranged as two eight-line stanzas. The first three words of line 6 conclude line 5. One word is altered:

7. Sparrow's] sparrow

792

Through the strait pass of suffering –
The Martyrs – even – trod.
Their feet – upon Temptation –
Their faces – upon God –

A stately – shriven – Company –
Convulsion – playing round –
Harmless – as streaks of Meteor –
Upon a Planet's Bond –

Their faith – the everlasting troth –
Their Expectation – fair –
The Needle – to the North Degree –
Wades – so – thro' polar Air!

MANUSCRIPTS: There are two, both written about 1863. A third, known to have been written, is now lost. That reproduced above (Bingham) is in a letter to an unidentified recipient, sent probably to Samuel Bowles. It is without signature, and the poem is preceded by the message:

Dear friend If you doubted my Snow – for a moment – you never will – again – I know –
Because I could not say it – I fixed it in the Verse – for you to read – when your thought wavers, for such a foot as mine –

The semifinal draft, of which the fair copy above and the lost copy are redactions, is in packet 18 (H 101a):

Through the Straight Pass of Suffering
The Martyrs even trod –
Their feet upon Temptation –
Their foreheads – upon God –

A Stately – Shriven Company –
Convulsion playing round –
Harmless as Streaks of Meteor –
Upon a Planet's Bond –

Their faith the Everlasting Troth –
Their Expectation – sure –
The Needle to the North Degree
Wades so – through Polar Air –

2. even] steady   10. sure] fair –
4. foreheads] faces

The text of the lost fair copy, discussed below, is that of the packet
copy with all suggested changes rejected, but with the spelling "strait"
(line 1). In the fair copy above ED adopted her suggested changes for
lines 4 and 10, but rejected that for line 2.

PUBLICATION: The poem first appeared in the *Independent*, XLIII (12
March 1891), 1, titled "The Martyrs." It derived from the lost copy to Sue
which she sent to the editor, Dr. William Hayes Ward. The exchange of
letters regarding it, written by Susan Dickinson and Dr. Ward, is in *AB*,
114–118. With the same title it was issued in *Poems* (1891), 33, and fol-
lows the text of the fair copy above, then in Mrs. Todd's possession. The
third word in line 1 is spelled "straight." In both printings, one word is
altered:

8. Bond] bound

793

Grief is a Mouse –
And chooses Wainscot in the Breast
For His Shy House –
And baffles quest –

Grief is a Thief – quick startled –
Pricks His Ear – report to hear
Of that Vast Dark –
That swept His Being – back –

Grief is a Juggler – boldest at the Play –
Lest if He flinch – the eye that way
Pounce on His Bruises – One – say – or Three –
Grief is a Gourmand – spare His luxury –

[599]

Best Grief is Tongueless – before He'll tell –
Burn Him in the Public Square –
His Ashes – will
Possibly – if they refuse – How then know –
Since a Rack could'nt coax a syllable – now

15. Ashes] embers –   17. a syllable] an answer –

MANUSCRIPT: About 1863, in packet 18 (H 102a).
PUBLICATION: *BM* (1945), 251–252. The text derives from a transcript made by Mrs. Todd, and is arranged as six quatrains. The suggested change for line 15 is adopted. One word is altered:

12. spare] span

794

┌ A Drop fell on the Apple Tree –
│ Another – on the Roof –
│ A Half a Dozen kissed the Eaves –
└ And made the Gables laugh –

A few went out to help the Brook
That went to help the Sea –
Myself Conjectured were they Pearls –
What Necklaces could be –

The Dust replaced, in Hoisted Roads –
The Birds jocoser sung –
The Sunshine threw his Hat away –
The Bushes – spangles flung –

The Breezes brought dejected Lutes –
And bathed them in the Glee –
Then Orient showed a single Flag,
And signed the Fete away –

6. That] Who   15] The East put out a single Flag /
8. could be] for Me –   Nature [put out a single Flag]
12. Bushes] Orchards – /   16. Feet] Show –
    Meadows –

MANUSCRIPT: The copy in packet 30 (H 159a), reproduced above, was written about 1863. A fair copy variant (H 332) of the last eight lines was made several years later, about 1874:

> The Dust replaced in hoisted Roads –
> The Birds redoubled sung –
> The Sunshine threw his Hat away,
> The Bushes spangles flung –
> The Breezes brought dejected Lutes
> And bathed them in the Sea –
> Then Nature raised a Colored Hand
> And signed the Van away –

ED did not adopt the changes suggested in the packet copy, and the new variant, which has never been published, seems to be intended as a complete poem. On a small scrap of paper (Bingham 98–4A–7), in the handwriting of 1863, ED has written:

> Myself computed were they Pearls
> What affluence could be –

On the inside of a slit open envelope (Bingham 98–4A–8), in the handwriting of about 1874, is another penciled trial:

> Myself computed were they Pearls
> What Legacy could be
>
> ———————————————
>
> Oh Magnanimity –
> My Visitor in Paradise –

PUBLICATION: *Poems* (1890), 81, titled "Summer Shower." It follows the packet copy, and adopts two suggested changes:

> 12. orchards   15] The East put out a single flag

One word is altered:

> 12. flung] hung

795

Her final Summer was it –
And yet We guessed it not –
If tenderer industriousness
Pervaded Her, We thought

[601]

A further force of life
Developed from within –
When Death lit all the shortness up
It made the hurry plain –

We wondered at our blindness
When nothing was to see
But Her Carrara Guide post –
At Our Stupidity –

When duller than our dullness
The Busy Darling lay –
So busy was she – finishing –
So leisurely – were We –

2] Yet we suspected not   7. shortness] limit –
5. force] Fund   7. shortness up] brevity

MANUSCRIPT: About 1863, in packet 30 (H 159b).
PUBLICATION: *Poems* (1891), 213, titled "At Length." All suggested
changes are rejected. One word is altered:

8. It] And

796

Who Giants know, with lesser Men
Are incomplete, and shy –
For Greatness, that is ill at ease
In minor Company –

A Smaller, could not be perturbed –
The Summer Gnat displays –
Unconscious that his single Fleet
Do not comprise the skies –

3. ill at ease] ill composed   7. Fleet] Bulk – / Sail –
4] With other quality –

MANUSCRIPT: About 1863, in packet 30 (H 159c).
PUBLICATION: *FP* (1929), 15. The last two words of line 1, arranged as

a separate line, are restored in later collections. One suggested change is adopted:

7. sail

Line 8 is altered to read:

Does not comprise the sky.

797

By my Window have I for Scenery
Just a Sea – with a Stem –
If the Bird and the Farmer – deem it a "Pine" –
The Opinion will do – for them –

It has no Port, nor a "Line" – but the Jays –
That split their route to the Sky –
Or a Squirrel, whose giddy Peninsula
May be easier reached – this way –

For Inlands – the Earth is the under side –
And the upper side – is the Sun –
And it's Commerce – if Commerce it have –
Of Spice – I infer from the Odors borne –

Of it's Voice – to affirm – when the Wind is within –
Can the Dumb – define the Divine?
The Definition of Melody – is –
That Definition is none –

It – suggests to our Faith –
They – suggest to our Sight –
When the latter – is put away
I shall meet with Conviction I somewhere met
That Immortality –

Was the Pine at my Window a "Fellow
Of the Royal" Infinity?
Apprehensions – are God's introductions –
To be hallowed – accordingly –

3. If] Grant
4. do] *serve*
6] [That] Ply between it, and the Sky

8. easier reached] Better attained – /
     easier gained –
14. define] divulge
25] Extended inscrutably –

MANUSCRIPT: About 1863, in packet 30 (H 160a).

PUBLICATION: *FP* (1929), 65. It adopts the suggested changes for lines 4, 8 (easier gained), 14, 25. Stanza 5 has been regularized to four lines by combining the first two. The last word in line 7 is spelled "peninsular." The last stanza, arranged in six lines, is restored to a quatrain in later collections. Compare the last two lines of stanza 4 with the poem beginning "The definition of Beauty is."

798

She staked her Feathers – Gained an Arc –
Debated – Rose again –
This time – beyond the estimate
Of Envy, or of Men –

And now, among Circumference –
Her steady Boat be seen –
At home – among the Billows – As
The Bough where she was born –

1. Feathers – Gained an Arc] Wings –
   and gained a Bush –

3. estimate] inference
7. home] ease

MANUSCRIPT: About 1863, in packet 30 (H 161b).

PUBLICATION: *Saturday Review of Literature*, XIII (9 November 1935), 12; *UP* (1935), 133. The suggested changes for lines 3 and 7 are adopted. The last word of line 7 is arranged as the first of line 8.

799

Despair's advantage is achieved
By suffering – Despair –
To be assisted of Reverse
One must Reverse have bore –

The Worthiness of Suffering like
The Worthiness of Death
Is ascertained by tasting –

As can no other Mouth

Of Savors – make us conscious –
As did ourselves partake –
Affliction feels impalpable
Until Ourselves are struck –

4. Reverse] itself
4. Reverse have] have previous

5. Worthiness] excellence – / quality
7. tasting] testing –

MANUSCRIPT: About 1863, in packet 30 (H 161c). Line 8 stands alone.
PUBLICATION: *UP* (1935), 144. The text, arranged as three quatrains,
adopts three suggested changes:

4. have previous
5. excellence

7. testing

The last word of line 5 is arranged as the first of line 6. One word is
altered:

4. bore] borne

800

Two – were immortal twice –
The privilege of few –
Eternity – obtained – in Time –
Reversed Divinity –

That our ignoble Eyes
The quality conceive
Of Paradise superlative –
Through their Comparative.

3] Eternity – in Time obtained –   6. conceive] perceive –

MANUSCRIPT: About 1863, in packet 30 (H 161d).
PUBLICATION: *BM* (1945), 199. Both suggested changes are adopted.
The text derives from a transcript made by Mrs. Todd.

I play at Riches – to appease
The Clamoring for Gold –
It kept me from a Thief, I think,
For often, overbold

With Want, and Opportunity –
I could have done a Sin
And been Myself that easy Thing
An independant Man –

But often as my lot displays
Too hungry to be borne
I deem Myself what I would be –
And novel Comforting

My Poverty and I derive –
We question if the Man –
Who own – Esteem the Opulence –
As We – Who never Can –

Should ever these exploring Hands
Chance Sovreign on a Mine –
Or in the long – uneven term
To win, become their turn –

How fitter they will be – for Want –
Enlightening so well –
I know not which, Desire, or Grant –
Be wholly beautiful –

6. could] might	21. How] 'Tis
7. easy] distant	21. they will be] I shall be –
12. novel Comforting] so much	21. for] by
comforting	23. Grant] Right – / sight
20. their] my	24. wholly] chiefest / utmost

MANUSCRIPT: About 1863, in packet 30 (H 163a).
PUBLICATION: *UP* (1935), 68. The suggested changes for lines 6, 7, 12 are adopted.

Time feels so vast that were it not
For an Eternity –
I fear me this Circumference
Engross my Finity –

To His exclusion, who prepare
By Processes of Size
For the Stupendous Vision
Of His Diameters –

6. Processes] Rudiments [of size]/   7] for the Stupendous Volume –
   Prefaces of size

MANUSCRIPT: About 1863, in packet 30 (H 162c).
PUBLICATION: *UP* (1935), 31. The suggested changes are adopted
("Rudiments" for line 6). The last four words of line 1 are transferred
to line 2; the last two of line 5 to line 6.

Who Court obtain within Himself
Sees every Man a King –
And Poverty of Monarchy
Is an interior thing –

No Man depose
Whom Fate Ordain –
And Who can add a Crown
To Him who doth continual
Conspire against His Own

3. And] So – / the   9. Conspire against] repudiate –
5–6] [No] Fate depose whom Trait
   [Ordain] –

MANUSCRIPT: About 1863, in packet 30 (H 163a).
PUBLICATION: *FP* (1929), 23. The text is arranged as two five-line
stanzas. Two suggested changes are adopted:

3. So   9. Repudiate

Lines 5 and 6 read:

> No fate depose
> Whom Fate ordain –

804

No Notice gave She, but a Change –
No Message, but a Sigh –
For Whom, the Time did not suffice
That She should specify.

She was not warm, though Summer shone
Nor scrupulous of cold
Though Rime by Rime, the steady Frost
Upon Her Bosom piled –

Of shrinking ways – she did not fright
Though all the Village looked –
But held Her gravity aloft –
And met the gaze – direct –

And when adjusted like a Seed
In careful fitted Ground
Unto the Everlasting Spring
And hindered but a Mound

Her Warm return, if so she chose –
And We – imploring drew –
Removed our invitation by
As Some She never knew –

3. suffice] remain
4. should] could
8. Bosom] Petals – / softness
9. she did not fright] Forebore her
   fright

17. Warm] straight – / good – /
    quick – / safe
17. chose] signed
20. Some] Us –

MANUSCRIPT: About 1863, in packet 30 (H 163b).
PUBLICATION: *UP* (1935), 124. Only the suggested change for line 9 is adopted. One word is altered:

13. And] Then

[608]

This Bauble was preferred of Bees –
By Butterflies admired
At Heavenly – Hopeless Distances –
Was justified of Bird –

Did Noon – enamel – in Herself
Was Summer to a Score
Who only knew of Universe –
It had created Her.

2. admired] adored – / desired   5. enamel] enable – / embellish
4] Of Bird – was justified –   8. created] afforded –

MANUSCRIPT: About 1863, in packet 30 (H 164b).
PUBLICATION: *UP* (1935), 63. Three suggested changes are adopted:

2. desired   5. embellish
4. Of Bird – was justified –

The text is arranged without stanza division. Two words are altered:

1. of] by   3. Distances] distance

805

806

A Plated Life – diversified
With Gold and Silver Pain
To prove the presence of the Ore
In Particles – 'tis when

A Value struggle – it exist –
A Power – will proclaim
Although Annihilation pile
Whole Chaoses on Him –

5. Value] Nature   8. Whole Chaoses] Oblivions –

MANUSCRIPT: About 1863, in packet 30 (H 164c).

PUBLICATION: *UP* (1935), 80. The suggested change for line 5 is adopted. The text is arranged without stanza division.

807

Expectation – is Contentment –
Gain – Satiety –
But Satiety – Conviction
Of Nescessity

Of an Austere trait in Pleasure –
Good, without alarm
Is a too established Fortune –
Danger – deepens Sum –

7. established Fortune] secure Possession – / too Contented Measure –

MANUSCRIPT: About 1863, in packet 30 (H 164d).
PUBLICATION: *FP* (1929), 31. A period concludes line 4. The two final lines read:

> Is a too serene possession –
> Danger deepens suns.

808

So set it's Sun in Thee
What Day be dark to me
What Distance far
So I the Ships may see
That touch how seldomly
Thy Shore?

MANUSCRIPTS: There are two, both written about 1864. The copy in packet 86 (Bingham 34e) is reproduced above. The other copy (H 315), in pencil, is addressed "Sue –" and signed "Emily." It is identical in text. Three lines differ in punctuation:

2] What Day be dark to me –   5] That touch – how seldomly –
3] What Distance, far –

PUBLICATION: *SH* (1914), 138. It derives from the copy to Sue. One word is altered:

2. be] is

809

Unable are the Loved to die
For Love is Immortality,
Nay, it is Deity –

Unable they that love – to die
For Love reforms Vitality
Into Divinity.

MANUSCRIPTS: The copy reproduced above, written about 1864, is in packet 86 (Bingham 36a). The first stanza only was sent to Sue (H B 18) perhaps in March 1865 on the occasion of the death of Sue's sister, Harriet Cutler:

Unable are the Loved – to die –
For Love is immortality –
Nay – it is Deity –

The lines, written in pencil, constitute the entire message.

PUBLICATION: The lines to Sue were first published in the *Atlantic Monthly*, CXV (1915), 40, where one word is altered:

1. Loved] dead

The text was corrected when the lines were printed in *FF* (1932), 263. The second stanza is now published for the first time.

810

Her Grace is all she has –
And that, so least displays –
One Art to recognize, must be,
Another Art, to praise.

MANUSCRIPTS: There are two, both written in 1864. That reproduced above (Bingham 36f) is in packet 86. It is identical in text with the penciled copy (H 264) sent to Sue, signed "Emily."

> Her Grace is all she has,
> And that, so least displays,
> One art, to recognize, must be,
> Another Art, to praise –

PUBLICATION: *SH* (1914), 135. One word is altered:

2. least] vast

Ralph Marcellino called attention to the correct reading in the *New York Herald Tribune Book Review* (3 May 1936) 22, from studying the facsimile reproduction of the copy to Sue in the Centenary edition of *Poems* (1930), facing page 266. It was this copy whence the printed text derived. Later issues of *Poems* did not incorporate the correction.

811

> The Veins of other Flowers
> The Scarlet Flowers are
> Till Nature leisure has for Terms
> As "Branch," and "Jugular."
>
> We pass, and she abides.
> We conjugate Her Skill
> While She creates and federates
> Without a syllable.

4. "Branch"] Trunk

MANUSCRIPTS: The two stanzas reproduced above are in packet 86 (Bingham 37e), written about 1864. A copy of the second stanza only (H 371), in pencil, written at the same time, was probably sent to Sue:

> We pass, and she – abides,
> We conjugate Her Skill,
> While She creates and federates
> Without a syllable.

PUBLICATION: *BM* (1945), 51, reproduces the packet copy. The suggested change is rejected.

A Light exists in Spring
Not present on the Year
At any other period –
When March is scarcely here

A Color stands abroad
On Solitary Fields
That Science cannot overtake
But Human Nature feels.

It waits upon the Lawn,
It shows the furthest Tree
Upon the furthest Slope you know
It almost speaks to you.

Then as Horizons step
Or Noons report away
Without the Formula of sound
It passes and we stay –

A quality of loss
Affecting our Content
As Trade had suddenly encroached
Upon a Sacrament.

MANUSCRIPTS: The copy reproduced above, written about 1864, is in packet 86 (Bingham 38a). Two words are marked for alternatives but none is given:

7. That   11. you

The concluding five lines of another copy (H 277) in pencil, written about 1867, are on a sheet which seems to be the second of two on which the poem was set down and sent to Sue. It is signed "Emily." The text and form are identical with those of the packet copy except that the final line is without punctuation. It is possible that the five lines were sent to Sue as a message after the departure of some guest. They are not separately published.

PUBLICATION: *Poems* (1896), 103–104. Four words are altered:

6. Fields] hills   11. you] we
8. feels] *feels*   12. you] me

813

This quiet Dust was Gentlemen and Ladies
And Lads and Girls –
Was laughter and ability and Sighing
And Frocks and Curls.

This Passive Place a Summer's nimble mansion
Where Bloom and Bees
Exist an Oriental Circuit
Then cease, like these –

Manuscripts: The copy reproduced above, in packet 86 (Bingham 39a), was written about 1864. The variant copy sent to Sue, signed "Emily –," is later and in pencil, about 1867; it is privately owned (A. Norcross):

> This quiet Dust was Gentlemen and Ladies
> And Lads and Girls
> Was Laughter and Ability and Sighing
> And Frocks and Curls –
> This passive place a Summer's nimble Mansion
> Where Bloom and Bees
> Fulfilled their Oriental Circuit
> Then ceased, like these.

It is variant in lines 7 and 8.

Publication: *SH* (1914), 80. It follows the copy to Sue.

814

One Day is there of the Series
Termed Thanksgiving Day.
Celebrated part at Table
Part in Memory.

[614]

Neither Patriarch nor Pussy
I dissect the Play
Seems it to my Hooded thinking
Reflex Holiday.

Had there been no sharp Subtraction
From the early Sum –
Not an Acre or a Caption
Where was once a Room –

Not a Mention, whose small Pebble
Wrinkled any Sea,
Unto Such, were such Assembly
Twere Thanksgiving Day.

MANUSCRIPTS: There are two. The copy reproduced above, in packet 87
(Bingham 42a), was written about 1864. The variant copy below to Sue
(H 303), headed "Sister" and signed "Emily.", is in pencil and was written
about 1869. The textual variants are in lines 5 and 6:

One Day is there of the series
Termed "Thanksgiving Day"
Celebrated part at table
Part in memory.
Neither Ancestor nor Urchin
I review the Play –
Seems it to my Hooded thinking
Reflex Holiday.

Had there been no sharp Subtraction
From the early Sum –
Not an Acre or a Caption
Where was once a Room
Not a mention whose small Pebble
Wrinkled any Sea,
Unto such, were such Assembly
'Twere "Thanksgiving Day" –

PUBLICATION: *Poems* (1896), 69, titled "Thanksgiving Day." It follows
the text of the packet copy. One word is altered:

14. Sea] bay

[615]

The Luxury to apprehend
The Luxury 'twould be
To look at Thee a single time
An Epicure of Me

In whatsoever Presence makes
Till for a further Food
I scarcely recollect to starve
So first am I supplied –

The Luxury to meditate
The Luxury it was
To banquet on thy Countenance
A Sumptuousness bestows

On plainer Days, whose Table far
As Certainty can see
Is laden with a single Crumb
The Consciousness of Thee.

MANUSCRIPTS: There are four fair copies. That reproduced above
(Bingham 42b), in packet 87, was written in 1864. A second copy (H 341),
in pencil and written at the same time, is addressed "Sue" and signed
"Emily." It is identical in text; in form it differs somewhat. It is without
stanza division; five words are not capitalized – "luxury" (lines 1, 2, 9,
10) and "food" (line 6); there is a comma after "Table" (line 13); and
lines 14 and 15 are punctuated with dashes at the end and after "Cer-
tainty." Line 13 is divided thus:

> On plainer Days,
> Whose Table, far

The copy to T. W. Higginson (BPL Higg 20) was enclosed in a note
(BPL Higg 63), postmarked 16 July 1868, that asks his critical guidance:

> The Luxury to apprehend
> The Luxury 'twould be
> To look at thee a single time
> An Epicure of me

[no stanza break]

In whatsoever presence makes
Till for a further food
I scarcely recollect to starve
So first am I supplied.
The Luxury to meditate
The Luxury it was
To banquet on thy Countenance
A sumptuousness supplies
To plainer Days whose table, far
As Certainty can see –
Is laden with a single Crumb –
The Consciousness of thee –

It quotes to him the title of his own January 1867 *Atlantic Monthly* article, and reads:

Bringing still my "plea for Culture."
Would it teach me now?

It is variant in two lines:

12. bestows] supplies   13. On] To

The fourth copy (Bingham 98–4B–18) was probably written in 1868 also, but somewhat earlier in the year. It is identical in text and form with the copy to Higginson except that "food" (line 6) is capitalized, and the last three lines lack punctuation.

PUBLICATION: *SH* (1914), 119. The text derives from the copy to Sue, and follows the text by printing it without stanza division as a seventeen-line poem. The same text is reproduced in *CP* (1924). In the Centenary edition (1930) and later collections, the text is changed to conform with the Higginson variant, which the editors evidently consulted in the Boston Public Library. Lines 12 and 13 read:

A sumptuousness supplies
To plainer days

816

A Death blow is a Life blow to Some
Who till they died, did not alive become –
Who had they lived, had died but when
They died, Vitality begun.

[617]

MANUSCRIPTS: The copy reproduced above (BPL Higg 17) was enclosed in a letter to T. W. Higginson (BPL Higg 59), postmarked 17 March 1866. There are two other fair copies, both written some two years earlier, about 1864. The text of all three is identical; differences are in form only. The copy to Sue (H B 81), written in pencil, is addressed "Sue –" and signed "Emily.":

> A Death blow – is a Life blow – to Some –
> Who, till they died –
> Did not alive – become –
> Who had they lived
> Had died, but when
> They died, Vitality begun –

The copy in packet 87 (Bingham 43b) reads thus:

> A Death blow is a Life blow, to Some,
> Who till they died, did not alive become
> Who had they lived had died, but when
> They died, Vitality begun.

PUBLICATION: The poem was first published in *Atlantic Monthly*, LXVIII (October 1891), 455, in an article which Higginson wrote dealing with the letters and poems he had received from ED. The same copy was later reproduced in *Letters* (ed. 1894), 319; (ed. 1931), 294; also *LL* (1924), 293. The poem was first collected in *Poems* (1891), 187, where it presumably derives from the same source, since at that time Mrs. Todd did not possess a copy (*AB*, 130).

817

> Given in Marriage unto Thee
> Oh thou Celestial Host –
> Bride of the Father and the Son
> Bride of the Holy Ghost.
>
> Other Betrothal shall dissolve –
> Wedlock of Will, decay –
> Only the Keeper of this Ring
> Conquer Mortality –

7. this Ring] the Seal

MANUSCRIPTS: There are two, both about 1864. The copy reproduced above is in packet 87 (Bingham 44e). A fair copy to Sue (H 257) is in pencil, signed "Emily –"; it omits the second stanza:

Given in Marriage unto Thee
Oh Thou Celestial Host –
Bride of the Father and the Son,
Bride of the Holy Ghost.

PUBLICATION: *Poems* (1896), 145. It derives from the packet copy. Part of the suggested change is adopted, so that line 7 reads:

Only the keeper of this seal

One word is altered:

8. Conquer] Conquers

818

I could not drink it, Sweet,
Till You had tasted first,
Though cooler than the Water was
The Thoughtfulness of Thirst.

MANUSCRIPTS: The copy reproduced above in packet 91 (Bingham 70f) was written about 1864. The variant copy (H B 139), addressed "Sue" and signed "Emily–," was written at the same time:

I could not drink it, Sue,
Till you had tasted first –
Though cooler than the Water – was
The Thoughtfulness of Thirst –

PUBLICATION: *FF* (1932), 270. The text follows the copy to Sue. The last word of line 3 is printed as the first of line 4.

819

All I may, if small,
Do it not display
Larger for the Totalness –
'Tis Economy

To bestow a World
And withold a Star –
Utmost, is Munificence –
Less, tho larger, poor.

MANUSCRIPTS: There are two, both written about 1864. The copy re-
produced above is that in packet 91 (Bingham 71d). The copy presumably
sent to Sue (H 232), in pencil, is variant in the third line:

> All I may – if small,
> Do it not display
> Larger for it's Totalness?
> 'Tis Economy
> To bestow a World
> And withold a Star,
> Utmost – is Munificence –
> Less – tho' Larger, Poor.

PUBLICATION: *SH* (1914), 121. It follows the copy to Sue.

820

All Circumstances are the Frame
In which His Face is set –
All Latitudes exist for His
Sufficient Continent –

The Light His Action, and the Dark
The Leisure of His Will –
In Him Existence serve or set
A Force illegible.

MANUSCRIPTS: There are two, both written about 1864. The above
text is that in packet 91 (Bingham 73b). The copy to Sue (H 231) is
identical in text and form with the above except that line 7 is punctuated:

> In Him, Existence serve, or set

It is in pencil, addressed "Sue –" and signed "Emily."
PUBLICATION: *SH* (1914), 149.

Away from Home are some and I –
An Emigrant to be
In a Metropolis of Homes
Is easy, possibly –

The Habit of a Foreign Sky
We – difficult – acquire
As Children, who remain in Face
The more their Feet retire.

MANUSCRIPTS: There are three, all written probably in 1864. The poem may have been inspired in a moment of longing for home shortly after she arrived in Cambridge in late April 1864 for eye treatment. The copy reproduced above (Library of Congress) presumably was sent to Sue; it is in pencil, signed "Emily." The copy in packet 92 (Bingham 77c), the only one in ink, is identical in text:

Away from Home are some and I –
An Emigrant to be
In a metropolis of Homes
Is easy possibly –

The Habit of a Foreign Sky
We – difficult acquire
As Children, who remain in Face
The more their Feet retire.

4. easy] common –

Neither of the fair copies adopts the suggested change. The second fair copy (Bingham 98–4B–6) is signed "Emily." It is also in pencil and may have been intended for or sent to some friend; it is variant in its first line:

Away from Home, are They and I –
An Emigrant to be
In a Metropolis of Homes
Is easy, possibly –

The Habit of a Foreign Sky
We – difficult acquire
As Children, who remain in Face
The more their Feet retire.

A fourth copy, the source of the published version, is now lost.

PUBLICATION: The lost copy is the one sent to Mrs. J. G. Holland, printed in *Letters* (ed. 1894), 178; (ed. 1931), 172; also *LL* (1924), 261. In the 1894 edition (and also in *LL*) it appears as an eight-line stanza, with the fourth line reading:

> Is common possibility.

In the 1931 edition the poem is printed as two quatrains with the same fourth line, but with a footnote referring to it saying:

> Alternative line, "Is easy, possibly."

Such an alternative reading in any fair copy is most unlikely. It is probable that Mrs. Todd, who had returned the Holland letters and poems to Mrs. Holland as soon as she had completed copy for the 1894 edition, used the packet copy as her source for the footnote, which appears only in the 1931 edition. In the copy to Mrs. Holland, ED evidently had substituted her original alternative "common" for "easy." But "possibility" is almost certainly a misreading; it renders the line meaningless and destroys the meter. The poem, derived from the 1931 edition of *Letters*, is in *LH* (1951), 68.

822

This Consciousness that is aware
Of Neighbors and the Sun
Will be the one aware of Death
And that itself alone

Is traversing the interval
Experience between
And most profound experiment
Appointed unto Men —

How adequate unto itself
It's properties shall be
Itself unto itself and none
Shall make discovery.

Adventure most unto itself
The Soul condemned to be –
Attended by a single Hound
It's own identity.

MANUSCRIPTS: The copy reproduced above, in packet 92 (Bingham 79a), was written about 1864. A copy of the fourth stanza only (H SH 2) is in pencil, addressed "Sue" and signed "Emily." It was written about the same time. This later copy was attached to the half title page in Martha Dickinson Bianchi's own copy of *The Single Hound* (1914). Sue had died in May of the previous year; Mrs. Bianchi has written above the poem an inscription to the memory of her mother:

> To my Dolly –
> From Aunt Emily
> and me.
> 1914

PUBLICATION: The stanza to Sue furnished the title for the first volume of poems edited by Mrs. Bianchi, and occupies the first place in the volume: *SH* (1914), 3. It was later included in *LL* (1924), 194, where it is dated 1854. The four stanzas of the packet copy are in *AB* (1945), 379–380.

823

Not what We did, shall be the test
When Act and Will are done
But what Our Lord infers We would
Had We diviner been –

MANUSCRIPTS: There are two, both written about 1864. The copy reproduced above is in packet 33 (H 176d). The variant below (Yale), in pencil, was sent to Sue, whose penciled note on the back reads: "Sent me in 1860 by Emily –."

> Not what We did, shall be the Test,
> When Act and Will are done,
> But what Our Lord inferred We would,
> Had we Diviner, been –

PUBLICATION: *FP* (1929), 193. The text derives from the packet copy. In line 3 "would" is italicized.

The Wind begun to knead the Grass –
As Women do a Dough –
He flung a Hand full at the Plain –
A Hand full at the Sky –
The Leaves unhooked themselves from Trees –
And started all abroad –
The Dust did scoop itself like Hands –
And throw away the Road –
The Wagons quickened on the Street –
The Thunders gossiped low –
The Lightning showed a Yellow Head –
And then a livid Toe –
The Birds put up the Bars to Nests –
The Cattle flung to Barns –
Then came one drop of Giant Rain –
And then, as if the Hands
That held the Dams – had parted hold –
The Waters Wrecked the Sky –
But overlooked my Father's House –
Just Quartering a Tree –

first version

The Wind begun to rock the Grass
With threatening Tunes and low –
He threw a Menace at the Earth –
A Menace at the Sky.

The Leaves unhooked themselves from Trees –
And started all abroad
The Dust did scoop itself like Hands
And threw away the Road.

The Wagons quickened on the Streets
The Thunder hurried slow –
The Lightning showed a Yellow Beak
And then a livid Claw.

The Birds put up the Bars to Nests –
The Cattle fled to Barns –
There came one drop of Giant Rain
And then as if the Hands

That held the Dams had parted hold
The Waters Wrecked the Sky,
But overlooked my Father's House –
Just quartering a Tree —

second version

MANUSCRIPTS: This poem survives in five fair copies, three of the first
version, two of the second. A sixth copy (a third copy of the second ver-
sion) is discussed below. The copy of the first version reproduced above
(Bingham) was written about 1864 and sent to Dr. and Mrs. Holland. It is
signed "Emily –." A second copy of the same version (Bingham 106–8),
identical in text, form, and signature, was written at the same time and sent
to an unidentified recipient. A third copy of the first version (H 356), writ-
ten about 1870, is addressed "Sue" and signed "Emily." It is variant in two
lines:

9. Street] Streets   10. Thunders] Thunder

PUBLICATION: *Poems* (1891), 158–159, titled "A Thunder-Storm." It
follows the text of the second version reproduced above, with two words
seemingly adopted from the first version:

3. threw] flung   8. threw] throw

In view of the fact that Mrs. Todd did not have copies of the poem in
the summer of 1891 when she was preparing the text for the Second Series,
and that the purpose of Higginson in sending his inventory (mentioned
above) was to make transcripts of his poems available, it seems probable
that the published version derives from the lost copy to Higginson. The
first version is unpublished.

825

An Hour is a Sea
Between a few, and me –
With them would Harbor be –

[625]

MANUSCRIPT: About 1864, in pencil (H B 78), in a letter to Sue.
PUBLICATION: *Atlantic Monthly*, CXV (1915), 37; *FF* (1932), 236.

826

Love reckons by itself – alone –
"As large as I" – relate the Sun
To One who never felt it blaze –
Itself is all the like it has –

MANUSCRIPT: About 1864, in pencil (H B 163a). It was probably sent to Sue, though it is without address or signature.
PUBLICATION: *SH* (1914), 122.

827

The Only News I know
Is Bulletins all Day
From Immortality.

The Only Shows I see –
Tomorrow and Today –
Perchance Eternity –

The Only One I meet
Is God – The Only Street –
Existence – This traversed

If Other News there be –
Or Admirabler Show –
I'll tell it You –

6] Three – with Eternity – / And
 some Eternity –

9. traversed] traverst
12. tell it You] Signify – / testify –

MANUSCRIPTS: The copy reproduced above, written in 1864, is in packet 39 (H 130a). The first stanza is incorporated in a letter (BPL Higg 57) written to T. W. Higginson in early June 1864. He was with his regiment in the South and she in Cambridge undergoing eye treatment. She is writing in pencil and comments on her imposed limitations. After inquiring for his health she says:

> The only News I know
> Is Bulletins all day
> From Immortality.

PUBLICATION: The letter to Higginson was first published in *Atlantic Monthly*, LXVIII (October 1891), 450, in an article which Higginson wrote dealing with the letters and poems he had received from ED. It was collected in *Letters* (ed. 1894), 311; (ed. 1931), 280; also *LL* (1924), 262. The four stanzas are in *FP* (1929), 115. All suggested changes are rejected.

828

> The Robin is the One
> That interrupt the Morn
> With hurried – few – express Reports
> When March is scarcely on –
>
> The Robin is the One
> That overflow the Noon
> With her cherubic quantity –
> An April but begun –
>
> The Robin is the One
> That speechless from her Nest
> Submit that Home – and Certainty
> And Sanctity, are best

MANUSCRIPT: About 1864, in packet 92 (Bingham 76a). Another copy, now lost, was sent to T. W. Higginson and is listed by him as among his papers in May 1891 (*AB*, 129). In his article discussed below he says that it came to him enclosed in a letter he received in the spring of 1863 while he was at camp in South Carolina. The packet copy is in handwriting clearly of a later date, sometime in 1864. Higginson was establishing his data from memory, nearly thirty years later, and there are instances where his memory as employed in that article was in error. It probably is in error here, for ED's custom was to send copies of her poems to friends after she had entered them in her packets, not before.

PUBLICATION: The poem was first published in *Atlantic Monthly*, LXVIII (October 1891), 450, titled "The Robin," in an article which Higginson wrote dealing with the letters and poems he had received from ED. It was first collected in *Poems* (1891), 117, also titled "The Robin." Unless the lost copy to Higginson is recovered, there can be no way of knowing whether the source of the texts, which are identical, was the packet copy or the copy to Higginson. In a letter which Mrs. Todd wrote Higginson on 18 May 1891 (*AB*, 130), she tells him that she did not at that time have a copy of the poem. In both printings the form of three words differs. The difference is of a nature to suggest editorial alteration rather than a variant source:

2. interrupt] interrupts   11. Submit] Submits
6. overflow] overflows

829

Ample make this Bed –
Make this Bed with Awe –
In it wait till Judgment break
Excellent and Fair.

Be it's Mattress straight –
Be it's Pillow round –
Let no Sunrise' yellow noise
Interrupt this Ground —

MANUSCRIPTS: There are four fair copies, identical in text but written in different years. The latest copy (Bingham), reproduced above, was enclosed in a letter to Thomas Niles, written in April 1883. ED titled the poem, in her letter, "Country Burial."

The earliest copy is that in packet 92 (Bingham 79d), written in 1864:

> Ample make this Bed
> Make this Bed with Awe
> In it wait till Judgment break
> Excellent and Fair
>
> Be it's Mattrass straight
> Be it's Pillow round
> Let no Sunrise' Yellow noise
> Interrupt this Ground.

The second copy (Bingham), in pencil, was written about 1864 and sent to an unidentified recipient. Its form is that of the packet copy except that dashes conclude lines 1, 2, 4, 5, 6; commas follow "it" (line 3) and "Excellent" (line 4); and "break" (line 3) is capitalized.

The third copy (BPL Higg 18) was one of four poems enclosed in a letter (BPL Higg 60) to T. W. Higginson, postmarked 9 June 1866:

> Ample make this Bed –
> Make this Bed with Awe –
> In it wait till Judgment – Break
> Excellent and Fair.
>
> Be it's Mattrass straight
> Be it's Pillow round –
> Let no Sunrise' yellow Noise
> Interrupt this Ground

By 1883, when ED sent the fourth copy to Niles, she evidently considered her spelling *mattrass* archaic.

PUBLICATION: *Poems* (1891), 207, titled "A Country Burial."

830

> To this World she returned.
> But with a tinge of that –
> A Compound manner,
> As a Sod
> Espoused a Violet,
> That chiefer to the Skies
> Than to Himself, allied,
> Dwelt hesitating, half of Dust,
> And half of Day, the Bride.

MANUSCRIPTS: The copy reproduced above (Collamore) was written in pencil in the summer of 1864. It is addressed "Mrs. Gertrude –" and signed "Emily." On 20 March 1864, Mrs. Vanderbilt was summoned to her back door by cries of distress and accidentally received a pistol shot intended for her maid. Her critical illness but ultimate recovery moved ED to send her two poems, this and the poem that follows. At the same time she sent the poem, she made a second copy in ink which she placed in

packet 33 (H 176c). Its text is identical with that of the copy to Mrs.
Vanderbilt, but it differs somewhat in form:

> To this World she returned
> But with a tinge of that
> A Compound manner as a Sod
> Espoused a Violet –
>
> That chiefer to the Skies
> Than to Himself allied
> Dwelt hesitating, half of Dust
> And half of Day the Bride.

PUBLICATION: The printed text, which derives from the copy to Mrs.
Vanderbilt, is in *Letters* (ed. 1894), 154; (ed. 1931), 152; also *LL* (1924),
259. One word is altered:

> 2. tinge] tingle

831

> Dying! To be afraid of thee
> One must to thine Artillery
> Have left exposed a Friend –
> Than thine old Arrow is a Shot
> Delivered straighter to the Heart
> The leaving Love behind.
>
> Not for itself, the Dust is shy,
> But, enemy, Beloved be
> Thy Batteries divorce.
> Fight sternly in a Dying eye
> Two Armies, Love and Certainty
> And Love and the Reverse.

MANUSCRIPTS: There are two, identical in text. The copy reproduced
above in packet 86 (Bingham 35d) was written about 1864; that below in
pencil (Collamore), addressed "Mrs. Vanderbilt –" and signed "Emily –,"
was written about 1866:

> Dying – to be afraid of Thee –
> One must to thine Artillery
> Have left exposed a friend –   [*no stanza break*]

Than thine old Arrow is a Shot
Delivered straighter to the Heart
The leaving Love behind –

Not for itself, the Dust is shy.
But Enemy – Beloved be –
Thy Batteries divorce –
Fight sternly in a dying eye
Two Armies – Love and Certainty,
And Love and the Reverse –

Though the packet copy of this poem was made in 1864, the copy to
Mrs. Vanderbilt almost certainly was sent some two years later.
PUBLICATION: *BM* (1945), 193. It derives from the packet copy.

832

Soto! Explore thyself!
Therein thyself shalt find
The "Undiscovered Continent" –
No Settler had the Mind.

MANUSCRIPTS: There are three autograph copies of this poem, all writ-
ten about 1864. That reproduced above is in packet 91 (Bingham 69d).
Another copy in pencil is addressed "Austin –" and signed "Emily."
(H B 19):

> "Soto" – Explore Thyself –
> Therein – Thyself shalt find
> The "Undiscovered Continent" –
> No Settler – had the Mind.

The third copy (Bingham 98–4A–13), also signed "Emily.", and evidently
intended for or sent to an unknown recipient, is identical with the copy to
Austin.
PUBLICATION: *FF* (1932), 245. The copy to Austin furnished the text.

833

Perhaps you think me stooping
I'm not ashamed of that
Christ – stooped until He touched the Grave –
Do those at Sacrament

Commemorate Dishonor
Or love annealed of love
Until it bend as low as Death
Redignified, above?

MANUSCRIPTS: There are two, both written about 1864. That repro-
duced above is in packet 87 (Bingham 41f). The other copy (Bingham), in
pencil and written at the same time, was sent to Samuel Bowles:

Perhaps you think me *stooping*!
I'm not ashamed – of *that*!
Christ – stooped – until he *touched the Grave*!
Do those at *Sacrament* –
Commemorate *dishonor* –
Or love – annealed of love –
Until it bend – as low as *Death*
Re-royalized – *above*?

It is variant in line 8.

PUBLICATION: The text of the copy to Bowles is in *Letters* (ed. 1894),
211; (ed. 1931), 200; also *LL* (1924), 245. The italics are not reproduced.
In the 1931 edition "Redignified" (line 8) is offered as an alternative read-
ing for "Re-royalized." Both copies of the poem were then in Mrs. Todd's
possession.

834

Before He comes we weigh the Time!
'Tis Heavy and 'tis Light.
When He depart, an Emptiness
Is the prevailing Freight.

MANUSCRIPTS: There are two, both written about 1864. That repro-
duced above is in packet 86 (Bingham 35g). A second copy (Bingham), in
pencil and signed "Emily –," was sent to Samuel Bowles. It is variant in the
last two lines:

Before He comes, We weigh the Time,
'Tis Heavy, and 'tis Light –
When He departs, An Emptiness
Is the superior Freight.

PUBLICATION: The copy to Bowles, arranged as a six-line stanza, is in *Letters* (ed. 1894), 208; (ed. 1931), 198; also *LL* (1924), 236. The alternative reading "Prevailing" (line 4), which Mrs. Todd gives in a footnote in the 1931 edition, she derived from the packet copy.

835

Nature and God – I neither knew
Yet Both so well knew me
They startled, like Executors
Of My identity.

Yet Neither told – that I could learn –
My Secret as secure
As Herschel's private interest
Or Mercury's affair –

MANUSCRIPTS: There are two, both written about 1864. That reproduced above is in packet 91 (Bingham 70a). The copy below (Bingham), in pencil and signed "Emily –," was sent to Samuel Bowles.

> Nature, and God, I neither knew
> Yet both, so well knew me
> They startled, like Executors
> Of an identity –
> Yet Neither – told – that I could learn –
> My secret, as secure
> As Herschel's private interest,
> Or Mercury's Affair –

It is variant in line 4. The reference to Herschel might be to either of the celebrated astronomers of that name: Sir William Herschel (1738–1822), who discovered the planet Uranus, or his son Sir John (1792–1871).

PUBLICATION: The text of the copy to Bowles is in *Letters* (ed. 1894), 213; (ed. 1931), 201; also *LL* (1924), 246.

836

Truth – is as old as God –
His Twin identity
And will endure as long as He
A Co-Eternity –

[633]

And perish on the Day
Himself is borne away
From Mansion of the Universe
A lifeless Deity.

MANUSCRIPTS: There are two, both written about 1864. That repro-
duced above is in packet 87 (Bingham 43a). The other copy (H H 99)
addressed "Doctor." and signed "Emily –," was sent to Dr. Holland. It is
variant in line 6:

> Truth – is as old as God –
> His Twin Identity –
> And will endure as long as He –
> A Co Eternity –
> And perish, on the Day
> That He is borne away
> From Mansion of the Universe –
> A lifeless Deity.

PUBLICATION: The copy sent to Dr. Holland is in *Letters* (ed. 1894),
162; (ed. 1931), 159; also *LL* (1924), 188. It is mistakenly dated late au-
tumn 1853. The text in *LH* (1951), 39, derived from *Letters*, since the
autograph of the poem was not then available.

837

How well I knew Her not
Whom not to know has been
A Bounty in prospective, now
Next Door to mine the Pain.

MANUSCRIPT: About 1864, in packet 91 (Bingham 70d). A second
copy, now lost, is discussed below.

PUBLICATION: *Letters* (ed. 1894), 335; (ed. 1931), 324; also *LL*
(1924), 311: among the letters to Maria Whitney. The poem, signed
"Emily," constitutes the entire letter; Maria Whitney's sister Sarah (Whit-
ney) Learned died 9 July 1864, at Plymouth, Connecticut. The first line
of the printed text reads:

How well I know her not

Impossibility, like Wine
Exhilirates the Man
Who tastes it; Possibility
Is flavorless – Combine

A Chance's faintest Tincture
And in the former Dram
Enchantment makes ingredient
As certainly as Doom –

MANUSCRIPT: About 1864, in packet 86 (Bingham 34d).
PUBLICATION: *BM* (1945), 277.

Always Mine!
No more Vacation!
Term of Light this Day begun!
Failless as the fair rotation
Of the Seasons and the Sun.

Old the Grace, but new the Subjects –
Old, indeed, the East,
Yet upon His Purple Programme
Every Dawn, is first.

MANUSCRIPT: About 1864, in packet 86 (Bingham 34g).
PUBLICATION: *BM* (1945), 141. The text is arranged as two quatrains.

I cannot buy it – 'tis not sold –
There is no other in the World –
Mine was the only one

I was so happy I forgot
To shut the Door And it went out
And I am all alone –

If I could find it Anywhere
I would not mind the journey there
Though it took all my store

But just to look it in the Eye –
"Did'st thou?" "Thou did'st not mean," to say,
Then, turn my Face away.

Manuscript: About 1864, in packet 86 (Bingham 34h).
Publication: *BM* (1945), 106.

841

A Moth the hue of this
Haunts Candles in Brazil.
Nature's Experience would make
Our Reddest Second pale.

Nature is fond, I sometimes think,
Of Trinkets, as a Girl.

Manuscript: About 1864, in packet 86 (Bingham 34i).
Publication: *BM* (1945), 72. The text is arranged as a six-line stanza.

842

Good to hide, and hear 'em hunt!
Better, to be found,
If one care to, that is,
The Fox fits the Hound –

Good to know, and not tell,
Best, to know and tell,
Can one find the rare Ear
Not too dull –

Manuscript: About 1864, in packet 86 (Bingham 34j).
Publication: *BM* (1945), 91.

843

I made slow Riches but my Gain
Was steady as the Sun
And every Night, it numbered more
Than the preceding One

All Days, I did not earn the same
But my perceiveless Gain
Inferred the less by Growing than
The Sum that it had grown.

MANUSCRIPT: About 1864, in packet 86 (Bingham 35e).
PUBLICATION: *BM* (1945), 106.

844

Spring is the Period
Express from God.
Among the other seasons
Himself abide,

But during March and April
None stir abroad
Without a cordial interview
With God.

MANUSCRIPT: About 1864, in packet 86 (Bingham 35f).
PUBLICATION: *BM* (1945), 34.

845

Be Mine the Doom —
Sufficient Fame —
To perish in Her Hand!

MANUSCRIPTS: There are two, both in packets, and both written about 1864. The copy reproduced above is in packet 91 (Bingham 70b). That in packet 86 (Bingham 34b) is identical in text and form except that the only punctuation is a period at the end. The lines were evidently written to accompany the gift of a flower.

PUBLICATION: *BM* (1945), 327. It is placed among the occasional or personal poems.

846

Twice had Summer her fair Verdure
Proffered to the Plain –
Twice a Winter's silver Fracture
On the Rivers been –

Two full Autumns for the Squirrel
Bounteous prepared –
Nature, Had'st thou not a Berry
For thy wandering Bird?

MANUSCRIPT: About 1864, in packet 86 (Bingham 35h).
PUBLICATION: *BM* (1945), 39.

847

Finite – to fail, but infinite to Venture –
For the one ship that struts the shore
Many's the gallant – overwhelmed Creature
Nodding in Navies nevermore –

MANUSCRIPT: About 1864, in packet 86 (Bingham 36b).
PUBLICATION: *Poems* (1896), 46, titled "Ventures."

848

Just as He spoke it from his Hands
This Edifice remain –
A Turret more, a Turret less
Dishonor his Design –

According as his skill prefer
It perish, or endure –
Content, soe'er, it ornament
His absent character.

MANUSCRIPT: About 1864, in packet 86 (Bingham 36c).
PUBLICATION: *BM* (1945), 236.

849

The good Will of a Flower
The Man who would possess
Must first present
Certificate
Of minted Holiness.

MANUSCRIPT: About 1864, in packet 86 (Bingham 36d).
PUBLICATION: *BM* (1945), 51. The text is arranged as a quatrain.

850

I sing to use the Waiting
My Bonnet but to tie
And shut the Door unto my House
No more to do have I

Till His best step approaching
We journey to the Day
And tell each other how We sung
To Keep the Dark away.

MANUSCRIPT: About 1864, in packet 86 (Bingham 36e).
PUBLICATION: *Poems* (1896), 170, titled "Waiting." One word is
altered:

7. sung] sang

When the Astronomer stops seeking
For his Pleiad's Face –
When the lone British Lady
Forsakes the Arctic Race

When to his Covenant Needle
The Sailor doubting turns –
It will be amply early
To ask what treason means.

MANUSCRIPT: About 1864, in packet 86 (Bingham 36g). Sir John
Franklin (1786–1847) started on his last Arctic exploration in 1845 and
never returned. His widow, Lady Jane Franklin, financed searching parties
for ten years until, in 1858, the fate of her husband was established.
PUBLICATION: *BM* (1945), 131.

852

Apology for Her
Be rendered by the Bee –
Herself, without a Parliament
Apology for Me.

MANUSCRIPT: About 1864, in packet 86 (Bingham 37b).
PUBLICATION: *BM* (1945), 326. It is placed among the personal and
occasional poems.

853

When One has given up One's life
The parting with the rest
Feels easy, as when Day lets go
Entirely the West

The Peaks, that lingered last
Remain in Her regret
As scarcely as the Iodine
Upon the Cataract.

MANUSCRIPT: About 1864, in packet 86 (Bingham 37d).
PUBLICATION: *BM* (1945), 177–178.

854

Banish Air from Air –
Divide Light if you dare –
They'll meet
While Cubes in a Drop
Or Pellets of Shape
Fit.
Films cannot annul
Odors return whole
Force Flame
And with a Blonde push
Over your impotence
Flits Steam.

MANUSCRIPT: About 1864, in packet 86 (Bingham 38b).
PUBLICATION: *BM* (1945), 280–281.

855

To own the Art within the Soul
The Soul to entertain
With Silence as a Company
And Festival maintain

Is an unfurnished Circumstance
Possession is to One
As an Estate perpetual
Or a reduceless Mine.

MANUSCRIPT: About 1864, in packet 86 (Bingham 39c).
PUBLICATION: *BM* (1945), 292.

856

There is a finished feeling
Experienced at Graves –
A leisure of the Future –
A Wilderness of Size.

By Death's bold Exhibition
Preciser what we are
And the Eternal function
Enabled to infer.

MANUSCRIPT: About 1864, in packet 86 (Bingham 39d).
PUBLICATION: *BM* (1945), 208.

857

Uncertain lease – developes lustre
On Time
Uncertain Grasp, appreciation
Of Sum –

The shorter Fate – is oftener the chiefest
Because
Inheritors upon a 'tenure
Prize –

MANUSCRIPT: About 1864, in packet 87 (Bingham 40a).
PUBLICATION: *BM* (1945), 267.

858

This Chasm, Sweet, upon my life
I mention it to you,
When Sunrise through a fissure drop
The Day must follow too.

If we demur, it's gaping sides
Disclose as 'twere a Tomb
Ourself am lying straight wherein
The Favorite of Doom.

When it has just contained a Life
Then, Darling, it will close
And yet so bolder every Day
So turbulent it grows

I'm tempted half to stitch it up
With a remaining Breath
I should not miss in yielding, though
To Him, it would be Death –

And so I bear it big about
My Burial – before
A Life quite ready to depart
Can harass me no more –

MANUSCRIPT: About 1864, in packet 87 (Bingham 40c).
PUBLICATION: *BM* (1945), 167.

859

A Doubt if it be Us
Assists the staggering Mind
In an extremer Anguish
Until it footing find.

An Unreality is lent,
A merciful Mirage
That makes the living possible
While it suspends the lives.

MANUSCRIPT: About 1864, in packet 87 (Bingham 41a).
PUBLICATION: *BM* (1945), 258.

860

Absence disembodies – so does Death
Hiding individuals from the Earth
Superstition helps, as well as love –
Tenderness decreases as we prove –

Manuscript: About 1864, in packet 87 (Bingham 41b).
Publication: *BM* (1945), 250.

861

Split the Lark – and you'll find the Music –
Bulb after Bulb, in Silver rolled –
Scantily dealt to the Summer Morning
Saved for your Ear when Lutes be old.

Loose the Flood – you shall find it patent –
Gush after Gush, reserved for you –
Scarlet Experiment! Sceptic Thomas!
Now, do you doubt that your Bird was true?

Manuscript: About 1864, in packet 87 (Bingham 41c). The Biblical
reference is to John 20.24–25:

But Thomas, one of the twelve, called Didymus, was not with them
when Jesus came. The other disciples therefore said unto him, We
have seen the Lord. But he said unto them, Except I shall see in
his hands the print of the nails, and put my finger into the print of
the nails, and thrust my hand into his side, I will not believe.

Publication: *Poems* (1896), 80, titled "Loyalty."

862

Light is sufficient to itself –
If Others want to see
It can be had on Window Panes
Some Hours in the Day.

But not for Compensation –
It holds as large a Glow
To Squirrel in the Himmaleh
Precisely, as to you.

Manuscripts: There are two. The copy reproduced above, in packet
87 (Bingham 41d), was written about 1864. A second fair copy (Bingham

98–4A–6), written at the same time, is on embossed notepaper. It is variant in lines 4 and 8:

> Light is sufficient to itself –
> If others want to see
> It can be had on Window panes
> Some Hours of the Day –
>
> But not for Compensation –
> It holds as large a Glow
> To Squirrel in the Himmaleh
> Precisely – as to Me –

PUBLICATION: *BM* (1945), 15. It is a composite of both copies. It adopts:

4. of   8. you

863

> That Distance was between Us
> That is not of Mile or Main –
> The Will it is that situates –
> Equator – never can –

MANUSCRIPT: About 1864, in packet 87 (Bingham 41e). Following "Equator" ED first wrote "can" but crossed it out.
PUBLICATION: *BM* (1945), 114.

864

> The Robin for the Crumb
> Returns no syllable
> But long records the Lady's name
> In Silver Chronicle.

MANUSCRIPT: About 1864, in packet 87 (Bingham 42c).
PUBLICATION: *BM* (1945), 65.

865

He outstripped Time with but a Bout,
He outstripped Stars and Sun
And then, unjaded, challenged God
In presence of the Throne.

And He and He in mighty List
Unto this present, run,
The larger Glory for the less
A just sufficient Ring.

MANUSCRIPT: About 1864, in packet 87 (Bingham 42d).
PUBLICATION: *BM* (1945), 133.

866

Fame is the tint that Scholars leave
Upon their Setting Names –
The Iris not of Occident
That disappears as comes –

MANUSCRIPT: About 1864, in packet 87 (Bingham 43d).
PUBLICATION: *BM* (1945), 237.

867

Escaping backward to perceive
The Sea upon our place –
Escaping forward, to confront
His glittering Embrace –

Retreating up, a Billow's hight
Retreating blinded down
Our undermining feet to meet
Instructs to the Divine.

MANUSCRIPT: About 1864, in packet 87 (Bingham 43e)
PUBLICATION: *BM* (1945), 121.

They ask but our Delight –
The Darlings of the Soil
And grant us all their Countenance
For a penurious smile.

MANUSCRIPT: About 1864, in packet 87 (Bingham 44b).
PUBLICATION: *BM* (1945), 47.

869

Because the Bee may blameless hum
For Thee a Bee do I become
List even unto Me.

Because the Flowers unafraid
May lift a look on thine, a Maid
Alway a Flower would be.

Nor Robins, Robins need not hide
When Thou upon their Crypts intrude
So Wings bestow on Me
Or Petals, or a Dower of Buzz
That Bee to ride, or Flower of Furze
I that way worship Thee.

MANUSCRIPT: About 1864, in packet 87 (Bingham 44c).
PUBLICATION: *BM* (1945), 149. The text is arranged as four triplets.

870

Finding is the first Act
The second, loss,
Third, Expedition for
the "Golden Fleece"

Fourth, no Discovery –
Fifth, no Crew –   [*no stanza break*]

Finally, no Golden Fleece –
Jason – sham – too.

MANUSCRIPT: About 1864, in packet 87 (Bingham 44d). The first word in line 4 is not capitalized.
PUBLICATION: *BM* (1945), 115–116.

871

The Sun and Moon must make their haste –
The Stars express around
For in the Zones of Paradise
The Lord alone is burned –

His Eye, it is the East and West –
The North and South when He
Do concentrate His Countenance
Like Glow Worms, flee away –

Oh Poor and Far –
Oh Hindered Eye
That hunted for the Day –
The Lord a Candle entertains
Entirely for Thee –

MANUSCRIPT: About 1864, in packet 87 (Bingham 45a).
PUBLICATION: *BM* (1945), 26. The last stanza is arranged as a quatrain.

872

As the Starved Maelstrom laps the Navies
As the Vulture teazed
Forces the Broods in lonely Valleys
As the Tiger eased

By but a Crumb of Blood, fasts Scarlet
Till he meet a Man
Dainty adorned with Veins and Tissues
And partakes – his Tongue

Cooled by the Morsel for a moment
Grows a fiercer thing
Till he esteem his Dates and Cocoa
A Nutrition mean

I, of a finer Famine
Deem my Supper dry
For but a Berry of Domingo
And a Torrid Eye.

MANUSCRIPT: About 1864, in packet 87 (Bingham 45b).
PUBLICATION: *BM* (1945), 104–105.

873

Ribbons of the Year –
Multitude Brocade –
Worn to Nature's Party once

Then, as flung aside
As a faded Bead
Or a Wrinkled Pearl –
Who shall charge the Vanity
Of the Maker's Girl?

MANUSCRIPT: About 1864, in packet 87 (Bingham 45c). The stanzaic
division is clear between lines 3 and 4.
PUBLICATION: *BM* (1945), 94. The text is arranged as two quatrains.

874

They wont frown always – some sweet Day
When I forget to teaze –
They'll recollect how cold I looked
And how I just said "Please."

Then They will hasten to the Door
To call the little Girl
Who cannot thank Them for the Ice
That filled the lisping full.

MANUSCRIPT: About 1864, in packet 91 (Bingham 69a).
PUBLICATION: *Poems* (1896), 147. Two lines are altered:

6. Girl] child   8] That on her lisping piled.

875

I stepped from Plank to Plank
A slow and cautious way
The Stars about my Head I felt
About my Feet the Sea.

I knew not but the next
Would be my final inch –
This gave me that precarious Gait
Some call Experience.

MANUSCRIPT: About 1864, in packet 91 (Bingham 69e).
PUBLICATION: *Poems* (1896), 68, titled "Experience." Line 2 is altered
to read:

So slow and cautiously;

876

It was a Grave, yet bore no Stone
Enclosed 'twas not of Rail
A Consciousness it's Acre, and
It held a Human Soul.

Entombed by whom, for what offence
If Home or Foreign born –
Had I the curiosity
'Twere not appeased of men

Till Resurrection, I must guess
Denied the small desire
A Rose upon it's Ridge to sow
Or take away a Briar.

[650]

MANUSCRIPTS: The fair copy reproduced above is in packet 86 (Bingham 34c), written about 1864. It is a redaction of an earlier semifinal draft in packet 30 (H 161a), written about 1863:

It was a Grave – yet bore no Stone –
Enclosed 'twas not – of Rail –
A Consciousness – it's Acre – And
It held a Human Soul –

Entombed by whom – for what offence –
If Home or foreign-born –
Had I the Curiosity –
'Twere not appeased of Man –

Till Resurrection, I must guess –
Denied the small desire
A Rose upon it's Ridge – to sow –
Or sacrificial Flower –

12. sacrificial Flower] palliate a Briar –

She substitutes "men" for "Man" (line 8) and creates a new final line, adopting "Briar" for it from the suggested change in the earlier packet copy.

PUBLICATION: *UP* (1935), 136. It derives from the earlier packet copy, and the suggested change is adopted. There are two alterations:

2. of] by   3. and] (*omitted*)

877

Each Scar I'll keep for Him
Instead I'll say of Gem
In His long Absence worn
A Costlier one

But every Tear I bore
Were He to count them o'er
His own would fall so more
I'll mis sum them.

MANUSCRIPT: About 1864, in packet 91 (Bingham 70c).
PUBLICATION: *BM* (1945), 303–304. It is placed among the incomplete or unfinished poems, but the packet text seems complete.

878

The Sun is gay or stark
According to our Deed.
If Merry, He is merrier –
If eager for the Dead

Or an expended Day
He helped to make too bright
His mighty pleasure suits Us not
It magnifies our Freight

MANUSCRIPT: About 1864, in packet 91 (Bingham 70g).
PUBLICATION: *BM* (1945), 241–242.

879

Each Second is the last
Perhaps, recalls the Man
Just measuring unconsciousness
The Sea and Spar between.

To fail within a Chance –
How terribler a thing
Than perish from the Chance's list
Before the Perishing!

MANUSCRIPT: About 1864, in packet 91 (Bingham 71a).
PUBLICATION: *BM* (1945), 185.

880

The Bird must sing to earn the Crumb
What merit have the Tune
No Breakfast if it guaranty

The Rose content may bloom
To gain renown of Lady's Drawer
But if the Lady come   [*no stanza break*]

But once a Century, the Rose
Superfluous become – ·

MANUSCRIPT: About 1864, in packet 91 (Bingham 71b).
PUBLICATION: BM (1945), 278. The text is arranged as two quatrains.

881

I've none to tell me to but Thee
So when Thou failest, nobody.
It was a little tie –
It just held Two, nor those it held
Since Somewhere thy sweet Face has spilled
Beyond my Boundary –

If things were opposite – and Me
And Me it were – that ebbed from Thee
On some unanswering Shore –
Would'st Thou seek so – just say
That I the Answer may pursue
Unto the lips it eddied through –
So – overtaking Thee –

MANUSCRIPT: About 1864, in packet 91 (Bingham 71c).
PUBLICATION: BM (1945), 151.

882

A Shade upon the mind there passes
As when on Noon
A Cloud the mighty Sun encloses
Remembering

That some there be too numb to notice
Oh God
Why give if Thou must take away
The Loved?

Manuscript: About 1864, in packet 91 (Bingham 73c).
Publication: *BM* (1945), 209–210.

883

The Poets light but Lamps –
Themselves – go out –
The Wicks they stimulate –
If vital Light

Inhere as do the Suns –
Each Age a Lens
Disseminating their
Circumference –

Manuscript: About 1864, in packet 91 (Bingham 75a).
Publication: *BM* (1945), 227.

884

An Everywhere of Silver
With Ropes of Sand
To keep it from effacing
The Track called Land.

Manuscript: About 1864, in packet 91 (Bingham 75b).
Publication: *Poems* (1891), 139, titled "The Sea."

885

Our little Kinsmen – after Rain
In plenty may be seen,
A Pink and Pulpy multitude
The tepid Ground upon.

A needless life, it seemed to me
Until a little Bird
As to a Hospitality
Advanced and breakfasted.

As I of He, so God of Me
I pondered, may have judged,
And left the little Angle Worm
With Modesties enlarged.

MANUSCRIPT: About 1864, in packet 91 (Bingham 75c).
PUBLICATION: *BM* (1945), 59.

886

These tested Our Horizon –
Then disappeared
As Birds before achieving
A Latitude.

Our Retrospection of Them
A fixed Delight,
But our Anticipation
A Dice – a Doubt –

MANUSCRIPT: About 1864, in packet 91 (Bingham 75e).
PUBLICATION: *BM* (1945), 212.

887

We outgrow love, like other things
And put it in the Drawer –
Till it an Antique fashion shows –
Like Costumes Grandsires wore.

MANUSCRIPT: About 1864, in packet 92 (Bingham 76c).
PUBLICATION: *Poems* (1896), 89.

888

When I have seen the Sun emerge
From His amazing House –
And leave a Day at every Door
A Deed, in every place –

Without the incident of Fame
Or accident of Noise –
The Earth has seemed to me a Drum,
Pursued of little Boys

MANUSCRIPT: About 1864, in packet 92 (Bingham 76d).
PUBLICATION: *BM* (1945), 13.

889

Crisis is a Hair
Toward which forces creep
Past which forces retrograde
If it come in sleep

To suspend the Breath
Is the most we can
Ignorant is it Life or Death
Nicely balancing.

Let an instant push
Or an Atom press
Or a Circle hesitate
In Circumference

It – may jolt the Hand
That adjusts the Hair
That secures Eternity
From presenting – Here –

MANUSCRIPT: About 1864, in packet 92 (Bingham 77a).
PUBLICATION: *BM* (1945), 190.

890

From Us She wandered now a Year,
Her tarrying, unknown,
If Wilderness prevent her feet
Or that Etherial Zone

No Eye hath seen and lived
We ignorant must be –
We only know what time of Year
We took the Mystery.

MANUSCRIPT: About 1864, in packet 92 (Bingham 79b). The only death among friends or relatives that ED might thus memorialize during the early sixties was that of her "Aunt Mira" (Mrs. Joel W.) Norcross, who died 4 May 1862. She was the young wife of Mrs. Dickinson's youngest brother, only seven years older than ED. He was much in the Dickinson home in the years before his marriage. The lines may have been sent to Louise and Frances Norcross, nieces of Lamira Norcross, and the cousins with whom ED maintained a steady correspondence. Louise had taken care of the Joel Norcross children when their mother died.

PUBLICATION: *Poems* (1896), 165, titled "Invisible."

891

To my quick ear the Leaves – conferred –
The Bushes – they were Bells –
I could not find a Privacy
From Nature's sentinels –

In Cave if I presumed to hide
The Walls – begun to tell –
Creation seemed a mighty Crack –
To make me visible –

MANUSCRIPT: About 1864, in packet 92 (Bingham 80b).
PUBLICATION: *Poems* (1896), 113. One word is altered:

6. begun] began

892

Who occupies this House?
A Stranger I must judge
Since No one knows His Circumstance –
'Tis well the name and age

Are writ upon the Door
Or I should fear to pause
Where not so much as Honest Dog
Approach encourages.

It seems a curious Town –
Some Houses very old,
Some – newly raised this Afternoon,
Were I compelled to build

It should not be among
Inhabitants so still
But where the Birds assemble
And Boys were possible.

Before Myself was born
'Twas settled, so they say,
A Territory for the Ghosts –
And Squirrels, formerly.

Until a Pioneer, as
Settlers often do
Liking the quiet of the Place
Attracted more unto –

And from a Settlement
A Capitol has grown
Distinguished for the gravity
Of every Citizen.

The Owner of this House
A Stranger He must be –
Eternity's Acquaintances
Are mostly so – to me.

MANUSCRIPT: About 1864, in packet 92 (Bingham 81a). ED has marked "Honest" (line 7) for an alternate, but none is given.

PUBLICATION: *BM* (1945), 205–206. The last word of line 21 is arranged as the first of line 22. In line 26 ED's "Capitol" is rendered "capital."

Drab Habitation of Whom?
Tabernacle or Tomb –
Or Dome of Worm –
Or Porch of Gnome –
Or some Elf's Catacomb?

MANUSCRIPT: About 1864, in packet 92 (Bingham 82b).
PUBLICATION: *Poems* (1896), 131, titled "Cocoon." A note added by
Mrs. Bianchi in later collections says: "Sent with a cocoon to her little
nephew." Ned was born 19 June 1861.

894

Of Consciousness, her awful Mate
The Soul cannot be rid –
As easy the secreting her
Behind the Eyes of God.

The deepest hid is sighted first
And scant to Him the Crowd –
What triple Lenses burn upon
The Escapade from God –

MANUSCRIPT: About 1864, in packet 92 (Bingham 83a).
PUBLICATION: *BM* (1945), 292.

895

A Cloud withdrew from the Sky
Superior Glory be
But that Cloud and it's Auxiliaries
Are forever lost to me

Had I but further scanned
Had I secured the Glow
In an Hermetic Memory
It had availed me now.

Never to pass the Angel
With a glance and a Bow
Till I am firm in Heaven
Is my intention now.

MANUSCRIPT: About 1864, in packet 92 (Bingham 83b). ED has marked "Memory" (line 7) for an alternate, but none is given.
PUBLICATION: *BM* (1945), 15–16.

896

Of Silken Speech and Specious Shoe
A Traitor is the Bee
His service to the newest Grace
Present continually

His Suit a chance
His Troth a Term
Protracted as the Breeze
Continual Ban propoundeth He
Continual Divorce.

MANUSCRIPTS: There are two, identical in text, both written about 1864. The copy reproduced above (Bingham 83c) is in packet 92. The copy below (Bingham 98–4A–11), in pencil, is on embossed stationery, signed "Emily."

> Of Silken Speech, and Specious Shoe –
> A Traitor is the Bee –
> His Service – to the newest Grace
> Present continually –
>
> His Suit, a Chance –
> His Troth, a Term
> Protracted as the Breeze –
> Continual Ban propoundeth He –
> Continual Divorce.

PUBLICATION: *BM* (1945), 69. The text is arranged as two quatrains.

897

How fortunate the Grave –
All Prizes to obtain –
Successful certain, if at last,
First Suitor not in vain.

MANUSCRIPT: About 1864, in packet 92 (Bingham 83d).
PUBLICATION: *BM* (1945), 206.

898

How happy I was if I could forget
To remember how sad I am
Would be an easy adversity
But the recollecting of Bloom

Keeps making November difficult
Till I who was almost bold
Lose my way like a little Child
And perish of the cold.

MANUSCRIPT: About 1864, in packet 92 (Bingham 83e).
PUBLICATION: *BM* (1945), 112–113.

899

Herein a Blossom lies –
A Sepulchre, between –
Cross it, and overcome the Bee –
Remain – 'tis but a Rind.

MANUSCRIPT: About 1864, in packet 92 (Bingham 84b).
PUBLICATION: *BM* (1945), 49.

What did They do since I saw Them?
Were They industrious?
So many questions to put Them
Have I the eagerness

That could I snatch Their Faces
That could Their lips reply
Not till the last was answered
Should They start for the Sky.

Not if Their Party were waiting,
Not if to talk with Me
Were to Them now, Homesickness
After Eternity.

Not if the Just suspect me
And offer a Reward
Would I restore my Booty
To that Bold Person, God –

MANUSCRIPT: About 1864, in packet 92 (Bingham 84c). The fourth stanza is written on a strip of paper that has been pinned onto the packet leaf over stanza 3. ED may have intended it as a substitute third stanza.

PUBLICATION: *BM* (1945), 211. The text is arranged, as above, in four stanzas; a note explains how the fourth stanza is attached and queries whether it may not be a substitute for the third.

Sweet, to have had them lost
For news that they be saved –
The nearer they departed Us
The nearer they, restored,

Shall stand to Our Right Hand –
Most precious are the Dead –
Next precious   [*no stanza break*]

Those that rose to go –
Then thought of Us, and stayed.

MANUSCRIPTS: There are two, both written about 1864. The fair copy
reproduced above (Bingham 97–5) is in pencil, signed "Emily."; it has
been folded as if enclosed in an envelope. It is a redaction of that in packet
33 (H 177b), which is a semifinal draft:

> Good to have had them lost
> For News that they be saved!
> The nearer they departed Us
> The nearer they, restored,
>
> Shall stand to Our Right Hand –
> Most precious – are the Dead.
> Next precious, those that turned to go
> Then thought of Us, and stayed.

7. turned] rose

In her fair copy ED adopted the suggested change in the packet copy.
PUBLICATION: *UP* (1935), 142. The text derives from the packet copy
and the suggested change is rejected. Two words are altered:

2. be] are   7. Next] Most

902

The first Day that I was a Life
I recollect it – How still –
The last Day that I was a Life
I recollect it – as well –

'Twas stiller – though the first
Was still –
'Twas empty – but the first
Was full –

This – was my finallest Occasion –
But then
My tenderer Experiment
Toward Men –

[663]

"Which choose I"?
That – I cannot say –
"Which choose They"?
Question Memory!

MANUSCRIPT: About 1864, in packet 39 (H 209a).
PUBLICATION: *BM* (1945), 302–303. The text derives from a transcript of the packet copy made by Mrs. Todd. It is placed among the unfinished poems, but the packet copy is complete. The spelling of "finallest" (line 9) is regularized. Line 13 omits the final word, and the line reads: "Which choose?"

903

I hide myself within my flower,
That fading from your Vase,
You, unsuspecting, feel for me –
Almost a loneliness.

MANUSCRIPTS: This one-stanza poem is one of the many that ED wrote to accompany the gift of a flower. The copy reproduced above (Bingham 110–5), written about 1864, is on note paper and may have accompanied such a gift. Identical in text is the copy in packet 39 (H 210a), written at the same time:

> I hide myself – within my flower,
> That fading from your Vase –
> You – unsuspecting – feel for me –
> Almost – a loneliness –

This version seems to be a redaction of an earlier version, written about 1859, in packet 1 (H 2h):

> I hide myself within my flower
> That wearing on your breast –
> You – unsuspecting, wear me too –
> And angels know the rest!

It is possible that other copies were made. Mary Adèle Allen, *Around a Village Green* (Northampton, Mass., 1939), page 76, says that ED once sent a bouquet to her mother and that one flower was bent back and a tiny note placed in it. "The note has long been lost, but I wonder if it might have been the poem in which she hides herself within her flower."

PUBLICATION: *Poems* (1890), 50, titled "With a Flower." The two versions are arranged as a poem of two quatrains, with the earlier version as the first stanza.

904

Had I not This, or This, I said,
Appealing to Myself,
In moment of prosperity —
Inadequate — were Life —

"Thou hast not Me, nor Me" — it said,
In Moment of Reverse —
"And yet Thou art industrious —
No need — hadst Thou — of us"?

My need — was all I had — I said —
The need did not reduce —
Because the food — exterminate —
The hunger — does not cease —

But diligence — is sharper —
Proportioned to the Chance —
To feed upon the Retrograde —
Enfeebles — the Advance —

MANUSCRIPT: About 1864, in packet 39 (H 210c).
PUBLICATION: *UP* (1935), 72. One word is altered:

5. nor] or

905

Between My Country — and the Others —
There is a Sea —
But Flowers — negotiate between us —
As Ministry.

MANUSCRIPT: About 1864, in packet 39 (H 210d).

PUBLICATION: *UP* (1935), 137. It is arranged as a six-line stanza with the notation: "In the old grave-yard."

906

The Admirations – and Contempts – of time –
Show justest – through an Open Tomb –
The Dying – as it were a Hight
Reorganizes Estimate
And what We saw not
We distinguish clear –
And mostly – see not
What We saw before –

'Tis Compound Vision –
Light – enabling Light –
The Finite – furnished
With the Infinite –
Convex – and Concave Witness –
Back – toward Time –
And forward –
Toward the God of Him –

MANUSCRIPT: About 1864, in packet 39 (H 211a). In lines 6, 7, and 13, the words "distinguish," "mostly," and "Witness" are marked for alternative readings, but none is given.

PUBLICATION: *FP* (1929), 119. There is no stanza division, and the poem is arranged as a twenty-line poem; in later editions as a poem of seventeen lines.

907

Till Death – is narrow Loving –
The scantest Heart extant
Will hold you till your privilege
Of Finiteness – be spent –

[666]

But He whose loss procures you
Such Destitution that
Your Life too abject for itself
Thenceforward imitate –

Until – Resemblance perfect –
Yourself, for His pursuit
Delight of Nature – abdicate –
Exhibit Love – somewhat –

MANUSCRIPT: About 1864, in packet 39 (H 211b).
PUBLICATION: *New York Herald Tribune Book Review,* 10 March 1929, page 4; *FP* (1929), 186. One word is altered:

2. scäntest] scantiest

The last word of line 3, printed as a separate line, is restored in later collections.

908

'Tis Sunrise – Little Maid – Hast Thou
No Station in the Day?
'Twas not thy wont, to hinder so –
Retrieve thine industry –

'Tis Noon – My little Maid –
Alas – and art thou sleeping yet?
The Lily – waiting to be Wed –
The Bee – Hast thou forgot?

My little Maid – 'Tis Night – Alas
That Night should be to thee
Instead of Morning – Had'st thou broached
Thy little Plan to Die –
Dissuade thee, if I c'd not, Sweet,
I might have aided – thee –

MANUSCRIPT: About 1864, in packet 39 (H 211c).
PUBLICATION: *Poems* (1896), 152, titled "Unwarned." The first word of line 6 is placed as the last of line 5. There are alterations in two lines:

8. Hast thou forgot] dost thou forget   12. Die] me

909

I make His Crescent fill or lack –
His Nature is at Full
Or Quarter – as I signify –
His Tides – do I control –

He holds superior in the Sky
Or gropes, at my Command
Behind inferior Clouds – or round
A Mist's slow Colonnade –

But since We hold a Mutual Disc –
And front a Mutual Day –
Which is the Despot, neither knows –
Nor Whose – the Tyranny –

MANUSCRIPT: About 1864, in packet 39 (H 213b).
PUBLICATION: FP (1929), 139. The last two words in line 7 begin
line 8.

910

Experience is the Angled Road
Preferred against the Mind
By – Paradox – the Mind itself –
Presuming it to lead

Quite Opposite – How Complicate
The Discipline of Man –
Compelling Him to Choose Himself
His Preappointed Pain –

MANUSCRIPT: About 1864, in packet 33 (H 175a).
PUBLICATION: FP (1929), 18. The text is arranged as a single eight-
line stanza. The sense of the poem is altered by the fact that the word
"Paradox," intended to be used adverbially – (By – Paradox) *paradoxically*
– is rendered substantively:

Preferred against the mind
By paradox, the mind itself
Presuming it to lead
Quite opposite.

911

Too little way the House must lie
From every Human Heart
That holds in undisputed Lease
A white inhabitant —

Too narrow is the Right between —
Too imminent the chance —
Each Consciousness must emigrate
And lose it's neighbor once —

MANUSCRIPT: About 1864, in packet 33 (H 175d).
PUBLICATION: *UP* (1935), 115. The misreading "For" for "Too" (line 5) is corrected in *Poems* (current).

912

Peace is a fiction of our Faith —
The Bells a Winter Night
Bearing the Neighbor out of Sound
That never did alight.

MANUSCRIPT: About 1864, in packet 33 (H 176b).
PUBLICATION: *BM* (1945), 278. The text derives from a transcript made by Mrs. Todd. One word is altered:

4. alight] delight

913

And this of all my Hopes
This, is the silent end
Bountiful colored, my Morning rose
Early and sere, it's end

Never Bud from a Stem
Stepped with so gay a Foot
Never a Worm so confident
Bored at so brave a Root

MANUSCRIPT: About 1864, in packet 33 (H 177a).
PUBLICATION: *Atlantic Monthly*, CXLIII (February 1929); *London Mercury*, XIX (February 1929), 358; *FP* (1929), 187.

914

I cannot be ashamed
Because I cannot see
The love you offer –
Magnitude
Reverses Modesty

And I cannot be proud
Because a Hight so high
Involves Alpine
Requirements
And Services of Snow.

MANUSCRIPT: About 1864, in packet 33 (H 177d). ED marked "Requirements" (line 9) for an alternative, but none is given.
PUBLICATION: *FP* (1929), 144. The text follows the stanza arrangement of the manuscript; in later collections it is altered to quatrains.

915

Faith – is the Pierless Bridge
Supporting what We see
Unto the Scene that We do not –
Too slender for the eye

It bears the Soul as bold
As it were rocked in Steel
With Arms of Steel at either side –
It joins – behind the Vail

To what, could We presume
The Bridge would cease to be
To Our far, vascillating Feet
A first Nescessity.

MANUSCRIPT: About 1864, in packet 33 (H 178a).
PUBLICATION: *FP* (1929), 129. Stanza 2, arranged as five lines, in later
collections is restored as a quatrain. One word is altered:

8. Vail (*veil*)] rail

916

His Feet are shod with Gauze –
His Helmet, is of Gold,
His Breast, a Single Onyx
With Chrysophras, inlaid.

His Labor is a Chant –
His Idleness – a Tune –
Oh, for a Bee's experience
Of Clovers, and of Noon!

MANUSCRIPT: About 1864, in packet 33 (H 178b). This is a separate
poem, although published in *Poems* (1890), 87, as the two final stanzas
of "Like trains of cars on tracks of plush." In packet 33 this follows "Faith
is the Pierless Bridge" and precedes "Love is anterior to Life" – all three
written on the same leaf. The poem "Like trains of cars" is in a different
packet and in the handwriting of about 1873. Although both poems apostro-
phize bees, they are quite differently conceived.

917

Love – is anterior to Life –
Posterior – to Death –
Initial of Creation, and
The Exponent of Earth –

MANUSCRIPT: About 1864, in packet 33 (H 178c).

PUBLICATION: *Poems* (1896), 75, titled "Love." The text derives from a transcript made by Mrs. Todd. One word is altered:

4. Earth] breath

918

Only a Shrine, but Mine –
I made the Taper shine –
Madonna dim, to whom all Feet may come,
Regard a Nun –

Thou knowest every Wo –
Needless to tell thee – so –
But can'st thou do
The Grace next to it – heal?
That looks a harder skill to us –
Still – just as easy, if it be thy Will
To thee – Grant me –
Thou knowest, though, so Why tell thee?

MANUSCRIPT: About 1864, in packet 33 (H 178d).
PUBLICATION: *London Mercury*, XIX (February 1929), 356; *FP* (1929), 172. The text is arranged as a single seventeen-line stanza. Words are omitted in two lines:

9. to us   11. To thee

919

If I can stop one Heart from breaking
I shall not live in vain
If I can ease one Life the Aching
Or cool one Pain

Or help one fainting Robin
Unto his Nest again
I shall not live in Vain.

MANUSCRIPT: About 1864, in packet 33 (H 178e).
PUBLICATION: *Poems* (1890), 18. It is printed without stanza division.

We can but follow to the Sun –
As oft as He go down
He leave Ourselves a Sphere behind –
'Tis mostly – following –

We go no further with the Dust
Than to the Earthen Door –
And then the Panels are reversed –
And we behold – no more

MANUSCRIPT: About 1864, in packet 33 (H 180c).
PUBLICATION: The second stanza is unpublished. The first stanza is
in *New England Quarterly*, XX (1947), 33, where it appears as stanza 1
of the poem beginning "Oh Shadow on the Grass!" It there derives from
a transcript made by Mrs. Todd. It is not clear why Mrs. Todd attached
the first stanza of this two-stanza poem, completed in 1864, to the other
two-stanza poem (in packet 38) which seems to have been written late
in 1871.

921

If it had no pencil
Would it try mine –
Worn – now – and *dull* – sweet,
Writing much to thee.
If it had no word,
Would it make the Daisy,
Most as big as I was,
When it plucked me?

MANUSCRIPT: About 1864, in pencil (Bingham 109–14). As the ac-
companying note states in *BM*, where it is published:

This slip of paper, pinned together around the stub of a pencil, was
signed "Emily."

PUBLICATION: *BM* (1945), 329. The text is arranged as two quatrains.

Those who have been in the Grave the longest –
Those who begin Today –
Equally perish from our Practise –
Death is the other way –

Foot of the Bold did least attempt it –
It – is the White Exploit –
Once to achieve, annuls the power
Once to communicate –

4. other] further

MANUSCRIPT: About 1864, in packet 86 (Bingham 34a).
PUBLICATION: *BM* (1945), 182. The suggested change is adopted.

923

How the Waters closed above Him
We shall never know –
How He stretched His Anguish to us
That – is covered too –

Spreads the Pond Her Base of Lilies
Bold above the Boy
Whose unclaimed Hat and Jacket
Sum the History –

3. Anguish] Spirit

MANUSCRIPT: About 1864, in packet 86 (Bingham 34f).
PUBLICATION: *BM* (1945), 185. The suggested change is rejected.

924

Love – is that later Thing than Death –
More previous – than Life –
Confirms it at it's entrance – And
Usurps it – of itself –

Tastes Death – the first – to hand the sting
The Second – to it's friend –
Disarms the little interval –
Deposits Him with God –

Then hovers – an inferior Guard –
Lest this Beloved Charge
Need – once in an Eternity –
A smaller than the Large –

5. hand] pass – / prove –   12. smaller] lesser –
11. Need] Miss

MANUSCRIPT: About 1864, in packet 86 (Bingham 35a).
PUBLICATION: *BM* (1945), 284. The suggested changes for lines 5
("prove") and 12 are adopted.

925

Struck, was I, nor yet by Lightning –
Lightning – lets away
Power to perceive His Process
With Vitality.

Maimed – was I – yet not by Venture –
Stone of stolid Boy –
Nor a Sportsman's Peradventure –
Who mine Enemy?

Robbed – was I – intact to Bandit –
All my Mansion torn –
Sun – withdrawn to Recognition –
Furthest shining – done –

Yet was not the foe – of any –
Not the smallest Bird
In the nearest Orchard dwelling
Be of Me – afraid.

[675]

Most – I love the Cause that slew Me.
Often as I die
It's beloved Recognition
Holds a Sun on Me –

Best – at Setting – as is Nature's –
Neither witnessed Rise
Till the infinite Aurora
In the other's eyes.

7. Peradventure] ruthless pleasure – /
wanton [pleasure –] / leisure
[pleasure –]
9. intact to Bandit] yet met no
Bandit –

15. dwelling] waiting
19. It's] That
22. witnessed] noticed –

MANUSCRIPT: About 1864, in packet 86 (Bingham 35b).
PUBLICATION: *BM* (1945), 139. The suggested changes for lines 7
("ruthless pleasure") and 9 are adopted.

926

Patience – has a quiet Outer –
Patience – Look within –
Is an Insect's futile forces
Infinites – between –

'Scaping one – against the other
Fruitlesser to fling –
Patience – is the Smile's exertion
Through the quivering –

7. Smile's exertion] Mouth's exertion – / Love's – [exertion –]

MANUSCRIPT: About 1864, in packet 86 (Bingham 35c). ED added to
her other suggested changes: "Mean of forces – stand by Her Wing," but
whether as a proposed substitute for line 8 and the latter part of line 7, or
for line 4 and the latter part of line 3 is not clear. Only "Smiles" is marked
for a substitute.
PUBLICATION: *BM* (1945), 251. The suggested changes are rejected.

Absent Place – an April Day –
Daffodils a-blow
Homesick curiosity
To the Souls that snow –

Drift may block within it
Deeper than without –
Daffodil delight but
Him it duplicate –

4. To the] Unto   8. Him] Whom

MANUSCRIPT: About 1864, in packet 86 (Bingham 37a).
PUBLICATION: *BM* (1945), 46. The text is without stanza division.
The suggested change for line 8 is adopted. One word is altered:

4. Souls] soul

928

The Heart has narrow Banks
It measures like the Sea
In mighty – unremitting Bass
And Blue Monotony

Till Hurricane bisect
And as itself discerns
It's insufficient Area
The Heart convulsive learns

That Calm is but a Wall
Of unattempted Gauze
An instant's Push demolishes
A Questioning – dissolves.

2. measures] paces

MANUSCRIPT: About 1864, in packet 86 (Bingham 37c).
PUBLICATION: *BM* (1945), 247. The suggested change is rejected.

929

How far is it to Heaven?
As far as Death this way –
Of River or of Ridge beyond
Was no discovery.

How far is it to Hell?
As far as Death this way –
How far left hand the Sepulchre
Defies Topography.

3. Of River or of Ridge] Of Fathom   8] Forbid that any know –
or of League

MANUSCRIPT: About 1864, in packet 86 (Bingham 38d).
PUBLICATION: *BM* (1945), 217. The suggested change for line 3 is
adopted.

930

There is a June when Corn is cut
And Roses in the Seed –
A Summer briefer than the first
But tenderer indeed

As should a Face supposed the Grave's
Emerge a single Noon
In the Vermillion that it wore
Affect us, and return –

Two Seasons, it is said, exist –
The Summer of the Just,
And this of Our's, diversified
With Prospect, and with Frost –

May not our Second with it's First
So infinite compare
That We but recollect the one
The other to prefer?

16. prefer] adore

MANUSCRIPT: About 1864, in packet 86 (Bingham 39b). In a letter which ED wrote Sue (H B 161), probably in June 1864 when she was in Boston undergoing eye treatment, she comments:

I knew it was "November," but then there is a June when Corn is cut, whose option is within.

The letter, in pencil, is published in part in *FF* (1932), 231.
PUBLICATION: *BM* (1945), 39–40. The suggested change is adopted.

931

Noon – is the Hinge of Day –
Evening – the Tissue Door –
Morning – the East compelling the sill
Till all the World is ajar –

2. Tissue] Folding

MANUSCRIPT: About 1864, in packet 87 (Bingham 40b).
PUBLICATION: *BM* (1945), 15. The suggested change is adopted.

932

My best Acquaintances are those
With Whom I spoke no Word –
The Stars that stated come to Town
Esteemed Me never rude
Although to their Celestial Call
I failed to make reply –
My constant – reverential Face
Sufficient Courtesy.

5–6] Though their repeated Grace
Elicit no reply

MANUSCRIPT: About 1864, in packet 87 (Bingham 40d).
PUBLICATION: *BM* (1945), 122. The suggested change is rejected. The text is arranged as two quatrains.

[679]

Two Travellers perishing in Snow
The Forests as they froze
Together heard them strengthening
Each other with the words

That Heaven if Heaven – must contain
What Either left behind
And then the cheer too solemn grew
For language, and the wind

Long steps across the features took
That Love had touched that Morn
With reverential Hyacinth –
The taleless Days went on

Till Mystery impatient drew
And those They left behind
Led absent, were procured of Heaven
As Those first furnished, said –

4. words] news   15. procured] obtained

MANUSCRIPT: About 1864, in packet 87 (Bingham 43c).
PUBLICATION: *BM* (1945), 188. The suggested change for line 4 is adopted.

That is solemn we have ended
Be it but a Play
Or a Glee among the Garret
Or a Holiday

Or a leaving Home, or later,
Parting with a World
We have understood for better
Still to be explained.

1. solemn] tender – / sacred   8. Still] Yet

MANUSCRIPT: About 1864, in packet 87 (Bingham 44a).

PUBLICATION: *Poems* (1896), 143, titled "Ending." The suggested changes are rejected. Three words are altered:

3. Garret] garrets   8. explained] unfurled
8. to] it

935

Death leaves Us homesick, who behind,
Except that it is gone
Are ignorant of it's Concern
As if it were not born.

Through all their former Places, we
like Individuals go
Who something lost, the seeking for
Is all that's left them, now —

5. their] it's   7. seeking] looking
7. lost] dropt

MANUSCRIPT: About 1864, in packet 87 (Bingham 45d). Though "like" (line 6) begins a line and is clearly intended to do so, it is not capitalized.

PUBLICATION: *BM* (1945), 198. The suggested change for line 5 is adopted.

936

This Dust, and it's Feature —
Accredited — Today —
Will in a second Future —
Cease to identify —

This Mind, and it's measure —
A too minute Area
For it's enlarged inspection's
Comparison — appear —

This World, and it's species
A too concluded show
For it's absorbed Attention's
Remotest scrutiny –

3. Future] Being   12. Remotest] Memorial –
9. species] Nations – /   Fashions – /
symbols – / standards

MANUSCRIPT: About 1864, in packet 87 (Bingham 46a).
PUBLICATION: *BM* (1945), 219. All suggested changes are rejected.

937

I felt a Cleaving in my Mind –
As if my Brain had split –
I tried to match it – Seam by Seam –
But could not make them fit.

The thought behind, I strove to join
Unto the thought before –
But Sequence ravelled out of Sound
Like Balls – upon a Floor.

5. strove] tried   7. Sound] reach –

MANUSCRIPT: About 1864, in packet 87 (Bingham 46b). For a variant
of the second stanza, see poem number 992.
PUBLICATION: *Poems* (1896), 37, titled "The Lost Thought." The
suggested change for line 7 is adopted. One word is altered:

1. Cleaving] clearing

In *CP* (1924) and later collections the word was again altered:

clearing] cleavage

938

Fairer through Fading – as the Day
Into the Darkness dips away –
Half Her Complexion of the Sun –
Hindering – Haunting – Perishing –

Rallies Her Glow, like a dying Friend –
Teazing with glittering Amend –
Only to aggravate the Dark
Through an expiring – perfect – look –

2. Darkness] Twilight – / Evening –   7. Only to aggravate] Just to intensify
5. Her Glow] The West   8. Through an] Nature's –
6. Teazing] Taunting –

Manuscript: About 1864, in packet 87 (Bingham 46c).
Publication: *BM* (1945), 25. All suggested changes are rejected.

939

What I see not, I better see –
Through Faith – my Hazel Eye
Has periods of shutting –
But, No lid has Memory –

For frequent, all my sense obscured
I equally behold
As someone held a light unto
The Features so beloved –

And I arise – and in my Dream –
Do Thee distinguished Grace –
Till jealous Daylight interrupt –
And mar thy perfectness –

1. What] When   7. unto] upon
5. frequent] often

Manuscript: About 1864, in packet 87 (Bingham 46d).
Publication: *BM* (1945), 159. The suggested changes for lines 1 and
5 are adopted. The first word in line 4 is placed as the last of line 3.

940

On that dear Frame the Years had worn
Yet precious as the House
In which We first experienced Light
The Witnessing, to Us –

[683]

Precious! It was conceiveless fair
As Hands the Grave had grimed
Should softly place within our own
Denying that they died.

8. Denying] Disputing

MANUSCRIPT: About 1864, in packet 91 (Bingham 69b).
PUBLICATION: *BM* (1945), 195–196. The suggested change is rejected.

941

The Lady feeds Her little Bird
At rarer intervals –
The little Bird would not dissent
But meekly recognize

The Gulf between the Hand and Her
And crumbless and afar
And fainting, on Her yellow Knee
Fall softly, and adore –

3. dissent] demur

MANUSCRIPT: About 1864, in packet 91 (Bingham 69c).
PUBLICATION: *BM* (1945), 92. The suggested change is adopted.

942

Snow beneath whose chilly softness
Some that never lay
Make their first Repose this Winter
I admonish Thee

Blanket Wealthier the Neighbor
We so new bestow
Than thine acclimated Creature
Wilt Thou, Austere Snow?

8. Austere] Russian

[684]

Manuscript: About 1864, in packet 91 (Bingham 70e).
Publication: *BM* (1945), 205. The suggested change is adopted.

943

A Coffin – is a small Domain,
Yet able to contain
A Citizen of Paradise
In it's diminished Plane.

A Grave – is a restricted Breadth –
Yet ampler than the Sun –
And all the Seas He populates
And Lands He looks upon

To Him who on it's small Repose
Bestows a single Friend –
Circumference without Relief –
Or Estimate – or End –

3. A Citizen] A Rudiment   9. small] low
5. a restricted] an inferior   10. Bestows] Conferred

Manuscript: About 1864, in packet 91 (Bingham 72a).
Publication: *BM* (1945), 204. The suggested changes for lines 3
and 9 are adopted.

944

I learned – at least – what Home could be –
How ignorant I had been
Of pretty ways of Covenant –
How awkward at the Hymn

Round our new Fireside – but for this –
This pattern – of the Way –
Whose Memory drowns me, like the Dip
Of a Celestial Sea –

What Mornings in our Garden – guessed –
What Bees – for us – to hum –
With only Birds to interrupt
The Ripple of our Theme –

And Task for Both –
When Play be done –
Your Problem – of the Brain –
And mine – some foolisher effect –
A Ruffle – or a Tune –

The Afternoons – Together spent –
And Twilight – in the Lanes –
Some ministry to poorer lives –
Seen poorest – thro' our gains –

And then Return – and Night – and Home –

And then away to You to pass –
A new – diviner – care –
Till Sunrise take us back to Scene –
Transmuted – Vivider –

This seems a Home –
And Home is not –
But what that Place could be –
Afflicts me – as a Setting Sun –
Where Dawn – knows how to be –

4. the Hymn] the Plan	17. Ruffle] Thimble
11. Birds] Bloom	22. Night] Trust
15. Problem] labor	25. take] call –

MANUSCRIPT: About 1864, in packet 91 (Bingham 72b). If ED intended line 22 as an alternative for the first line of the succeeding stanza, she gives no sign; the line stands complete in itself.

PUBLICATION: *BM* (1945), 152–153. The text is arranged as seven quatrains. The suggested change for line 25 is adopted. Line 22 is selected as an alternative for line 23, which is omitted.

This is a Blossom of the Brain –
A small – italic Seed
Lodged by Design or Happening
The Spirit fructified –

Shy as the Wind of his Chambers
Swift as a Freshet's Tongue
So of the Flower of the Soul
It's process is unknown.

When it is found, a few rejoice
The Wise convey it Home
Carefully cherishing the spot
If other Flower become.

When it is lost, that Day shall be
The Funeral of God,
Upon his Breast, a closing Soul
The Flower of our Lord.

5. Chambers] Lodgings

MANUSCRIPT: About 1864, in packet 91 (Bingham 73a).
PUBLICATION: BM (1945), 230–231. The suggested change is rejected.

946

It is an honorable Thought
And makes One lift One's Hat
As One met sudden Gentlefolk
Upon a daily Street

That We've immortal Place
Though Pyramids decay
And Kingdoms, like the Orchard
Flit Russetly away

3. met sudden] encountered

MANUSCRIPT: About 1864, in packet 91 (Bingham 73d).
PUBLICATION: *Poems* (1896), 148. The suggested change is adopted.
In all subsequent editions the opening words "It is" are altered to " 'Tis."

947

Of Tolling Bell I ask the cause?
"A Soul has gone to Heaven"
I'm answered in a lonesome tone –
Is Heaven then a Prison?

That Bells should ring till all should know
A Soul had gone to Heaven
Would seem to me the more the way
A Good News should be given.

5. know] hear

MANUSCRIPT: About 1864, in packet 91 (Bingham 75d).
PUBLICATION: *Poems* (1896), 181, titled "Joy in Death." The alterations
in the published text are many. The text reads:

If tolling bell I ask the cause
  "A soul has gone to God,"
I'm answered in a lonesome tone;
  Is heaven then so sad?

That bells should joyful ring to tell
  A soul had gone to heaven,
Would seem to me the proper way
  A good news should be given.

948

'Twas Crisis – All the length had passed –
That dull – benumbing time
There is in Fever or Event –
And now the Chance had come –

The instant holding in it's claw
The privilege to live   [*no stanza break*]

[688]

Or warrant to report the Soul
The other side the Grave.

The Muscles grappled as with leads
That would not let the Will –
The Spirit shook the Adamant –
But could not make it feel.

The Second poised – debated – shot –
Another had begun –
And simultaneously, a Soul
Escaped the House unseen –

7. report] present   12. feel] tell –
9. grappled] struggled

MANUSCRIPT: About 1864, in packet 92 (Bingham 76b).
PUBLICATION: *BM* (1945), 189. The suggested changes are rejected.

949

Under the Light, yet under,
Under the Grass and the Dirt,
Under the Beetle's Cellar
Under the Clover's Root,

Further than Arm could stretch
Were it Giant long,
Further than Sunshine could
Were the Day Year long,

Over the Light, yet over,
Over the Arc of the Bird –
Over the Comet's chimney –
Over the Cubit's Head,

Further than Guess can gallop
Further than Riddle ride –
Oh for a Disc to the Distance
Between Ourselves and the Dead!

4. Root] Foot

MANUSCRIPT: About 1864, in packet 92 (Bingham 77b).
PUBLICATION: *BM* (1945), 207–208. The suggested change is adopted.

950

The Sunset stopped on Cottages
Where Sunset hence must be
For treason not of His, but Life's,
Gone Westerly, Today –

The Sunset stopped on Cottages
·Where Morning just begun –
What difference, after all, Thou mak'st
Thou supercilious Sun?

1. stopped] dropped   6. Morning] Sunrise

MANUSCRIPT: About 1864, in packet 92 (Bingham 79c).
PUBLICATION: *BM* (1945), 23. Both suggested changes are rejected.

951

As Frost is best conceived
By force of it's Result –
Affliction is inferred
By subsequent effect –

If when the sun reveal,
The Garden keep the Gash –
If as the Days resume
The wilted countenance

Cannot correct the crease
Or counteract the stain –
Presumption is Vitality
Was somewhere put in twain.

2. force of it's Result] scanning it's
   Result –
5. when] as
6. Garden keep] Landscape show – /
   own – / hold

7. resume] increase
8. wilted] Blackened
9. correct] efface –

MANUSCRIPT: About 1864, in packet 92 (Bingham 80a).
PUBLICATION: *BM* (1945), 259. The suggested change for line 9 is
adopted.

952

A Man may make a Remark –
In itself – a quiet thing
That may furnish the Fuse unto a Spark
In dormant nature – lain –

Let us divide – with skill –
Let us discourse – with care –
Powder exists in Charcoal –
Before it exists in Fire.

1. make] drop
2. quiet] tranquil
3. the Fuse] ignition
5. divide] deport

6. discourse] disclose
7. Charcoal] Elements – / sulphurets
8. exists] express

MANUSCRIPT: About 1864, in packet 92 (Bingham 80c).
PUBLICATION: *BM* (1945), 233. The suggested changes for lines 1
and 5 are adopted.

953

A Door just opened on a street –
I – lost – was passing by –
An instant's Width of Warmth disclosed –
And Wealth – and Company.

The Door as instant shut – And I –
I – lost – was passing by –
Lost doubly – but by contrast – most –
Informing – misery –

[691]

1. just opened on a street] there   8. Informing] Enlightening – / Ena-
   opened – to a House –   bling –
5. instant] sudden

MANUSCRIPT: About 1864, in packet 92 (Bingham 80d).
PUBLICATION: *Poems* (1896), 42, titled "Contrast." Two suggested changes are adopted:

> 5. sudden   8. Enlightening

954

The Chemical conviction
That Nought be lost
Enable in Disaster
My fractured Trust –

The Faces of the Atoms
If I shall see
How more the Finished Creatures
Departed me!

> 8. Departed] Entrusted

MANUSCRIPT: About 1864, in packet 92 (Bingham 81b).
PUBLICATION: *BM* (1945), 209. The suggested change is rejected.

955

The Hollows round His eager Eyes
Were Pages where to read
Pathetic Histories – although
Himself had not complained.
Biography to All who passed
Of Unobtrusive Pain
Except for the italic Face
Endured, unhelped – unknown.

4. not complained] hitherto concealed –   8. unhelped] resigned –

MANUSCRIPT: About 1864, in packet 92 (Bingham 81c).
PUBLICATION: *BM* (1945), 129. The text is arranged as two quatrains.
The suggested changes are rejected.

956

What shall I do when the Summer troubles –
What, when the Rose is ripe –
What when the Eggs fly off in Music
From the Maple Keep?

What shall I do when the Skies a'chirrup
Drop a Tune on me –
When the Bee hangs all Noon in the Buttercup
What will become of me?

Oh, when the Squirrel fills His Pockets
And the Berries stare
How can I bear their jocund Faces
Thou from Here, so far?

'Twould'nt afflict a Robin –
All His Goods have Wings –
I – do not fly, so wherefore
My Perennial Things?

15. do not fly] fly not

MANUSCRIPT: About 1864, in packet 92 (Bingham 82a).
PUBLICATION: *BM* (1945), 162. The suggested change is rejected.

957

As One does Sickness over
In convalescent Mind,
His scrutiny of Chances
By blessed Health obscured –

As One rewalks a Precipice
And whittles at the Twig   [*no stanza break*]

[693]

That held Him from Perdition
Sown sidewise in the Crag

A Custom of the Soul
Far after suffering
Identity to question
For evidence 't has been –

9. Custom] Habit   11. question] handle –

MANUSCRIPT: About 1864, in packet 92 (Bingham 82c).
PUBLICATION: *BM* (1945), 246. The suggested change for line 11 is
adopted.

958

We met as Sparks – Diverging Flints
Sent various – scattered ways –
We parted as the Central Flint
Were cloven with an Adze –
Subsisting on the Light We bore
Before We felt the Dark –
We knew by change between itself
And that etherial Spark.

7–8] A Flint unto this Day – perhaps –
        But for that single Spark.

MANUSCRIPT: About 1864, in packet 92 (Bingham 82d). The alterna-
tive reading for lines 7–8 has been set down on a scrap of paper that is
pinned onto the packet leaf.
PUBLICATION: *BM* (1945), 158. The text is arranged as two quatrains.
The suggested change is adopted.

959

A loss of something ever felt I –
The first that I could recollect
Bereft I was – of what I knew not
Too young that any should suspect

A Mourner walked among the children
I notwithstanding went about
As one bemoaning a Dominion
Itself the only Prince cast out –

Elder, Today, a session wiser
And fainter, too, as Wiseness is –
I find myself still softly searching
For my Delinquent Palaces –

And a Suspicion, like a Finger
Touches my Forehead now and then
That I am looking oppositely
For the site of the Kingdom of Heaven –

5. walked] lurked   6. went] stole

MANUSCRIPT: About 1864, in packet 92 (Bingham 84a).
PUBLICATION: *BM* (1945), 101–102. Both suggested changes are
adopted.

960

As plan for Noon and plan for Night
So differ Life and Death
In positive Prospective –
The Foot upon the Earth

At Distance, and Achievement, strains,
The Foot upon the Grave
Makes effort at conclusion
Assisted faint of Love.

8. faint] slow

MANUSCRIPT: About 1864, in packet 92 (Bingham 84d).
PUBLICATION: *BM* (1945), 202. The suggested change is rejected.

Wert Thou but ill – that I might show thee
How long a Day I could endure
Though thine attention stop not on me
Nor the least signal, Me assure –

Wert Thou but Stranger in ungracious country –
And Mine – the Door
Thou paused at, for a passing bounty –
No More –

Accused – wert Thou – and Myself – Tribunal –
Convicted – Sentenced – Ermine – not to Me
Half the Condition, thy Reverse – to follow –
Just to partake – the infamy –

The Tenant of the Narrow Cottage, wert Thou –
Permit to be
The Housewife in thy low attendance
Contenteth Me –

No Service hast Thou, I would not achieve it –
To die – or live –
The first – Sweet, proved I, ere I saw thee –
For Life – be Love –

4. Me] Mine	17. achieve] attempt –
7. passing] doubtful	19. proved I] That was
11. Condition] distinction	20. be] is – / means –

MANUSCRIPT: About 1864, in packet 39 (H 130b).

PUBLICATION: *BM* (1945), 165–166. The text derives from a transcript made by Mrs. Todd. The suggested changes for lines 4, 7, 11, and 20 ("means") are adopted. Line 8 reads:

Thou'd pause no more

962

Midsummer, was it, when They died –
A full, and perfect time –
The Summer closed upon itself
In Consummated Bloom –

The Corn, her furthest kernel filled
Before the coming Flail –
When These – leaned into Perfectness –
Through Haze of Burial –

7. These – leaned into] These Two – leaned in –

MANUSCRIPT: About 1864, in packet 39 (H 130c).
PUBLICATION: *FP* (1929), 97. The suggested change is rejected.

963

A nearness to Tremendousness –
An Agony procures –
Affliction ranges Boundlessness –
Vicinity to Laws

Contentment's quiet Suburb –
Affliction cannot stay
In Acres – It's Location
Is Illocality –

7–8] In Acre – Or Location –
It rents Immensity –

MANUSCRIPT: About 1864, in packet 39 (H 209b).
PUBLICATION: *UP* (1935), 148. The suggested changes are adopted;
there is no stanza division.

964

"Unto Me?" I do not know you –
Where may be your House?

"I am Jesus – Late of Judea –
Now – of Paradise" –

Wagons – have you – to convey me?
This is far from Thence –

"Arms of Mine – sufficient Phaeton –
Trust Omnipotence" –

I am spotted – "I am Pardon" –
I am small – "The Least
Is esteemed in Heaven the Chiefest –
Occupy my House" –

12. House] Breast –

MANUSCRIPT: About 1864, in packet 39 (H 209c).
PUBLICATION: FP (1929), 49. The suggested change is rejected. The
text is arranged as five stanzas 3, 3, 3, 3, 7 lines. In later editions the
stanzas are further altered.

965

Denial – is the only fact
Perceived by the Denied –
Whose Will – a numb significance –
The Day the Heaven died –

And all the Earth strove common round –
Without Delight, or Beam –
What Comfort was it Wisdom – was –
The spoiler of Our Home?

3. numb significance] Blank intelli-   6. Beam] aim –
gence

MANUSCRIPT: About 1864, in packet 39 (H 209d).
PUBLICATION: FP (1929), 165. The text is arranged as a single eight-
line stanza. Both suggested changes are adopted. One word is altered:

2. Perceived] Received

[698]

All forgot for recollecting
Just a paltry One –
All forsook, for just a Stranger's
New Accompanying –

Grace of Wealth, and Grace of Station
Less accounted than
An unknown Esteem possessing –
Estimate – Who can –

Home effaced – Her faces dwindled –
Nature – altered small –
Sun – if shone – or Storm – if shattered –
Overlooked I all –

Dropped – my fate – a timid Pebble –
In thy bolder Sea –
Prove – me – Sweet – if I regret it –
Prove Myself – of Thee –

1. for] through –
5] Grace of Rank – and Grace of
   Fortune

7. Esteem] content
15. Prove] Ask –

MANUSCRIPT: About 1864, in packet 39 (H 210a).
PUBLICATION: *FP* (1929), 149. All suggested changes except the first
are adopted. "One" (line 2) is italicized.

967

Pain – expands the Time –
Ages coil within
The minute Circumference
Of a single Brain –

Pain contracts – the Time –
Occupied with Shot
Gammuts of Eternities
Are as they were not –

2. coil] lurk   8. Are] flit – / Show –
7. Gammuts] Triplets

MANUSCRIPT: About 1864, in packet 39 (H 211d).
PUBLICATION: *FP* (1929), 118. One suggested change is adopted:

7. Triplets

The text remained unchanged in the Centenary edition (1930), but in
the next and final edition, *Poems* (1937) and later printings, "Triplets" is
replaced by "Gamuts" – with the spelling regularized.

968

Fitter to see Him, I may be
For the long Hindrance – Grace – to Me –
With Summers, and with Winters, grow,
Some passing Year – A trait bestow

To make Me fairest of the Earth –
The Waiting – then – will seem so worth
I shall impute with half a pain
The blame that I was chosen – then –

Time to anticipate His Gaze –
It's first – Delight – and then – Surprise –
The turning o'er and o'er my face
For Evidence it be the Grace –

He left behind One Day – So less
He seek Conviction, That – be This –

I only must not grow so new
That He'll mistake – and ask for me
Of me – when first unto the Door
I go – to Elsewhere go no more –

I only must not change so fair
He'll sigh – "The Other – She – is Where?"
The Love, tho, will array me right
I shall be perfect – in His sight –

[700]

If He perceive the other Truth –
Upon an Excellenter Youth –

How sweet I shall not lack in Vain –
But gain – thro' loss – Through Grief – obtain –
The Beauty that reward Him most –
The Beauty of Demand – at Rest –

4. trait] charm	20. Other] Real One
8. chosen] common	21. array] instruct
9. Time] Time's	26. Grief] pain
10. It's] the	27. most] best
16. He'll] He –	28. Demand] Belief –

MANUSCRIPT: About 1864, in packet 39 (H 212a).
PUBLICATION: *Poems* (Centenary edition, 1930), 276. The text is
arranged as six stanzas of 4, 4, 6, 4, 4, 6 lines. The suggested changes for
lines 20, 27, and 28 are adopted. One line is altered:

20] He'll sigh "the Real One where is she?"

969

He who in Himself believes –
Fraud cannot presume –
Faith is Constancy's Result –
And assumes – from Home –

Cannot perish, though it fail
Every second time –
But defaced Vicariously –
For Some Other Shame –

| 2. Fraud] Lie | 7. But] When – / if – |
| 4. assumes] infers | 8. Some Other Shame] Another Shame – |

MANUSCRIPT: About 1864, in packet 39 (H 212b).
PUBLICATION: *BM* (1945), 237. The text derives from a transcript of
the packet copy made by Mrs. Todd. All suggested changes are rejected.

Color – Caste – Denomination –
These – are Time's Affair –
Death's diviner Classifying
Does not know they are –

As in sleep – All Hue forgotten –
Tenets – put behind –
Death's large – Democratic fingers
Rub away the Brand –

If Circassian – He is careless –
If He put away
Chrysalis of Blonde – or Umber –
Equal Butterfly –

They emerge from His Obscuring –
What Death – knows so well –
Our minuter intuitions –
Deem unplausible

16. unplausible] incredible –

MANUSCRIPT: About 1864 (H 213a).
PUBLICATION: *Nation*, CXXIII (13 March 1929), 315; *FP* (1929),
10. The suggested change is adopted. In line 3 the misreading of "division"
for "diviner" is corrected in *Poems* (current). One word is altered:

5. Hue] here

Robbed by Death – but that was easy –
To the failing Eye
I could hold the latest Glowing –
Robbed by Liberty

For Her Jugular Defences –
This, too, I endured –   [*no stanza break*]

Hint of Glory – it afforded –
For the Brave Beloved –

Fraud of Distance – Fraud of Danger,
Fraud of Death – to bear –
It is Bounty – to Suspense's
Vague Calamity –

Staking our entire Possession
On a Hair's result –
Then – Seesawing – coolly – on it –
Trying if it split –

2. failing] Dying – / clouding   13. entire] divine –
8. Brave] bold   16] As to estimate

MANUSCRIPT: About 1864, in packet 39 (H 213c).
PUBLICATION: *BM* (1945), 151–152. The text derives from a transcript
of the packet copy made by Mrs. Todd. All suggested changes are rejected.

972

Unfulfilled to Observation –
Incomplete – to Eye –
But to Faith – a Revolution
In Locality –

Unto Us – the Suns extinguish –
To our Opposite –
New Horizons – they embellish –
Fronting Us – with Night.

7. embellish] Replenish   8] Turning us – their Night.

MANUSCRIPT: About 1864, in packet 39 (H 213d).
PUBLICATION: *UP* (1935), 75. The stanza division is not retained. The
suggested change for line 7 is adopted. One word is altered:

3. Revolution] revelation

[703]

'Twas awkward, but it fitted me –
An Ancient fashioned Heart –
It's only lore – it's Steadfastness –
In Change – unerudite –

It only moved as do the Suns –
For merit of Return –
Or Birds – confirmed perpetual
By Alternating Zone –

I only have it not Tonight
In it's established place –
For technicality of Death –
Omitted in the Lease –

5. moved] swerved –

MANUSCRIPT: About 1864, in packet 33 (H 175b).
PUBLICATION: *UP* (1935), 119. The suggested change is adopted. One word is altered:

3. lore] love

974

The Soul's distinct connection
With immortality
Is best disclosed by Danger
Or quick Calamity –

As Lightning on a Landscape
Exhibits Sheets of Place –
Not yet suspected – but for Flash –
And Click – and Suddenness.

6. Exhibits] Developes   7. Flash] Fork
7. Not yet suspected] Still unsuspected   8. Click] Bolt –

MANUSCRIPT: About 1864, in packet 33 (H 175c).

PUBLICATION: *FP* (1929), 116. The suggested change for line 8 is adopted. The text, arranged as two stanzas of 6 and 5 lines, is restored to quatrains in later collections.

975

The Mountain sat upon the Plain
In his tremendous Chair –
His observation omnifold,
His inquest, everywhere –

The Seasons played around his knees
Like Children round a sire –
Grandfather of the Days is He
Of Dawn, the Ancestor –

2. tremendous] Eternal – / enormous –

MANUSCRIPT: About 1864, in packet 33 (H 176a).
PUBLICATION: *Poems* (1890), 93, titled "The Mountain." The suggested change "Eternal" is adopted. One word is altered:

5. played] prayed

976

Death is a Dialogue between
The Spirit and the Dust.
"Dissolve" says Death – The Spirit "Sir
I have another Trust["] –

Death doubts it – Argues from the Ground –
The Spirit turns away
Just laying off for evidence
An Overcoat of Clay.

5. Argues] Reasons

MANUSCRIPT: About 1864 (H 176e).
PUBLICATION: *Poems* (1890), 143. The suggested change is not adopted.

Besides this May
We know
There is Another –
How fair
Our Speculations of the Foreigner!

Some know Him whom We knew –
Sweet Wonder –
A Nature be
Where Saints, and our plain going Neighbor
Keep May!

6. Him] it   8. Nature] Section

MANUSCRIPT: About 1864, in packet 33 (H 177c).
PUBLICATION: *BM* (1945), 222. The text derives from a transcript made by Mrs. Todd. The suggested changes are rejected and the stanzas are arranged as quatrains.

978

It bloomed and dropt, a Single Noon –
The Flower – distinct and Red –
I, passing, thought another Noon
Another in it's stead

Will equal glow, and thought no More
But came another Day
To find the Species disappeared –
The Same Locality –

The Sun in place – no other fraud
On Nature's perfect Sum –
Had I but lingered Yesterday –
Was my retrieveless blame –

Much Flowers of this and further Zones
Have perished in my Hands
For seeking it's Resemblance –
But unapproached it stands –

The single Flower of the Earth
That I, in passing by
Unconscious was – Great Nature's Face
Passed infinite by Me –

10. perfect Sum] General Sum
15. Resemblance] similitude –

19–20] Was ignorant that Nature
    closed / My Opportunity
20] Went infinite by Me –

MANUSCRIPT: About 1864, in packet 33 (H 180a).
PUBLICATION: The first nine lines only are published in *BM* (1945), 301, among the incomplete poems. The text derives from a transcript of the packet copy made by Mrs. Todd. In line 9, "fraud" is misread as "brand."

979

This Merit hath the worst –
It cannot be again –
When Fate hath taunted last
And thrown Her furthest Stone –

The Maimed may pause, and breathe,
And glance securely round –
The Deer attracts no further
Than it resists – the Hound –

7. attracts no further] invites no
    longer –

8. Than it resists] than it evades – /
    eludes –

MANUSCRIPT: About 1864, in packet 33 (H 180b).
PUBLICATION: *Poems* (1891), 75. The suggested changes are adopted, with choice of "eludes" for line 8.

Purple – is fashionable twice –
This season of the year,
And when a soul perceives itself
To be an Emperor.

MANUSCRIPT: About 1864 (Bingham 102–42). It is a pencil draft
jotted down on a small scrap of paper.
PUBLICATION: *BM* (1945), 254.

As Sleigh Bells seem in summer
Or Bees, at Christmas show –
So fairy – so fictitious
The individuals do
Repealed from observation –
A Party that we knew –
More distant in an instant
Than Dawn in Timbuctoo.

1. seem] sound   6. that] whom
3. fairy] foreign   8. in] on

MANUSCRIPT: This rough draft (Bingham 102–12) is written in pencil
on a slit-open envelope. The handwriting is that of about 1864.
PUBLICATION: *BM* (1945), 197. The suggested changes for lines 3 and
6 are adopted. The text is arranged as two quatrains.

No Other can reduce
Our mortal Consequence
Like the remembering it be nought
A Period from hence
But Contemplation for
Cotemporaneous Nought
Our Single Competition
Jehovah's Estimate.

MANUSCRIPTS: There are three. The fair copy reproduced above (H 295), probably sent to Sue, is signed "Emily –," and was written in 1865. It seems to be a final redaction of two earlier semifinal packet copies. The earlier of the two, in packet 18 (H 97a), was written in late 1863:

> No Other can reduce Our
> Mortal Consequence
> Like the remembering it be nought –
> A Period from hence –
>
> But Contemplation for
> Cotemporaneous Nought –
> Our Mutual Fame – that haply
> Jehovah – recollect –
>
> No Other can exalt Our
> Mortal Consequence
> Like the remembering it exist –
> A Period from hence –
>
> Invited from Itself
> To the Creator's House –
> To tarry an Eternity –
> His — shortest Consciousness –

Many months later, sometime in 1865, ED returned to this poem and transcribed the first two stanzas only into packet 90 (Bingham 60d). At the same time, though the text of the stanzas is identical with that in the earlier packet, she suggested changes for two lines:

> No other can reduce
> Our mortal Consequence
> Like the remembering it be nought
> A period from hence
>
> But Contemplation for
> Cotemporaneous nought –
> Our mutual fame that haply
> Jehovah recollect
>
> 7–8] Our only Competition
> Jehovah's Estimate.

The fair copy to Sue, evidently written soon after this second packet copy was set down, adopts the suggested changes. One may infer from the development that ED considered the draft to Sue final, and had permanently discarded the eight lines that constitute the two final stanzas of the earlier packet copy.

PUBLICATION: *SH* (1914), 17. It reproduces the copy to Sue. The later packet copy, with the suggested changes adopted, is in *New England Quarterly*, XX (1947), 29. Added to them are the two final stanzas of the earlier packet copy, reproduced from a transcript made by Mrs. Todd.

983

Ideals are the Fairy Oil
With which we help the Wheel
But when the Vital Axle turns
The Eye rejects the Oil.

MANUSCRIPTS: There are two, ·both written about 1865. The copy in packet 90 (Bingham 61d) is reproduced above. The other copy (H 270) is addressed "Sue –" and signed "Emily –." They are identical in text; in form, in the copy to Sue, lines 2–4 end with dashes and a comma follows "Ideals."

PUBLICATION: *BM* (1945), 231.

984

'Tis Anguish grander than Delight
'Tis Resurrection Pain –
The meeting Bands of smitten Face
We questioned to, again.

'Tis Transport wild as thrills the Graves
When Cerements let go
And Creatures clad in Miracle
Go up by Two and Two.

MANUSCRIPTS: The copy reproduced above, in packet 90 (Bingham 63c), was written about 1865. A quatrain sent to Sue some four years earlier (H B 191), about 1861, was used in the later poem as a variant second stanza. The copy to Sue is headed "Dear Sue –" and signed "Emily."

I'm thinking on that other morn –
When Cerements – let go –
And Creatures – clad in Victory –
Go up – by two – and two!

PUBLICATION: The stanza to Sue is in *SH* (1914), 96. Two lines are altered:

1] I'm thinking of that other morn   4] Go up in two by two

This text was reproduced in *CP* (1924). In the Centenary edition (1930) the lines are reproduced in facsimile on page xiii, and the text corrected. The two-stanza redaction is in *BM* (1945), 215.

985

The Missing All, prevented Me
From missing minor Things.
If nothing larger than a World's
Departure from a Hinge
Or Sun's extinction, be observed
'Twas not so large that I
Could lift my Forehead from my work
For Curiosity.

MANUSCRIPTS: There are two, both written about 1865. That reproduced above (Bingham 52e) is in packet 88. The other copy (H 342) is in pencil; it is addressed "Sue." and is signed "Emily." In text and form it is identical with the packet copy except that dashes conclude lines 4 and 5, and a dash replaces the comma in line 1. "Things" (line 2) is not capitalized.

PUBLICATION: *SH* (1914), 23; also *LL* (1924), 195. Both derive from the copy to Sue. In *LL* the poem is dated 1854.

986

A narrow Fellow in the Grass
Occasionally rides –
You may have met Him – did you not
His notice sudden is –

[711]

The Grass divides as with a Comb –
A spotted shaft is seen –
And then it closes at your feet
And opens further on –

He likes a Boggy Acre
A Floor too cool for Corn –
Yet when a Boy, and Barefoot –
I more than once at Noon
Have passed, I thought, a Whip lash
Unbraiding in the Sun
When stooping to secure it
It wrinkled, and was gone –

Several of Nature's People
I know, and they know me –
I feel for them a transport
Of cordiality –

But never met this Fellow
Attended, or alone
Without a tighter breathing
And Zero at the Bone –

MANUSCRIPTS: There are two fair copies. That reproduced above, in
packet 88 (Bingham 53a), was written in 1865. The other copy (H B 193),
written about 1872, is incorporated in a note to Sue:

A narrow Fellow in the Grass
Occasionally rides –
You may have met him? Did you not
His notice instant is –

The Grass divides as with a Comb –
A spotted shaft is seen,
And then it closes at your Feet
And opens further on –

He likes a Boggy Acre –
A Floor too cool for Corn –
But when a Boy and Barefoot
I more than once at Noon

Have passed I thought a Whip Lash
Unbraiding in the Sun
When stooping to secure it
It wrinkled and was gone –

Several of Nature's People
I know and they know me
I feel for them a transport
Of Cordiality

But never met this Fellow
Attended or alone
Without a tighter Breathing
And Zero at the Bone.

A question mark is here substituted for the dash in line 3, and two words are variant:

4. sudden] instant   11. Yet] But

The note to Sue makes no comment about the poem. It merely says:

Loo and Fanny will come tonight, but need that make a difference?
Space is as the Presence –

Thus one learns that the cousins Louise and Frances Norcross were expected, and infers that Sue had just sent a note to inquire whether she might make an evening call and whether ED would send her a copy of the poem, which she obviously knew well.

PUBLICATION: This is the poem which, titled "The Snake," had been anonymously published on 14 February 1866 in the columns of the *Springfield Daily Republican*. The fact that Sue lacked a copy tends to confirm the conjecture that it was Sue who had forwarded her own copy to Samuel Bowles because he had expressed his admiration for it. "How did that girl ever know that a boggy field wasn't good for corn?" he is reported to have exclaimed (*FF*, 27).

The impression that Sue's copy was used is strengthened by ED's comment to T. W. Higginson in a letter to him, postmarked 17 March 1866. She evidently enclosed a clipping from the *Republican*, protesting:

Lest you meet my Snake and suppose I deceive it was robbed of me – defeated too of the third line by the punctuation. The third and fourth were one – I had told you I did not print – I feared you might think me ostensible.

No copy of "The Snake" survives among the Higginson papers, but the inference is inescapable that she must have sent him a copy since he would otherwise not have penetrated the anonymity of the published poem. The *Republican* had printed the poem as three 8-line stanzas and had rendered the third and fourth lines

> You may have met him — did you not,
> His notice instant is.

Otherwise the text conforms to that of the packet copy. When the poem was again issued in *Poems* (1891), 142–143, titled "The Snake," the editors followed the packet copy by the readings "sudden" (line 4) and "Yet" (line 11), but they too introduced a comma at the end of line 3:

> You may have met him, — did you not,
> His notice sudden is.

In *CP* (1924), and in all subsequent gatherings, the reading of the lines compounded the error by substituting a question mark for the final comma in line 3:

> You may have met him, — did you not?
> His notice sudden is.

The 1872 version to Sue makes perfectly clear ED's intention regarding the way she expected the lines to be read. Two words were altered in *Poems* (1891) and later printings:

11. Boy] child   12. Noon] morn

987

The Leaves like Women, interchange
Sagacious Confidence –
Somewhat of nods and somewhat
Portentous inference.

The Parties in both cases
Enjoining secrecy –
Inviolable compact
To notoriety.

[714]

MANUSCRIPTS: The copy reproduced above is in packet 88 (Bingham 53c). The copy to Sue (H B 187), in pencil, is signed "Emily." Both were written in 1865. In form they are identical, except that the copy to Sue lacks a comma after "Women" (line 1). In text one word is variant:

2. Sagacious] Exclusive

PUBLICATION: *Poems* (1891), 153, titled "Gossip." The text derives from the packet copy. The third line is altered by the addition, at the end, of the word "of."

988

The Definition of Beauty is
That Definition is none –
Of Heaven, easing Analysis,
Since Heaven and He are one.

MANUSCRIPTS: The copy is packet 88 (Bingham 55c), reproduced above, was written about 1865. Another copy (H 328), written at the same time and sent to Sue, is signed "Emily." It is identical in text and form except that it has a comma after "Beauty," and the last two words, arranged as a final line, are capitalized. In the poem beginning "By my Window have I for Scenery," written about 1863, occur the lines

The Definition of Melody – is –
That Definition is none –

PUBLICATION: The copy to Sue furnished the text in *LL* (1924), 49, where it is printed as prose with one alteration:

3. easing Analysis] easier

The packet copy is followed in *New England Quarterly*, XX (1947), 46, where a note calls attention to the variant two words.

989

Gratitude – is not the mention
Of a Tenderness,
But it's still appreciation
Out of Plumb of Speech.

When the Sea return no Answer
By the Line and Lead
Proves it there's no Sea, or rather
A remoter Bed?

MANUSCRIPTS: There are two, both written in 1865. That reproduced above (Bingham 55e) is in packet 88. A penciled copy of the first stanza only (H B 53), identical in text and form with that above, was sent to Sue, signed "Emily."

PUBLICATION: The copy to Sue is in *FF* (1932), 227. One word is altered:

4. of Speech] by speech

The packet copy is reproduced in *New England Quarterly*, XX (1947), 38.

990

Not all die early, dying young –
Maturity of Fate
Is consummated equally
In Ages, or a Night –

A Hoary Boy, I've known to drop
Whole statured – by the side
Of Junior of Fourscore – 'twas Act
Not Period – that died.

MANUSCRIPTS: There are three, identical in text, all written about 1865. That reproduced above (Bingham 78c) is in packet 92. A second copy (H 298), signed "Emily –," and presumably sent to Sue, differs in form only in the punctuation of the last line:

"Not Period, that died – "

A third copy (H H 98), in pencil, addressed "Doctor." and signed "Emily –," was sent to Dr. Holland. It is without stanza division, "Hoary" (line 5) is not capitalized, a dash concludes line 7, and the punctuation of line 8 is the same as that in the copy to Sue.

PUBLICATION: The text of the copy to Dr. Holland is in *Letters* (ed.

1894), 177; (ed. 1931), 171; also *LL* (1924), 261. The text in *LH* (1951), 72, reproduces that in *Letters*.

991

She sped as Petals of a Rose
Offended by the Wind –
A frail Aristocrat of Time
Indemnity to find –
Leaving on nature – a Default
As Cricket or as Bee –
But Andes in the Bosoms where
She had begun to lie –

MANUSCRIPTS: Two are extant; a third, known to have been made, is now missing. The fair copy reproduced above (Bingham 100–8) is a redaction of a worksheet draft (Bingham 100–9) reproduced below. Both are in pencil, written on scraps of paper in early November 1865.

She sped as Petals from a Rose –
Offended by the Wind
A fleet Aristocrat of Time
Indemnity to find –
Leaving an attitude on Time
Of Monad or of Fly –
But Andes, in the Bosoms where
[She had begun to lie]

1. from] of	3. fleet] frail – / brief
2. Offended] insulted – / assaulted	5. an attitude] a magnitude

The final line of the worksheet draft is missing. The redaction adopts two suggested changes in lines 1 and 3, and introduces a new reading for lines 5 and 6. The published text derives from the missing copy, sent to Sue on the occasion of the death of Martha Gilbert Smith's two-year-old daughter Susan, 3 November 1865.

PUBLICATION: *FF* (1932), 253–254. It is prefaced by the note:

Addressed 'Sue,' whose baby niece,
named for her, had just died

The text is identical with that of the fair copy above with one exception:

1. of] from

The Dust behind I strove to join
Unto the Disk before –
But Sequence ravelled out of Sound
Like Balls upon a Floor –

MANUSCRIPT: This unpublished variant of the second stanza of poem
937, written about 1865 (H 331), was probably sent to Sue.

993

We miss Her, not because We see –
The Absence of an Eye –
Except it's Mind accompany
Abridge Society

As slightly as the Routes of Stars –
Ourselves – asleep below –
We know that their superior Eyes
Include Us – as they go –

MANUSCRIPTS: The fair copy reproduced above (H 370) is addressed
"Sue –" and signed "Emily –"; it was written about 1865. An earlier semi-
final draft (H 133c) is in packet 24, written about 1863:

> We miss Her – not because We see –
> The Absence of an Eye –
> Except it's Mind accompany –
> Abridge Society
>
> As slightly as the Routes of Stars –
> Ourselves – asleep below –
> We know that their Superior Eyes
> Include Us – as they go –

2. Absence] Journey
4. Abridge] impair / debar – / deprive –
5. slightly] scarcely

5. Routes] flights
8. include Us] Scan better – / Convey
us –

ED rejected all the suggested changes when she later made the fair copy
she sent to Sue.

PUBLICATION: *BM* (1945), 194. The text derives from a transcript Mrs. Todd made of the packet copy. One suggested change is adopted:

4. Impair

994

Partake as doth the Bee,
Abstemiously.
The Rose is an Estate –
In Sicily.

MANUSCRIPTS: There are two. The fair copy (Bingham 98–4A–12) in pencil, reproduced above, was written about 1865. The diary of ED's cousin, Perez Dickinson Cowan, who was graduated from Amherst College in 1866, under date of 26 April 1864, records that ED presented him with a bouquet of flowers with this poem enclosed as a note. The diary is privately owned (Davies). The variant copy in packet 88 (Bingham 52c), below, was written about 1865:

Partake as doth the Bee –
Abstemiously –
A Rose is an Estate
In Sicily.

3–4] I know the Family
in Tripoli.

PUBLICATION: *BM* (1945), 331. It follows the text of the packet copy. The suggested change is rejected.

995

This was in the White of the Year –
That – was in the Green –
Drifts were as difficult then to think
As Daisies now to be seen –

Looking back is best that is left
Or if it be – before –
Retrospection is Prospect's half,
Sometimes, almost more.

MANUSCRIPT: About 1865, in packet 90 (Bingham 61b). A second copy, now lost, was sent to the Norcross cousins; it appears to have been identical in text with the copy reproduced above.

PUBLICATION: The letter to the Norcross cousins is in *Letters* (ed. 1894), 254; (ed. 1931), 234; also *LL* (1924), 266. It is printed without stanza division and dated 1865. It is included in *CP* (1924), 235, and later collections, arranged as two quatrains. If the text in *CP* derived from a holograph copy, it must have been from yet a third, since the copy in packet 90 was not available to Mrs. Bianchi, and the copy to the Norcrosses had presumably been destroyed.

996

We'll pass without the parting
So to spare
Certificate of Absence –
Deeming where

I left Her I could find Her
If I tried –
This way, I keep from missing
Those that died.

MANUSCRIPT: About 1865, in packet 88 (Bingham 48c).

PUBLICATION: *Letters* (ed. 1894), 154; (ed. 1931), 152; also *LL* (1924), 259. It is introduced by the note:

On the occasion of Mrs. Maria Avery Howard's departure from Amherst after a visit, Emily's good-by was embodied in the following lines, accompanied by an oleander blossom tied with black ribbon.

The text is arranged without stanza division. Two words are variant:

1. the] a   8. that] who

Crumbling is not an instant's Act
A fundamental pause
Delapidation's processes
Are organized Decays.

'Tis first a Cobweb on the Soul
A Cuticle of Dust
A Borer in the Axis
An Elemental Rust –

Ruin is formal – Devils work
Consecutive and slow –
Fail in an instant, no man did
Slipping – is Crashe's law.

MANUSCRIPT: About 1865, in packet 90 (Bingham 60a).
PUBLICATION: *BM* (1945), 258. The spelling slip of "Crashe's" (line 12) is corrected. The holograph is reproduced in facsimile in *AB* (1945), plate XVI.

998

Best Things dwell out of Sight
The Pearl – the Just – Our Thought.

Most shun the Public Air
Legitimate, and Rare –

The Capsule of the Wind
The Capsule of the Mind

Exhibit here, as doth a Burr –
Germ's Germ be where?

MANUSCRIPT: About 1865, in packet 90 (Bingham 60c).
PUBLICATION: *BM* (1945), 274.

Superfluous were the Sun
When Excellence be dead
He were superfluous every Day
For every Day be said

That syllable whose Faith
Just saves it from Despair
And whose "I'll meet You" hesitates
If Love inquire "Where"?

Upon His dateless Fame
Our Periods may lie
As Stars that drop anonymous
From an abundant sky.

MANUSCRIPT: About 1865, in packet 90 (Bingham 61a).
PUBLICATION: *Poems* (1896), 172. Two words are altered:

2. be] is   4. be] is

The Fingers of the Light
Tapped soft upon the Town
With "I am great and cannot wait
So therefore let me in."

"You're soon," the Town replied,
"My Faces are asleep –
But swear, and I will let you by
You will not wake them up."

The easy Guest complied
But once within the Town
The transport of His Countenance
Awakened Maid and Man

The Neighbor in the Pool
Upon His Hip elate
Made loud obeisance and the Gnat
Held up His Cup for Light.

MANUSCRIPT: About 1865, in packet 90 (Bingham 61c).
PUBLICATION: *BM* (1945), 11.

1001

The Stimulus, beyond the Grave
His Countenance to see
Supports me like imperial Drams
Afforded Day by Day.

MANUSCRIPT: About 1865, in packet 90 (Bingham 62a).
PUBLICATION: *Poems* (1896), 144. One line is altered:

4] Afforded royally

The reading "royally" appears also in *CP* (1924); in the Centenary edition
(1930) and in subsequent collections, the reading is altered to "royalty."
The poem is correctly published in a footnote in *Ancestors' Brocades*
(1945), 341, with the comment: "In search of a rhyme Mrs. Todd substi-
tuted 'royally' for 'day by day'. . ."

1002

Aurora is the effort
Of the Celestial Face
Unconsciousness of Perfectness
To simulate, to Us.

MANUSCRIPT: About 1865, in packet 90 (Bingham 62b).
PUBLICATION: *BM* (1945), 220.

1003

Dying at my music!
Bubble! Bubble!
Hold me till the Octave's run!
Quick! Burst the Windows!
Ritardando!
Phials left, and the Sun!

MANUSCRIPT: About 1865, in packet 90 (Bingham 62c).
PUBLICATION: *BM* (1945), 234.

1004

There is no Silence in the Earth – so silent
As that endured
Which uttered, would discourage Nature
And haunt the World.

MANUSCRIPT: About 1865, in packet 90 (Bingham 62d).
PUBLICATION: *BM* (1945), 250.

1005

Bind me – I still can sing –
Banish – my mandolin
Strikes true within –

Slay – and my Soul shall rise
Chanting to Paradise –
Still thine.

MANUSCRIPT: About 1865, in packet 90 (Bingham 62e).
PUBLICATION: *BM* (1945), 148.

1006

The first We knew of Him was Death –
The second – was – Renown –
Except the first had justified
The second had not been.

MANUSCRIPT: About 1865, in packet 90 (Bingham 62f).
PUBLICATION: *BM* (1945), 238.

1007

Falsehood of Thee could I suppose
'Twould undermine the Sill
To which my Faith pinned Block by Block
Her Cedar Citadel.

MANUSCRIPT: About 1865, in packet 90 (Bingham 62g).
PUBLICATION: *BM* (1945), 147.

1008

How still the Bells in Steeples stand
Till swollen with the Sky
They leap upon their silver Feet
In frantic Melody!

MANUSCRIPT: About 1865, in packet 90 (Bingham 62h).
PUBLICATION: *Poems* (1896), 22.

1009

I was a Phebe – nothing more –
A Phebe – nothing less –
The little note that others dropt
I fitted into place –

I dwelt too low that any seek –
Too shy, that any blame –
A Phebe makes a little print
Upon the Floors of Fame –

MANUSCRIPT: About 1865, in packet 90 (Bingham 63a).
PUBLICATION: *BM* (1945), 63.

1010

Up Life's Hill with my little Bundle
If I prove it steep –
If a Discouragement with[h]old me –
If my newest step

Older feel than the Hope that prompted –
Spotless be from blame
Heart that proposed as Heart that accepted
Homelessness, for Home –

MANUSCRIPT: About 1865, in packet 90 (Bingham 64b).
PUBLICATION: *BM* (1945), 104.

1011

She rose as high as His Occasion
Then sought the Dust –
And lower lay in low Westminster
For Her brief Crest –

MANUSCRIPT: About 1865, in packet 90 (Bingham 64c).
PUBLICATION: *BM* (1945), 212.

1012

Which is best? Heaven –
Or only Heaven to come
With that old Codicil of Doubt?
I cannot help esteem

The "Bird within the Hand"
Superior to the one
The "Bush" may yield me
Or may not
Too late to choose again.

MANUSCRIPT: About 1865, in packet 90 (Bingham 64e).

PUBLICATION: *BM* (1945), 276–277. The text is arranged as two quatrains.

1013

Too scanty 'twas to die for you,
The merest Greek could that.
The living, Sweet, is costlier –
I offer even that –

The Dying, is a trifle, past,
But living, this include
The dying multifold – without
The Respite to be dead.

MANUSCRIPT: About 1865, in packet 90 (Bingham 65b).
PUBLICATION: *BM* (1945), 167.

1014

Did We abolish Frost
The Summer would not cease –
If Seasons perish or prevail
Is optional with Us –

MANUSCRIPT: About 1865, in packet 90 (Bingham 65c).
PUBLICATION: *BM* (1945), 38.

1015

Were it but Me that gained the Hight –
Were it but They, that failed!
How many things the Dying play
Might they but live, they would!

MANUSCRIPT: About 1865, in packet 90 (Bingham 65d).
PUBLICATION: *BM* (1945), 306. It is placed among unfinished poems, but the packet copy from which the text derives seems to be complete.

The Hills in Purple syllables
The Day's Adventures tell
To little Groups of Continents
Just going Home from School.

MANUSCRIPT: About 1865, in packet 90 (Bingham 65e).
PUBLICATION: *BM* (1945), 92.

To die – without the Dying
And live – without the Life
This is the hardest Miracle
Propounded to Belief.

MANUSCRIPT: About 1865, in packet 90 (Bingham 65f).
PUBLICATION: *BM* (1945), 175.

Who saw no Sunrise cannot say
The Countenance 'twould be.
Who guess at seeing, guess at loss
Of the Ability.

The Emigrant of Light, it is
Afflicted for the Day.
The Blindness that beheld and blest –
And could not find it's Eye.

MANUSCRIPT: About 1865, in packet 90 (Bingham 66a).
PUBLICATION: *BM* (1945), 13.

1019

My Season's furthest Flower –
I tenderer commend
Because I found Her Kinsmanless,
A Grace without a Friend.

MANUSCRIPT: About 1865, in packet 90 (Bingham 66c).
PUBLICATION: BM (1945), 331.

1020

Trudging to Eden, looking backward,
I met Somebody's little Boy
Asked him his name – He lisped me "Trotwood" –
Lady, did He belong to thee?

Would it comfort – to know I met him –
And that He did'nt look afraid?
I could'nt weep – for so many smiling
New Acquaintance – this Baby made –

MANUSCRIPT: About 1865, in packet 90 (Bingham 66d). *David Copperfield*, from which she frequently quoted, was one of ED's favorite books.
PUBLICATION: BM (1945), 91.

1021

Far from Love the Heavenly Father
Leads the Chosen Child,
Oftener through Realm of Briar
Than the Meadow mild.

Oftener by the Claw of Dragon
Than the Hand of Friend
Guides the Little One predestined
To the Native Land.

MANUSCRIPT: About 1865, in packet 90 (Bingham 66e).
PUBLICATION: *Poems* (1896), 196.

1022

I knew that I had gained
And yet I knew not how
By Diminution it was not
But Discipline unto

A Rigor unrelieved
Except by the Content
Another bear it's Duplicate
In other Continent.

MANUSCRIPT: About 1865, in packet 90 (Bingham 67a).
PUBLICATION: *BM* (1945), 117–118.

1023

It rises – passes – on our South
Inscribes a simple Noon –
Cajoles a Moment with the Spires
And infinite is gone –

MANUSCRIPT: About 1865, in packet 90 (Bingham 67b).
PUBLICATION: *BM* (1945), 26.

1024

So large my Will
The little that I may
Embarrasses
Like gentle infamy –

Affront to Him
For whom the Whole were small
Affront to me
Who know His Meed of all.

Earth at the best
Is but a scanty Toy –   [*no stanza break*]

Bought, carried Home
To Immortality.

It looks so small
We chiefly wonder then
At our Conceit
In purchasing.

MANUSCRIPT: About 1865, in packet 90 (Bingham 67c).
PUBLICATION: *BM* (1945), 107.

1025

The Products of my Farm are these
Sufficient for my Own
And here and there a Benefit
Unto a Neighbor's Bin.

With Us, 'tis Harvest all the Year
For when the Frosts begin
We just reverse the Zodiac
And fetch the Acres in.

MANUSCRIPT: About 1865, in packet 90 (Bingham 67d).
PUBLICATION: *BM* (1945), 39.

1026

The Dying need but little, Dear,
A Glass of Water's all,
A Flower's unobtrusive Face
To punctuate the Wall,

A Fan, perhaps, a Friend's Regret
And Certainty that one
No color in the Rainbow
Perceive, when you are gone.

[731]

MANUSCRIPT: About 1865, in packet 90 (Bingham 67e).
PUBLICATION: *Poems* (1896), 175. Two words are altered:

6. certainty] certainly   8. Perceive] Perceives

1027

My Heart upon a little Plate
Her Palate to delight
A Berry or a Bun, would be,
Might it an Apricot!

MANUSCRIPT: About 1865, in packet 90 (Bingham 68b). Evidently this
was written to accompany the gift of fruit.
PUBLICATION: *BM* (1945), 330.

1028

'Twas my one Glory –
Let it be
Remembered
I was owned of Thee –

MANUSCRIPT: About 1865, in packet 90 (Bingham 68c). This is prob-
ably a flower poem.
PUBLICATION: *BM* (1945), 168.

1029

Nor Mountain hinder Me
Nor Sea –
Who's Baltic –
Who's Cordillera?

MANUSCRIPT: About 1865, in packet 90 (Bingham 68d). This verse
likewise may have been written to accompany the gift of a flower.
PUBLICATION: *BM* (1945), 168.

That Such have died enable Us
The tranquiller to die—
That Such have lived,
Certificate for Immortality.

MANUSCRIPT: About 1865, in packet 88 (Bingham 47b).
PUBLICATION: *Poems* (1896), 146. The first word of line 4 concludes
line 3. One word is altered:

1. enable] enables

1031

Fate slew Him, but He did not drop—
She felled—He did not fall—
Impaled Him on Her fiercest stakes—
He neutralized them all—

She stung Him—sapped His firm Advance—
But when Her Worst was done
And He—unmoved regarded Her—
Acknowledged Him a Man.

MANUSCRIPT: About 1865, in packet 88 (Bingham 47d).
PUBLICATION: *Poems* (1896), 45, titled "A Man."

1032

Who is the East?
The Yellow Man
Who may be Purple if He can
That carries in the Sun.

Who is the West?
The Purple Man
Who may be Yellow if He can
That lets Him out again.

[733]

Manuscript: About 1865, in packet 88 (Bingham 47e).
Publication: *BM* (1945), 21–22. The text is arranged as two triplets.

1033

Said Death to Passion
"Give of thine an Acre unto me."
Said Passion, through contracting Breaths
"A Thousand Times Thee Nay."

Bore Death from Passion
All His East
He – sovreign as the Sun
Resituated in the West
And the Debate was done.

Manuscript: About 1865, in packet 88 (Bingham 48a).
Publication: *BM* (1945), 1900. The text is arranged as two quatrains.

1034

His Bill an Augur is
His Head, a Cap and Frill
He laboreth at every Tree
A Worm, His utmost Goal.

Manuscript: About 1865, in packet 88 (Bingham 48d).
Publication: *Poems* (1896), 122, titled "The Woodpecker."

1035

Bee! I'm expecting you!
Was saying Yesterday
To Somebody you know
That you were due –

The Frogs got Home last Week –
Are settled, and at work –
Birds, mostly back –
The Clover warm and thick –

You'll get my Letter by
The seventeenth; Reply
Or better, be with me –
Yours, Fly.

MANUSCRIPT: About 1865, in packet 88 (Bingham 50a).
PUBLICATION: BM (1945), 67.

1036

Satisfaction – is the Agent
Of Satiety –
Want – a quiet Comissary
For Infinity.

To possess, is past the instant
We achieve the Joy –
Immortality contented
Were Anomaly.

MANUSCRIPT: About 1865, in packet 88 (Bingham 50b).
PUBLICATION: BM (1945), 277–278. The spelling of "Comissary" is
regularized.

1037

Here, where the Daisies fit my Head
'Tis easiest to lie
And every Grass that plays outside
Is sorry, some, for me.

Where I am not afraid to go
I may confide my Flower –
Who was not Enemy of Me
Will gentle be, to Her.

Nor separate, Herself and Me
By Distances become –
A single Bloom we constitute
Departed, or at Home –

[735]

MANUSCRIPT: About 1865, in packet 88 (Bingham 50c).
PUBLICATION: *BM* (1945), 49.

1038

Her little Parasol to lift
And once to let it down
Her whole Responsibility –
To imitate be Mine.

A Summer further I must wear,
Content if Nature's Drawer
Present me from sepulchral Crease
As blemishless, as Her.

MANUSCRIPT: About 1865, in packet 88 (Bingham 50d).
PUBLICATION: *BM* (1945), 328. A note reads: "With a morning-glory."

1039

I heard, as if I had no Ear
Until a Vital Word
Came all the way from Life to me
And then I knew I heard.

I saw, as if my Eye were on
Another, till a Thing
And now I know 'twas Light, because
It fitted them, came in.

I dwelt, as if Myself were out,
My Body but within
Until a Might detected me
And set my kernel in.

And Spirit turned unto the Dust
"Old Friend, thou knowest me,"
And Time went out to tell the News
And met Eternity

[736]

MANUSCRIPTS: The text reproduced above (Bingham 51a) is in packet 88, written about 1865. A variant of the last stanza is in the penciled draft of a letter (Bingham), written late in 1870 to an unidentified recipient, probably T. W. Higginson.

> The Spirit said unto the Dust
> Old Friend, thou knewest me
> And Time went out to tell the news
> Unto Eternity

PUBLICATION: The four stanzas are in *BM* (1945), 124.

1040

Not so the infinite Relations – Below
Division is Adhesion's forfeit – On High
Affliction but a Speculation – And Wo
A Fallacy, a Figment, We knew –

MANUSCRIPT: About 1865, in packet 88 (Bingham 51b).
PUBLICATION: *BM* (1945), 219. It is arranged as an eight-line stanza.

1041

Somewhat, to hope for,
Be it ne'er so far
Is Capital against Despair –

Somewhat, to suffer,
Be it ne'er so keen –
If terminable, may be borne.

MANUSCRIPT: About 1865, in packet 88 (Bingham 51c).
PUBLICATION: *BM* (1945), 242. The text is arranged as two quatrains.

1042

Spring comes on the World –
I sight the Aprils –
Hueless to me until thou come
As, till the Bee   [*no stanza break*]

Blossoms stand negative,
Touched to Conditions
By a Hum.

MANUSCRIPT: About 1865, in packet 88 (Bingham 51d).
PUBLICATION: *BM* (1945), 141. Line 7 is printed as the conclusion
to line 6.

1043

Lest this be Heaven indeed
An Obstacle is given
That always guages a Degree
Between Ourself and Heaven.

MANUSCRIPT: About 1865, in packet 88 (Bingham 51e).
PUBLICATION: *BM* (1945), 255.

1044

A Sickness of this World it most occasions
When Best Men die.
A Wishfulness their far Condition
To occupy.

A Chief indifference, as Foreign
A World must be
Themselves forsake – contented,
For Deity

MANUSCRIPT: About 1865, in packet 88 (Bingham 52b).
PUBLICATION: *Poems* (1896), 171. Lines 7–8 read:

> Themselves forsake contented,
> For Deity.

1045

Nature rarer uses Yellow
Than another Hue.
Saves she all of that for Sunsets
Prodigal of Blue

Spending Scarlet, like a Woman
Yellow she affords
Only scantly and selectly
Like a Lover's Words.

MANUSCRIPT: About 1865, in packet 88 (Bingham 54a).
PUBLICATION: *Poems* (1891), 152.

1046

I've dropped my Brain – My Soul is numb –
The Veins that used to run
Stop palsied – 'tis Paralysis
Done perfecter on stone.

Vitality is Carved and cool.
My nerve in Marble lies –
A Breathing Woman
Yesterday – Endowed with Paradise.

Not dumb – I had a sort that moved –
A Sense that smote and stirred –
Instincts for Dance – a caper part –
An Aptitude for Bird –

Who wrought Carrara in me
And chiselled all my tune
Were it a Witchcraft – were it Death –
I've still a chance to strain

To Being, somewhere – Motion – Breath –
Though Centuries beyond,
And every limit a Decade –
I'll shiver, satisfied.

MANUSCRIPT: About 1865, in packet 88 (Bingham 54c).
PUBLICATION: *BM* (1945), 164–165. "Yesterday" (line 8) concludes
line 7.

1047

The Opening and the Close
Of Being, are alike
Or differ, if they do,
As Bloom upon a Stalk.

That from an equal Seed
Unto an equal Bud
Go parallel, perfected
In that they have decayed.

MANUSCRIPT: About 1865, in packet 88 (Bingham 54d).
PUBLICATION: *BM* (1945), 202.

1048

Reportless Subjects, to the Quick
Continual addressed –
But foreign as the Dialect
Of Danes, unto the rest.

Reportless Measures, to the Ear
Susceptive – stimulus –
But like an Oriental Tale
To others, fabulous –

MANUSCRIPT: About 1865, in packet 88 (Bingham 55b).
PUBLICATION: *BM* (1945), 276.

1049

Pain has but one Acquaintance
And that is Death –
Each one unto the other
Society enough.

Pain is the Junior Party
By just a Second's right –
Death tenderly assists Him
And then absconds from Sight.

MANUSCRIPT: About 1865, in packet 88 (Bingham 55d).
PUBLICATION: *BM* (1945), 189.

1050

As willing lid o'er weary eye
The Evening on the Day leans
Till of all our nature's House
Remains but Balcony

MANUSCRIPT: About 1865, in packet 92 (Bingham 78b).
PUBLICATION: *BM* (1945), 25. The last word of line 2 is printed as
the first of line 3.

1051

I cannot meet the Spring unmoved –
I feel the old desire –
A Hurry with a lingering, mixed,
A Warrant to be fair –

A Competition in my sense
With something hid in Her –
And as she vanishes, Remorse
I saw no more of Her.

MANUSCRIPTS: There are two, both in pencil, written about 1865. That reproduced above (Bingham 102–26) is a two-stanza version. The second stanza only (H 221) is slightly variant:

> A competition in my sense
> With something hid in her,
> And when she vanishes, remorse –
> I saw no more of her –

PUBLICATION: The two stanzas are in *BM* (1945), 34–35.

1052

> I never saw a Moor –
> I never saw the Sea –
> Yet know I how the Heather looks
> And what a Billow be.
>
> I never spoke with God
> Nor visited in Heaven –
> Yet certain am I of the spot
> As if the Checks were given –

MANUSCRIPT: About 1865 (Bingham 98–3–14). It is written in pencil on the back of a discarded piece of embossed stationery. ED's use of the word "Checks" perplexed the early editors, who altered it. She seems to be using it in the accepted colloquial sense of railroad tickets: "My assurance of the existence of Heaven is as great as though, having surrendered my checks to the conductor, I knew I had arrived there."

PUBLICATION: This was one of fourteen poems selected for publication in an article contributed by T. W. Higginson to the *Christian Union*, XLII (25 September 1890), 393. Three words are altered:

4. a Billow] the billows   8. Checks] chart

When it appeared in *Poems* (1890), 126, the alteration of line 8 remained, but that in line 4 was altered again, so that the line reads:

And what a wave must be

All succeeding editions have followed the text of *Poems* (1890).

1053

It was a quiet way –
He asked if I was his –
I made no answer of the Tongue
But answer of the Eyes –
And then He bore me on
Before this mortal noise
With swiftness, as of Chariots
And distance, as of Wheels.
This World did drop away
As Acres from the feet
Of one that leaneth from Balloon
Upon an Ether street.
The Gulf behind was not,
The Continents were new –
Eternity it was before
Eternity was due.
No Seasons were to us –
It was not Night nor Morn –
But Sunrise stopped upon the place
And fastened it in Dawn.

MANUSCRIPTS: The copy reproduced above (Bingham 98–4B–10), written about 1865, is in pencil, signed "Emily." It has been folded as if enclosed in an envelope. Evidently it is a redaction of the copy in packet 16 (H 86c), written in 1862:

It was a quiet way –
He asked if I was His –
I made no answer of the Tongue,
But answer of the Eyes –

And then he bore me high
Before this mortal noise
With swiftness as of Chariots –
And distance – as of Wheels –

The World did drop away
As Counties – from the feet
Of Him that leaneth in Balloon –
Upon an Ether Street –

[743]

The Gulf behind – was not –
The Continents – were new –
Eternity – it was – before
Eternity was due –

No Seasons were – to us –
It was not Night – nor Noon –
For Sunrise – stopped upon the Place –
And fastened it – in Dawn.

Seven words have been changed in the redaction:

5. high] on	11. Him] one
9. The] This	11. in] from
10. Counties] Acres	18. Noon] Morn
	19. For] But

PUBLICATION: *London Mercury*, XIX (February 1929), 353; *FP* (1929), 137. It derives from the text of the packet copy. Stanzas 1, 3, and 5, arranged as 5, 5, and 6 lines respectively, are restored as quatrains in later collections. One word is altered:

10. Counties] countries

1054

Not to discover weakness is
The Artifice of strength –
Impregnability inheres
As much through Consciousness

Of faith of others in itself
As Pyramidal Nerve
Behind the most unconscious clock
What skilful Pointers move –

2. Artifice] Mystery	6. Pyramidal] Elemental – / plupoten-
4-5] [As much through] Conscious	tial
faith	7. unconscious] Consummate
of others in it's ableness	8. skilful] Anxious

MANUSCRIPT: About 1865, in packet 90 (Bingham 60b).

PUBLICATION: *BM* (1945), 277. The suggested changes for lines 2, 6 (elemental), 7 are adopted.

1055

The Soul should always stand ajar
That if the Heaven inquire
He will not be obliged to wait
Or shy of troubling Her

Depart, before the Host have slid
The Bolt unto the Door –
To search for the accomplished Guest,
Her Visitor, no more –

6. unto] upon   7. search] seek

MANUSCRIPT: About 1865, in packet 90 (Bingham 64a).
PUBLICATION: *Poems* (1896), 177. Both suggested changes are adopted.
A period at the end of line 4 destroys the sense. The error is noted in
Ancestors' Brocades (1945), 340, and the poem identically reprinted except
that the period is deleted. One word is altered:

5. have] has

1056

There is a Zone whose even Years
No Solstice interrupt –
Whose Sun constructs perpetual Noon
Whose perfect Seasons wait –

Whose Summer set in Summer, till
The Centuries of June
And Centuries of August cease
And Consciousness – is Noon.

5. Whose] Where   7. cease] fuse – / lapse – / blend

MANUSCRIPT: About 1865, in packet 90 (Bingham 64d).
PUBLICATION: *BM* (1945), 218. Only "fuse" among the suggested
changes is adopted.

1057

I had a daily Bliss
I half indifferent viewed
Till sudden I perceived it stir –
It grew as I pursued

Till when around a Hight
It wasted from my sight
Increased beyond my utmost scope
I learned to estimate.

7. Increased] Enlarged

MANUSCRIPT: About 1865, in packet 90 (Bingham 66b).
PUBLICATION: *Poems* (1896), 52, titled "Lost Joy." The suggested
change is adopted. Words in two lines are altered:

5. Hight] crag   8. to estimate] its sweetness right

1058

Bloom – is Result – to meet a Flower
And casually glance
Would cause one scarcely to suspect
The minor Circumstance

Assisting in the Bright Affair
So intricately done
Then offered as a Butterfly
To the Meridian –

To pack the Bud – oppose the Worm –
Obtain it's right of Dew –
Adjust the Heat – elude the Wind –
Escape the prowling Bee

Great Nature not to disappoint
Awaiting Her that Day –
To be a Flower, is profound
Responsibility –

3. cause one scarcely] scarcely cause [one]

MANUSCRIPT: About 1865, in packet 90 (Bingham 68a).
PUBLICATION: *BM* (1945), 46. The suggested change is rejected.

1059

Sang from the Heart, Sire,
Dipped my Beak in it,
If the Tune drip too much
Have a tint too Red

Pardon the Cochineal –
Suffer the Vermillion –
Death is the Wealth
Of the Poorest Bird.

Bear with the Ballad –
Awkward – faltering –
Death twists the strings –
'Twas'nt my blame –

Pause in your Liturgies –
Wait your Chorals –
While I repeat your
Hallowed name –

15. repeat] recite

MANUSCRIPT: About 1865, in packet 88 (Bingham 47c).
PUBLICATION: *BM* (1945), 144. The last word of line 15 is printed as
the first of line 16. The suggested change is rejected.

1060

Air has no Residence, no Neighbor,
No Ear, no Door,
No Apprehension of Another
Oh, Happy Air!

[747]

Etherial Guest at e'en an Outcast's Pillow –
Essential Host, in Life's faint, wailing Inn,
Later than Light thy Consciousness accost me
Till it depart, persuading Mine –

8. persuading] conveying

MANUSCRIPT: About 1865, in packet 88 (Bingham 48b).
PUBLICATION: *BM* (1945), 281. The suggested change is adopted.
One word is altered:

8. conveying] convoying

1061

Three Weeks passed since I had seen Her –
Some Disease had vext
'Twas with Text and Village Singing
I beheld Her next

And a Company – our pleasure
To discourse alone –
Gracious now to me as any –
Gracious unto none –

Borne without dissent of Either
To the Parish night –
Of the Separated Parties
Which be out of sight?

3. Village] Antique   11. Parties] People
9. Either] any

MANUSCRIPT: About 1865, in packet 88 (Bingham 52a).
PUBLICATION: *Poems* (1896), 178. The suggested change for line 11
is adopted. One word is altered:

12. be] are

He scanned it – staggered –
Dropped the Loop
To Past or Period –
Caught helpless at a sense as if
His Mind were going blind –

Groped up, to see if God were there –
Groped backward at Himself
Caressed a Trigger absently
And wandered out of Life.

6. were] was

MANUSCRIPT: About 1865, in packet 88 (Bingham 52d).
PUBLICATION: *BM* (1945), 186. The text is arranged as two quatrains.
The suggested change is adopted.

1063

Ashes denote that Fire was –
Revere the Grayest Pile
For the Departed Creature's sake
That hovered there awhile –

Fire exists the first in light
And then consolidates
Only the Chemist can disclose
Into what Carbonates.

2. Revere] Respect

MANUSCRIPT: About 1865, in packet 88 (Bingham 53b).
PUBLICATION: *Poems* (1896), 44, titled "Fire." The suggested change
is adopted.

1064

To help our Bleaker Parts
Salubrious Hours are given
Which if they do not fit for Earth
Drill silently for Heaven –

4. Drill silently] Arrange the Heart

MANUSCRIPT: About 1865, in packet 88 (Bingham 54b).
PUBLICATION: *Poems* (1896), 61. The suggested change is rejected.

1065

Let down the Bars, Oh Death –
The tired Flocks come in
Whose bleating ceases to repeat
Whose wandering is done –

Thine is the stillest night
Thine the securest Fold
Too near Thou art for seeking Thee
Too tender, to be told.

6. securest] Paternal   8] too willing, to be called

MANUSCRIPT: About 1865, in packet 88 (Bingham 55a).
PUBLICATION: *Poems* (1891), 181. Both suggested changes are rejected.

1066

Fame's Boys and Girls, who never die
And are too seldom born –

MANUSCRIPT: About 1865 (Bingham 102–17). It is a penciled scrap,
a jotting perhaps intended for further use.
PUBLICATION: *BM* (1945), 319. It is placed among incomplete poems.

1067

Except the smaller size
No lives are round –
These – hurry to a sphere
And show and end –
The larger – slower grow
And later hang –
The Summers of Hesperides
Are long.

MANUSCRIPTS: The copy reproduced above (BPL Higg 59) is incorporated in a letter written to T. W. Higginson; it is enclosed in an envelope postmarked 17 March 1866. A second fair copy (H 250), written about the same time, is addressed "Sue" and signed "Emily." It perhaps accompanied a gift of apples. The copies are identical in text:

Except the smaller size
No Lives are Round –
These – hurry to a Sphere –
And show – and end –

The Larger – slower grow –
And later hang –
The Summers of Hesperides
Are long –

The semifinal draft from which the fair copies derive is in packet 84 (Bingham 27d) and was written some years earlier, about 1862:

Except the smaller size –
No Lives – are Round –
These – hurry to a Sphere –
And show – and end –

The Larger – slower grow –
And later – hang –
The Summers of Hesperides
Are long –

Hugest of Core
Present the awkward Rind –
Yield Groups of Ones –
No Cluster – ye shall find –

But far after Frost –
And Indian Summer Noon –
Ships – offer these –
As West-Indian –

7. of] in   12. ye] you
9. Hugest] The Huge   14. Noon] Sun –

The text of the first eight lines is identical with that of the two fair copies.
It should be noted that all suggested changes are confined to the two final
stanzas, the ones that ED discarded in the two fair copies.

PUBLICATION: The letter to Higginson was first published in *Atlantic
Monthly*, LXVIII (October 1891), 451, in an article which Higginson
wrote dealing with the letters and poems he had received from ED. It was
collected in *Letters* (ed. 1894), 312; (ed. 1931), 282; also *LL* (1924),
268–269. The copy to Sue furnished the text in *SH* (1914), 5, where the
lines are arranged as a single quatrian. The packet copy is reproduced in
New England Quarterly, XX (1947), 16; the suggested changes are re-
jected.

1068

Further in Summer than the Birds
Pathetic from the Grass
A minor Nation celebrates
It's unobtrusive Mass.

No Ordinance be seen
So gradual the Grace
A pensive Custom it becomes
Enlarging Loneliness.

Antiquest felt at Noon
When August burning low
Arise this spectral Canticle
Repose to typify

Remit as yet no Grace
No Furrow on the Glow
Yet a Druidic Difference
Enhances Nature now

MANUSCRIPTS: There are three holographs of this poem which apparently was written sometime early in 1866. The copy reproduced above (BPL Higg 13) was enclosed in a letter to T. W. Higginson (BPL Higg 64) postmarked 27 January 1866. The letter (*Letters* [ed. 1931 only], 281) tersely announces the death of her dog and requests Higginson's criticism of the poem:

> Amherst
>
> Carlo died.
>
> E – Dickinson
>
> Would you instruct me now?

Higginson has tentatively titled it by a penciled query in the upper left margin: "Insect-Sounds?"

The copy sent to Higginson was preceded — very possibly in the same month of January — by a semifinal draft (Bingham 109–3):

> Further in Summer than the Birds
> Pathetic from the Grass
> A minor Nation celebrates
> It's unobtrusive Mass
>
> No Ordinance be seen
> So gradual the Grace
> A pensive Custom it becomes
> Enlarging Loneliness
>
> Antiquest felt at Noon
> When August burning low
> Arise this spectral Canticle
> Repose to typify.
>
> Remit as yet no Grace
> No Furrow on the Glow
> Yet a Druidic – Difference
> Enhances Nature now

"Antiquest" she first wrote "Antiquer," but in pencil she overlaid the final "r" with "st," and to confirm her decision she wrote "Antiquest" in pencil above the original word. It was the only alteration she judged necessary and, with its adoption, the fair copy to Higginson is identical with it in text. Some seventeen years later, in mid-March 1883 she chose this as the poem to enclose in a letter (Bingham 106) to Thomas Niles, editor of the publishing house of Roberts Brothers. She arranged it as two eight-line stanzas and introduced variants in lines 7, 11, and 15:

Further in Summer than the Birds –
Pathetic from the Grass
A minor Nation celebrates
It's unobtrusive Mass –
No Ordinance be seen –
So gradual the Grace
A gentle Custom it becomes –
Enlarging loneliness.

Antiquest felt at Noon
When August burning low
Arise the Spectral Canticle
Repose to typify –
Remit as yet no Grace –
No furrow on the Glow –
But a Druidic Difference
Enhances Nature now –

Niles had recently sent her a copy of Mathilde Blind's life of George Eliot
just issued by his firm. She acknowledges receipt of the volume and thanks
him by transcribing two of her poems (*Letters* [ed. 1931], 406):

I bring you a chill Gift – My Cricket – and the Snow –

Thus she indicates a title for this poem. "Snow" is her poem beginning
"It sifts from leaden sieves."

Though no other holographs exist, there is a transcript of this poem
which contains new third, fourth, and fifth stanzas. Mrs. Millicent Todd
Bingham, who published it, believes the transcript to have been made by
ED's cousin Frances Norcross:

Further in summer than the birds
Pathetic from the grass
A minor nation celebrates
Its unobtrusive mass.

No ordinance be seen,
So gradual the grace
A gentle custom it becomes,
Enlarging loneliness.

'Tis audibler at dusk
When day's attempt is done
And nature nothing waits to do
But terminate in tune;

Nor difference it knows
Of cadence or of pause
But simultaneous as sound
The service emphasize;

Nor know I when it cease,
At candle it is here;
When sunrise is, that is it not.
Than this, I know no more.

Antiquest felt at noon
When August burning low
Arise this spectral canticle
Repose to typify.

Remit as yet no grace,
No furrow on the glow,
But a druidic difference
Enhances nature now.

One might assume that the original of this version was written late from the fact that two of the three variants correspond to those in the Niles copy. (Stanzas 3, 4, 5 of the Norcross transcript are not reckoned in the line count.)

Semifinal	*Higginson*	*Niles*	*Norcross transcript*
7. pensive	pensive	gentle	gentle
11. this	this	the	this
15. Yet	Yet	But	But

But a more compelling argument that it was an early version stems from the fact that ED always shortened her poems if she made stanza changes in later fair copies — never lengthened them.

PUBLICATION: *Poems* (1891), 167, titled "My Cricket." The text follows either the semifinal copy or the copy to Higginson. Three alterations have been introduced which have no warrant in the extant manuscripts or the Norcross transcript:

    1. Further] Farther   11. Arise this] Calls forth
    5. be] is

The Norcross transcript is published in *New England Quarterly*, XX (1947), 12–13.

1069

Paradise is of the option.
Whosoever will
Own in Eden notwithstanding
Adam and Repeal.

MANUSCRIPTS: There are two. The fair copy reproduced above con-
cludes a letter (BPL Higg 60) to T. W. Higginson, postmarked 9 June
1866. Except that there the two sentences are arranged each as a para-
graph, it is here exactly rendered. The lines are preceded by the thought:
"To escape enchantment, one must always flee." The poem is a redaction
of a penciled draft (Bingham 100–7) written at the same time:

> Paradise is of the option.
> Whosoever will
> Dwell in Eden notwithstanding
> Adam and Repeal.

3. Dwell in] Own in

The suggested change is adopted in the fair copy.

PUBLICATION: The letter to Higginson is in *Letters* (ed. 1931 only),
282–283, where the prose arrangement is retained. The rough draft is re-
produced in *BM* (1945), 318, where it is placed among the fragments.
The suggested change is rejected.

1070

To undertake is to achieve
Be Undertaking blent
With fortitude of obstacle
And toward encouragement

That fine Suspicion, Natures must
Permitted to revere
Departed Standards and the few
Criterion Sources here

MANUSCRIPTS: There are three copies, two written in 1866, and one
written about a year earlier. That reproduced above (BPL Higg 19) was

enclosed with three other poems in a letter to T. W. Higginson (BPL Higg 60) postmarked 9 June 1866. The letter (not the poem) is published in *Letters* (ed. 1931 only), 282–283. A second fair copy (Bingham 98–4A–19) was made about the same time. It is identical in text and form with that sent to Higginson, except that it entirely lacks punctuation. Both copies are redactions of that in packet 88 (Bingham 48e) written about a year earlier, in 1865. It is identical in text with the other copies, except for the final line:

Criterion Natures here –

Its form is that of the second fair copy except for line 8, above.

PUBLICATION: The copy to Higginson is in *New England Quarterly*, V (1932), 219. The second fair copy is reproduced in *BM* (1945), 274.

1071

Perception of an object costs
Precise the Object's loss –
Perception in itself a Gain
Replying to it's Price –
The Object Absolute – is nought –
Perception sets it fair
And then upbraids a Perfectness
That situates so far –

MANUSCRIPTS: There are two, both written about 1866. The copy reproduced above (H B 192) is addressed "Sue –" and signed "Emily." The copy below is in packet 35 (H 188b):

Perception of an Object costs
Precise the Object's loss –
Perception in itself a Gain
Replying to it's price –

The Object Absolute, is nought –
Perception sets it fair
And then upbraids a Perfectness
That situates so far –

2. Precise] More oft –   8] that 'tis so Heavenly far –

[757]

The changes ED suggests in the packet copy she does not adopt in the fair copy to Sue; the texts are identical.

PUBLICATION: *SH* (1914), 16. It follows the copy to Sue in that it is without stanza division.

1072

Title divine – is mine!
The Wife – without the Sign!
Acute Degree – conferred on me –
Empress of Calvary!
Royal – all but the Crown!
Betrothed – without the swoon
God sends us Women –
When you – hold – Garnet to Garnet –
Gold – to Gold –
Born – Bridalled – Shrouded –
In a Day –
"My Husband" – women say –
Stroking the Melody –
Is *this* – the way?

MANUSCRIPTS: There are two. That reproduced above (Bingham) was written about 1862 on two pages of a folded sheet of stationery and sent probably to Samuel Bowles. At the end of the poem ED has written:

Here's – what I had to "tell you" –
You will tell no other?
Honor – is it's own pawn –

A second copy (H 361), signed "Emily." was sent to Sue. On the evidence of handwriting it was clearly written at a later date, perhaps as late as 1866. It is variant in line 7, and a further line is added after line 11.

Title divine, is mine.
The Wife without the Sign –
Acute Degree conferred on me –
Empress of Calvary –
Royal, all but the Crown –
Betrothed, without the Swoon
God gives us Women –   [*no stanza break*]

[758]

When You hold Garnet to Garnet –
Gold – to Gold –
Born – Bridalled – Shrouded –
In a Day –
Tri   Victory –
"My Husband" – Women say
Stroking the Melody –
Is this the Way –

PUBLICATION: The copy to Sue is in *LL* (1924), 49–50; *CP* (1924),
176–177, and later collections. The text is arranged as twenty-one lines. In
line 8, "You" is altered to "two."

1073

Experiment to me
Is every one I meet
If it contain a Kernel?
The Figure of a Nut

Presents upon a Tree
Equally plausibly
But Meat within, is requisite
To Squirrels and to Me

MANUSCRIPTS: There are three fair copies, identical in text. The copy
reproduced above (Bingham 98–4B–8) was written about 1866. It has been
folded as if enclosed in an envelope. A second fair copy (H 253), written
in pencil about the same time, is signed "Emily."; it was probably sent to
Sue:

Experiment to me
is every one I meet
If it contain a Kernel?
The Figure of a Nut
Presents upon a Tree
Equally plausibly,
But Meat within, is requisite
To Squirrels, and to Me.

The first word of line 2 is not capitalized. Both these copies derive from
the copy in packet 88 (Bingham 47a), evidently written somewhat earlier,
about 1865:

Experiment to me
Is Every one I meet
If It contain a Kernel –
The figure of a Nut

Presents upon a Tree
Equally plausibly
But Meat within is requisite
To Squirrels, and to Me.

PUBLICATION: *Poems* (1891), 51. The text reproduces the Bingham
1866 copy.

1074

Count not that far that can be had,
Though sunset lie between –
Nor that adjacent, that beside,
Is further than the sun.

MANUSCRIPT: No holograph survives. The lines are included in a letter
now lost to Mrs. J. G. Holland, written in early May 1866. There is also a
transcript made by Sue (H ST 23a), presumably from another copy now
lost; the text is that of the Holland copy.
PUBLICATION: *Letters* (ed. 1894), 172; (ed. 1931), 166; also *LL*
(1924), 202; and *LH* (1951), 75: in all instances an exact transcription
of the copy to Mrs. Holland.

1075

The Sky is low – the Clouds are mean.
A Travelling Flake of Snow
Across a Barn or through a Rut
Debates if it will go –

A Narrow Wind complains all Day
How some one treated him
Nature, like Us is sometimes caught
Without her Diadem.

6] How Parties treated him

[760]

MANUSCRIPT: About 1866 (Bingham 98–3–30). It is a penciled draft on a scrap of paper.

PUBLICATION: *Poems* (1890), 103, titled "Beclouded." The suggested change is rejected. It is also in *LH* (1951), 77, among letters to Mrs. J. G. Holland, written probably about November 1866. The letter here printed that incorporates the poem is reproduced from *Letters* (ed. 1931), 174, where the poem is omitted from the letter and the reader referred to *Poems* (1890).

1076

Just Once! Oh least Request!
Could Adamant refuse
So small a Grace
So scanty put,
Such agonizing terms?
Would not a God of Flint
Be conscious of a sigh
As down His Heaven dropt remote
"Just Once" Sweet Deity?

MANUSCRIPTS: There are three. The copy reproduced above (Bingham 98–4A–25) was written about 1866 on the first and third pages of a sheet of notepaper. Identical in text is a second fair copy (Bingham 98–4A–24), written about the same time and signed "Emily." It has been folded as if enclosed in an envelope:

Just Once – Oh Least Request –
Could Adamant refuse
So small a Grace –
So scanty put –
Such agonizing terms?

Would not a God of Flint
Be conscious of a sigh
As down His Heaven dropt remote –
"Just Once" – Sweet Deity?

Both fair copies are redactions of a semifinal draft in packet 19 (H 108d), written late in 1862:

[761]

Just Once! Oh Least Request!
Could Adamant – refuse?
So small – a Grace – so scanty – put –
So agonized Urged?

Would not a God of Flint –
Be conscious of a Sigh –
As down his Heaven – echoed faint –
"Just Once!" Sweet Deity!

4] Such agonizing Terms –   7. echoed faint] Dropt – remote –

A fourth copy now lost was sent to Samuel Bowles.

PUBLICATION: The copy to Bowles is in *Letters* (ed. 1894), 217; (ed. 1931), 205; also *LL* (1924), 256. The text is arranged without stanza division and is identical with that of the fair copies. The packet copy is reproduced in *FP* (1929), 202. The text is arranged as a ten-line stanza and both suggested changes are adopted.

1077

These are the Signs to Nature's Inns –
Her invitation broad
To Whosoever famishing
To taste her mystic Bread –

These are the rites of Nature's House –
The Hospitality
That opens with an equal width
To Beggar and to Bee

For Sureties of her staunch Estate
Her undecaying Cheer
The Purple in the East is set
And in the North, the Star –

MANUSCRIPT: About 1866, in packet 35 (H 189a).
PUBLICATION: *FP* (1929), 74. Words in two lines are altered:

3. To Whosoever] For whomsoever   8. and] or

1078

The Bustle in a House
The Morning after Death
Is solemnest of industries
Enacted upon Earth –

The Sweeping up the Heart
And putting Love away
We shall not want to use again
Until Eternity.

MANUSCRIPT: About 1866, in packet 35 (H 189c).
PUBLICATION: *Poems* (1890), 133.

1079

The Sun went down – no Man looked on –
The Earth and I, alone,
Were present at the Majesty –
He triumphed, and went on –

The Sun went up – no Man looked on –
The Earth and I and One
A nameless Bird – a Stranger
Were Witness for the Crown –

MANUSCRIPT: About 1866, in packet 35 (H 189d).
PUBLICATION: *London Mercury*, XIX (February, 1929), 350; *FP*
(1929), 53. The text is arranged as two five-line stanzas.

1080

When they come back – if Blossoms do –
I always feel a doubt
If Blossoms can be born again
When once the Art is out –

When they begin, if Robins may,
I always had a fear
I did not tell, it was their last Experiment
Last Year,

When it is May, if May return,
Had nobody a pang
Lest in a Face so beautiful
He might not look again?

If I am there – One does not know
What Party – One may be
Tomorrow, but if I am there
I take back all I say –

MANUSCRIPT: About 1866, in packet 35 (H 190a).
PUBLICATION: *London Mercury*, XIX (1929), 351; FP (1929), 67.
The text is arranged as four stanzas of 7, 7, 5, and 6 lines; in later collec-
tions, as four five-line stanzas. In line 15 "am" is italicized. One word is
altered:

11. in] on

1081

Superiority to Fate
Is difficult to gain
'Tis not conferred of Any
But possible to earn

A pittance at a time
Until to Her surprise
The Soul with strict economy
Subsist till Paradise.

MANUSCRIPT: About 1866, in packet 35 (H 190b).
PUBLICATION: *Poems* (1896), 14, titled "Superiority to Fate." Three
words are altered:

2. gain] learn   8. Subsist] Subsists
3. of] by

Revolution is the Pod
Systems rattle from
When the Winds of Will are stirred
Excellent is Bloom

But except it's Russet Base
Every Summer be
The Entomber of itself,
So of Liberty –

Left inactive on the Stalk
All it's Purple fled
Revolution shakes it for
Test if it be dead.

MANUSCRIPT: About 1866, in packet 35 (H 190c).
PUBLICATION: *Nation*, CXXVIII (13 March 1929), 315; *FP* (1929), 33. The text, arranged as five-line stanzas, in later collections is restored as quatrains.

We learn in the Retreating
How vast an one
Was recently among us –
A Perished Sun

Endear in the departure
How doubly more
Than all the Golden presence
It was – before –

MANUSCRIPT: About 1866, in packet 35 (H 190d).
PUBLICATION: *Outlook*, LIII (25 January 1896), 140, titled "Departing." In *Poems* (1896), 140, the title is omitted. One word is altered:

5. Endear] Endears

At Half past Three, a single Bird
Unto a silent Sky
Propounded but a single term
Of cautious melody.

At Half past Four, Experiment
Had subjugated test
And lo, Her silver Principle
Supplanted all the rest.

At Half past Seven, Element
Nor Implement, be seen –
And Place was where the Presence was
Circumference between.

MANUSCRIPTS: There are four, identical in text, all written about 1866. That reproduced above (H 191a) is in packet 35. A second copy (H H 97), in pencil, addressed "Doctor –" and signed "Emily –," was sent to Dr. Holland. It is identical in form with the packet copy except that line 10 has no punctuation at the end, a comma follows "Place" (line 11), and four words are not capitalized:

5. experiment	9. element
7. her	10. implement

A third copy, in pencil (Bingham), signed "Emily –," was sent to an un-identified friend. It is identical in form with the packet copy except that the same four words are not capitalized as in the Holland copy. A fourth copy (Bingham 98–4B–5) has an altered line arrangement:

At Half past Three
A single Bird
Unto a silent sky
Propounded but a single term
Of cautious melody.

At Half past Four
Experiment had subjugated test
And lo, her silver principle
Supplanted all the rest.

At Half past Seven
Element nor implement be seen
And Place was where the Presence was
Circumference between

PUBLICATION: *Poems* (1891), 114. The text derives from the packet copy. One word is altered:

10. be] was

1085

If Nature smiles – the Mother must
I'm sure, at many a whim
Of Her eccentric Family –
Is She so much to blame?

MANUSCRIPT: About 1866, in packet 35 (H 191c).
PUBLICATION: *FP* (1929), 63.

1086

What Twigs We held by –
Oh the View
When Life's swift River striven through
We pause before a further plunge
To take Momentum –
As the Fringe

Upon a former Garment shows
The Garment cast,
Our Props disclose
So scant, so eminently small
Of Might to help, so pitiful
To sink, if We had labored, fond
The diligence were not more blind

How scant, by everlasting Light
The Discs that satisfied Our Sight –
How dimmer than a Saturn's Bar
The Things esteemed, for Things that are!

[767]

MANUSCRIPT: About 1866, in packet 35 (H 192a).

PUBLICATION: *UP* (1935), 24. The text is arranged in fourteen lines with stanza division for the last four lines only. The misreading "another" for "a further" (line 4) is corrected in *Poems* (current).

1087

We miss a Kinsman more
When warranted to see
Than when with[h]eld of Oceans
From possibility

A Furlong than a League
Inflicts a pricklier pain,
Till We, who smiled at Pyrrhenees –
Of Parishes, complain.

MANUSCRIPT: About 1866, in packet 35 (H 192b).

PUBLICATION: *FP* (1929), 14. One word is altered:

3. of] by

1088

Ended, ere it begun –
The Title was scarcely told
When the Preface perished from Consciousness
The Story, unrevealed –

Had it been mine, to print!
Had it been your's, to read!
That it was not Our privilege
The interdict of God –

MANUSCRIPT: About 1866, in packet 35 (H 192c).

PUBLICATION: *FF* (1932), 224.

1089

Myself can read the Telegrams
A Letter chief to me
The Stock's advance and Retrograde
And what the Markets say

The Weather – how the Rains
In Counties have begun.
'Tis News as null as nothing,
But sweeter so – than none.

MANUSCRIPT: About 1866, in packet 35 (H 192d).
PUBLICATION: *BM* (1945), 104. The text derives from a transcript
of the packet copy made by Mrs. Todd.

1090

I am afraid to own a Body –
I am afraid to own a Soul –
Profound – precarious Property –
Possession, not optional –

Double Estate – entailed at pleasure
Upon an unsuspecting Heir –
Duke in a moment of Deathlessness
And God, for a Frontier.

MANUSCRIPT: About 1866, in packet 35 (H 193a).
PUBLICATION: *UP* (1935), 19.

1091

The Well upon the Brook
Were foolish to depend –
Let Brooks – renew of Brooks –
But Wells – of failless Ground!

MANUSCRIPT: About 1866, in packet 35 (H 193b).

PUBLICATION: *BM* (1945), 232. The text derives from a transcript made by Mrs. Todd.

1092

It was not Saint – it was too large –
Nor Snow – it was too small –
It only held itself aloof
Like something spiritual –

MANUSCRIPT: About 1866, in packet 35 (H 193c).
PUBLICATION: *London Mercury*, XIX (February 1929), 352; *FP* (1929), 121. The text is arranged as a seven-line stanza.

1093

Because 'twas Riches I could own,
Myself had earned it – Me,
I knew the Dollars by their names –
It feels like Poverty

An Earldom out of sight to hold,
An Income in the Air,
Possession – has a sweeter chink
Unto a Miser's Ear –

MANUSCRIPT: About 1866, in packet 35 (H 193d).
PUBLICATION: *UP* (1935), 120.

1094

Themself are all I have –
Myself a freckled – be –
I thought you'd choose a Velvet Cheek
Or one of Ivory –
Would you – instead of Me?

MANUSCRIPT: About 1866, in packet 35 (H 193e). It was written to accompany a flower.

PUBLICATION: *UP* (1935), 60. One word is altered:

1. Themself] Themselves

1095

To Whom the Mornings stand for Nights,
What must the Midnights – be!

MANUSCRIPT: About 1866, in packet 35 (H 193f).
PUBLICATION: *UP* (1935), 15.

1096

These Strangers, in a foreign World,
Protection asked of me –
Befriend them, lest Yourself in Heaven
Be found a Refugee –

MANUSCRIPT: About 1866 (Bingham 102–64). It is a penciled message,
signed "Emily – ."
PUBLICATION: *BM* (1945), 60.

1097

Dew – is the Freshet in the Grass –
'Tis many a tiny Mill
Turns unperceived beneath our feet
And Artisan lies still –

We spy the Forests and the Hills
The Tents to Nature's Show
Mistake the Outside for the in
And mention what we saw.

Could Commentators on the Sign
Of Nature's Caravan
Obtain "Admission" as a Child
Some Wednesday Afternoon.

4. Artisan lies] Small Estate stands –

MANUSCRIPTS: There are two, both written about 1866. The copy reproduced above is in packet 35 (H 188a). The other copy (H 373) is in pencil, addressed "Sue –" and signed "Emily –." There may have been a first page, now missing:

We spy the Forests, and the Hills,
The Tents to Nature's Show,
Mistake the Outside for the in –
And mention what We saw –

Could Commentators on the Sign
Of Nature's Caravan
Obtain "Admission" as a Child
Some Wednesday – Afternoon –

PUBLICATION: SH (1914), 47. The text derives from the copy to Sue, and the first stanza is wanting. Stanza 1 is reproduced in AB (1945), 379. All three stanzas are in New England Quarterly, XX (1947), 30, printed from a transcript made by Mrs. Todd of the packet copy.

1098

Of the Heart that goes in, and closes the Door
Shall the Playfellow Heart complain
Though the Ring is unwhole, and the Company broke
Can never be fitted again?

4. fitted] matched

MANUSCRIPT: About 1866, in packet 35 (H 188d).
PUBLICATION: BM (1945), 247. The text derives from a transcript made by Mrs. Todd. It is arranged as a six-line stanza. The suggested change is rejected.

1099

My Cocoon tightens – Colors teaze –
I'm feeling for the Air –
A dim capacity for Wings
Demeans the Dress I wear –

[772]

A power of Butterfly must be –
The Aptitude to fly
Meadows of Majesty concedes
And easy Sweeps of Sky –

So I must baffle at the Hint
And cipher at the Sign
And make much blunder, if at last
I take the clue divine –

4. Demeans] Degrades   7. concedes] implies –

MANUSCRIPT: About 1866, in packet 35 (H 189b).
PUBLICATION: *Poems* (1890), 115, titled "From the Chrysalis." The
first suggested change is adopted.

1100

The last Night that She lived
It was a Common Night
Except the Dying – this to Us
Made Nature different

We noticed smallest things –
Things overlooked before
By this great light upon our Minds
Italicized – as 'twere.

As We went out and in
Between Her final Room
And Rooms where Those to be alive
Tomorrow were, a Blame

That Others could exist
While She must finish quite
A Jealousy for Her arose
So nearly infinite –

We waited while She passed –
It was a narrow time –   [*no stanza break*]

[773]

Too jostled were Our Souls to speak
At length the notice came.

She mentioned, and forgot –
Then lightly as a Reed
Bent to the Water, struggled scarce –
Consented, and was dead –

And We – We placed the Hair –
And drew the Head erect –
And then an awful leisure was
Belief to regulate –

22. lightly] softly   28. Belief to] With nought to – / Our
23. struggled] shivered –   faith to –

MANUSCRIPT: About 1866, in packet 35 (H 191b). On Thursday,
3 May 1866, Laura Dickey (Mrs. Frank W.) of Michigan, youngest
daughter of Mr. and Mrs. L. M. Hills, died at her parents' home in
Amherst. The Hills land lay next to the Dickinsons on the east.
    PUBLICATION: *Poems* (1890), 130–131. The third stanza is omitted.
Two suggested changes are adopted:

23. shivered   28. Our faith to

1101

Between the form of Life and Life
The difference is as big
As Liquor at the Lip between
And Liquor in the Jug
The latter – excellent to keep –
But for extatic need
The corkless is superior –
I know for I have tried

5. keep] have

MANUSCRIPT: About 1866, in pencil (Bingham 102–13). It is a rough draft. After line 6, ED wrote "Give me the corkless" and crossed it out, continuing with the two final lines as above.

PUBLICATION: *BM* (1945), 269. The text is arranged as two quatrains. The suggested change is adopted.

1102

His Bill is clasped—his Eye forsook—
His Feathers wilted low—
The Claws that clung, like lifeless Gloves
Indifferent hanging now—
The Joy that in his happy Throat
Was waiting to be poured
Gored through and through with Death, to be
Assassin of a Bird
Resembles to my outraged mind
The firing in Heaven,
On Angels—squandering for you
Their Miracles of Tune—

1. clasped] locked   6. Was waiting] Assembled
1. forsook] estranged   12. Miracles of] unsuspecting / [unsus-]
4. hanging] gathered   picious

MANUSCRIPT: About 1866 (Bingham 98–1–3). This penciled work-sheet draft is written on part of a tradesman's bill.

PUBLICATION: *BM* (1945), 66. The text is arranged as three quatrains; the suggested changes for line 1 are adopted.

1103

The spry Arms of the Wind
If I could crawl between
I have an errand imminent
To an adjoining Zone—

I should not care to stop
My Process is not long
The Wind could wait without the Gate
Or stroll the Town among.

To ascertain the House
And is the soul at Home
And hold the Wick of mine to it
To light, and then return –

10] And if the soul's within

MANUSCRIPT: About 1866 (Bingham 98–1–10). It is a penciled work-
sheet draft jotted down on the inside of a slit-open envelope which on
the face has been addressed in her father's hand "Miss Emily Dickinson."
ED began by writing "The long Arms," then crossed the words out, turned
the sheet bottom side up, and began again.
PUBLICATION: *BM* (1945), 230. The suggested change is adopted.

1104

The Crickets sang
And set the Sun
And Workmen finished one by one
Their Seam the Day upon.

The low Grass loaded with the Dew
The Twilight stood, as Strangers do
With Hat in Hand, polite and new
To stay as if, or go.

A Vastness, as a Neighbor, came,
A Wisdom, without Face, or Name,
A Peace, as Hemispheres at Home
And so the Night became.

MANUSCRIPTS: There are three: two fair copies and a semifinal packet
copy. That reproduced above (H 325) is signed "Emily–" and was prob-
ably sent to Sue; it is the latest of the three, written about 1867. Both
fair copies, identical in text, are redactions of the copy in packet 35 (H
188c), written about 1866:

> The Crickets sang
> And set the Sun
> And Workmen finished one by one
> Their Seams the Day upon –

The Bee had perished from the Scene
And distant as an Order done
And doubtful as Report upon
The Multitudes of Noon –

The low Grass loaded with the Dew
The Twilight leaned as Strangers do
With Hat in Hand, polite and new
To stay as if, or go –

A Vastness, as a Neighbor, came –
A Wisdom without Face or Name –
A Peace, as Hemispheres at Home
And so, the Night became.

10. leaned] stood

The fair copies are not variants. ED has deleted from them the second stanza of the packet copy, perhaps conscious of its vagueness, and has adopted the suggested change. The other fair copy (Bingham 98–4B–15), written about the same time as the packet copy in 1866, is also signed "Emily." Like the copy to Sue, it has been folded as if enclosed in an envelope. There are several punctuation changes:

The Crickets sang
And set the Sun
And Workmen finished, one by one
Their Seam the Day upon.

The low Grass loaded with the Dew,
The Twilight stood as Strangers do –
With Hat in Hand, polite and new
To stay as if, or go.

A Vastness, as a Neighbor, came –
A Wisdom without Face or Name –
A Peace, as Hemispheres at Home –
And so, the Night became.

PUBLICATION: *Poems* (1896), 130, titled "Evening." It follows the text of the fair copies and probably derives from the earlier of the two. One word is altered:

1. Crickets] cricket

The second stanza of the longer version is unpublished.

1105

Like Men and Women Shadows walk
Upon the Hills Today –
With here and there a mighty Bow
Or trailing Courtesy
To Neighbors doubtless of their own
Not quickened to perceive
Minuter landscape as Ourselves
And Boroughs where we live –

MANUSCRIPTS: There are two. The copy reproduced above (H 285),
written about 1867 in pencil, is addressed "Sue –" and signed "Emily."
It is a redaction of the semifinal draft in packet 86 (Bingham 38c), written
about 1864:

> Like Men and Women Shadows walk,
> Upon the Hills Today –
> With here and there a mighty Bow
> Or trailing Courtesy
>
> To Neighbors doubtless of their own
> Not quickened to perceive
> Minuter Landscape as Ourselves
> And Boroughs where We live

4. trailing] sweeping   8. Boroughs] limits

The text of the fair copy is identical with that of the packet copy; the
suggested changes are rejected.
PUBLICATION: SH (1914), 44. The text derives from the copy to Sue.

1106

We do not know the time we lose –
The awful moment is
And takes it's fundamental place
Among the certainties –

A firm appearance still inflates
The card – the chance – the friend –

[778]   [*no stanza break*]

The spectre of solidities
Whose substances are sand –

MANUSCRIPT: About 1867 (H B 159). It is a penciled draft presumably sent to Sue.
PUBLICATION: *FF* (1932), 264. One word is altered:

6. card] word

1107

The Bird did prance – the Bee did play –
The Sun ran miles away
So blind with joy he could not choose
Between his Holiday

The morn was up – the meadows out
The Fences all but ran,
Republic of Delight, I thought
Where each is Citizen –

From Heavy laden Lands to thee
Were seas to cross to come
A Caspian were crowded –
Too near thou art for Fame –

4. his] the   12. near] close
9. Lands] Climes

MANUSCRIPTS: The copy reproduced above (Bingham 102–50) is a semifinal redaction of the worksheet draft below (Bingham 102–51). ED wrote "blind with" (line 3) after crossing out "full of." She first wrote "between" at the end of the line, crossed it out, and began line 4. The worksheet draft proving unsatisfactory, ED turned over the half-sheet of stationery and began again. Both are in pencil, written about 1867.

The Bird did prance – the ~~Bird~~ Bee did play –
The Sun ran miles away
So blind with joy he could not choose
Between the Holiday –
The morn was up – the meadow /s out   [*no stanza break*]

The Fences all but ran
~~What hindered me~~
Republic of Delight, I thought
Where each is Citizen
From Heavy laden Lands to thee
~~As Emigrants we come~~
~~Or Pass~~
~~Too uncertain Passengers~~

PUBLICATION: *BM* (1945), 14. It follows the semifinal draft; the suggested changes are rejected.

1108

A Diamond on the Hand
To Custom Common grown
Subsides from it's significance
The Gem were best unknown –
Within a Seller's Shrine
How many sight and sigh
And cannot, but are mad with fear
That any other buy.

7. with] for   8] lest some one else should [buy]/
                              Lest Richer people buy –

MANUSCRIPT: About 1867, in pencil (H 223). Apparently it is a work-sheet. The first word was crossed out, "The" substituted and crossed out, and "A" restored.
PUBLICATION: *FF* (1932), 244, arranged as two quatrains. The final lines read:

And cannot, but are mad for fear
Lest richer people buy.

1109

I fit for them –
I seek the Dark
Till I am thorough fit.
The labor is a sober one
With the austerer sweet – an – this –
With this sufficient sweet

That abstinence of mine produce
A purer food for them, if I succeed,
If not I had
The transport of the Aim —

7. mine] me

MANUSCRIPT: About 1867, in pencil (H 271). This worksheet is quite
unfinished. Line 1 may be intended as a partial substitute for line 3; evi-
dently the "an – this –" of line 5 are alternates for "the" of the same line;
and line 6 is certainly a suggested change for the entire line 5.

PUBLICATION: *SH* (1914), 88. It is reconstructed thus:

I fit for them,
I seek the dark till I am thorough fit.
The labor is a solemn one,
With this sufficient sweet —
That abstinence as mine produce
A purer good for them,
If I succeed, —
If not, I had
The transport of the Aim.

1110

None who saw it ever told it
'Tis as hid as Death
Had for that specific treasure
A departing breath —
Surfaces may be invested
Did the Diamond grow
General as the Dandelion
Would you serve it so?

1. None] They	5. invested] related
5. may] can	8. serve] seek

MANUSCRIPT: About 1867 (Bingham 102–37). It is a penciled work-
sheet draft written on the back of part of a discarded handbill. On the
same sheet is the poem beginning "The Merchant of the Picturesque."

PUBLICATION: *BM* (1945), 247. The suggested change for line 8 is
adopted. The text is arranged as two quatrains.

1111

Some Wretched creature, savior take
Who would exult to die
And leave for thy sweet mercy's sake
Another Hour to me

3. mercy's] patience'   4] My earthly Hour to me/ [My] human Life [to me]

MANUSCRIPT: About 1867 (Bingham 104–38). It is a penciled work-sheet draft jotted down on a scrap of envelope.
PUBLICATION: *BM* (1945), 125. The suggested changes are rejected.

1112

That this should feel the need of Death
The same as those that lived
Is such a ~~stroke~~
     ~~Hight~~ – *Feat* – ~~pass~~ –
Of Irony
As never was ~~beheld~~ – achieved –
~~As makes one hide it's head –~~
      ~~hang~~

Not satisfied to ape the Great in his simplicity
The small must die, the same as he – as well as He –
    ~~do~~
~~What a Pomposity –~~
    ~~an absurdity –~~
     ~~Perversity –~~
~~Oh the pomposity~~
Oh the Audacity –

MANUSCRIPT: About 1867 (Bingham 104–43). It is a penciled work-sheet draft.
PUBLICATION: *BM* (1945), 213. The text is arranged as two quatrains. The final four words in the second line of stanza 2 are rejected.

There is a strength in proving that it can be bourne
Although it tear –
What are the sinews of such cordage for
Except to bear
The ship might be of satin had it not to fight –
To walk on seas requires cedar Feet

1. a] good   6. seas] tides
1. proving] knowing

MANUSCRIPT: About 1867, in pencil (Bingham 104–49). It is a rough draft.

PUBLICATION: BM (1945), 242. The second and third suggested changes are adopted.

1114

The largest Fire ever known
Occurs each Afternoon –
Discovered is without surprise
Proceeds without concern –
Consumes and no report to men
An Occidental Town,
Rebuilt another morning
To be burned down again

MANUSCRIPTS: The fair copy reproduced above (H 339) was written in pencil about 1868; it is signed "Emily –" and was probably sent to Sue. It is a redaction of a semifinal draft in packet 33 (H 176f), written about 1864:

> The largest Fire ever known
> Occurs each Afternoon –
> Discovered is without Surprise
> Proceeds, without concern –
>
> Consumes without Report to Men
> An Occidental Town –
> Rebuilt in time next Morning
> To be burned down again.

7. in time next Morning] Another Morning / Without insurance – / to the Horizon –

A change is introduced into line 5 of the fair copy, and the first of the suggested changes for line 7 is adopted.

PUBLICATION: *SH* (1914), 50. It follows the text of the fair copy. Line 8 is altered to read:

> To be again burned down.

1115

The murmuring of Bees, has ceased
But murmuring of some
Posterior, prophetic,
Has simultaneous come.
The lower metres of the Year
When Nature's laugh is done
The Revelations of the Book
Whose Genesis was June.
Appropriate Creatures to her change
The Typic Mother sends
As Accent fades to interval
With separating Friends
Till what we speculate, has been
And thoughts we will not show
More intimate with us become
Than Persons, that we know.

MANUSCRIPTS: The fair copy reproduced above (H 345) is in pencil, signed "Emily." It was written about 1868 and probably sent to Sue. The worksheet draft (Bingham 98–1–7), also in pencil and written at the same time, is identical in its final text:

> The murmuring of Bees has ceased
> But murmuring of some
> Posterior, prophetic
> Has simultaneous come –
>
> The lower metres of the Year
> When Nature's Laugh is done –
> The Revelations of the Book
> Whose Genesis was June

Appropriate Creatures to her change
The Typic Mother sends –
As Accent ~~wanes~~ fades to interval
With separating Friends

Till what we ~~could not see has come~~ speculate has been

~~face~~

~~name~~   ~~been~~

~~choose~~

~~prove~~

And thoughts we will not show
More intimate with us become
Than Persons that we know.

PUBLICATION: The first stanza only was published in Frederick H. Hitchcock, ed., *The Handbook of Amherst, Massachusetts* (Amherst, 1891), page 21. The first two quatrains are in *Poems* (1896), 136, titled "Aftermath." In the Centenary edition (1930) and later collections the lines are without stanza division. Mrs. Todd made a transcript of the poem in the late 1880's, presumably of the worksheet draft in her possession, and the eight lines printed in *Poems* derive presumably from that transcript. In both manuscripts and in Mrs. Todd's transcript line 8 reads:

Whose Genesis was June

In *Poems* one word is altered:

was] is

All four stanzas are published in *New England Quarterly*, XX (1947), 26, from the worksheet draft. In line 8 "was" is restored.

1116

There is another Loneliness
That many die without –
Not want of friend occasions it
Or circumstance of Lot

But nature, sometimes, sometimes thought
And whoso it befall
Is richer than could be revealed
By mortal numeral –

MANUSCRIPT: About 1868 (Bingham 97–14). It is a rough penciled draft, although a finished copy. A variant fair còpy sent to Sue, now lost, is discussed below.

PUBLICATION: *SH* (1914), 20; *LL* (1924), 195. It reproduces the text of the copy to Sue in which three words apparently are variant:

3. of] or   7. revealed] divulged
4. of] or

The rough draft, then in the possession of Mrs. Todd, was not the source of the text. The variant in line 7 of the published text is clearly a different word. One suspects that those words which appear to be variants in lines 3 and 4 are in fact misreadings. The sense of the lines calls for "of," not "or." In ED's handwriting the words can be easily confused.

1117

A Mine there is no Man would own
But must it be conferred,
Demeaning by exclusive wealth
A Universe beside –

Potosi never to be spent
But hoarded in the mind
What Misers wring their hands tonight
For Indies in the Ground!

MANUSCRIPT: About 1868, in pencil (H 234). Signed "Emily – ."
PUBLICATION: *FF* (1932), 240.

1118

Exhiliration is the Breeze
That lifts us from the Ground
And leaves us in another place
Whose statement is not found –

Returns us not, but after time
We soberly descend   *[no stanza break]*

A little newer for the term
Upon Enchanted Ground –

MANUSCRIPT: About 1868, in pencil (H 252a).
PUBLICATION: *SH* (1914), 13. The text is arranged as a single eight-line stanza.

1119

Paradise is that old mansion
Many owned before –
Occupied by each an instant
Then reversed the Door –
Bliss is frugal of her Leases
Adam taught her Thrift
Bankrupt once through his excesses –

MANUSCRIPT: About 1868, in pencil (Bingham 102–41). This unfinished poem is written on a half-sheet of embossed stationery.
PUBLICATION: *BM* (1945), 307. It is placed among the unfinished poems.

1120

This slow Day moved along –
I heard it's axles go
As if they could not hoist themselves
They hated motion so –

I told my soul to come –
It was no use to wait –
We went and played and came again
And it was out of sight

MANUSCRIPT: About 1868 (Bingham 107–78). It is a penciled draft.
PUBLICATION: *BM* (1945), 26.

1121

Time does go on –
I tell it gay to those who suffer now –
They shall survive –
There is a sun –
They dont believe it now –

MANUSCRIPT: About 1868 (Bingham 102–66). It is a penciled draft
jotted down on a scrap of paper.
PUBLICATION: *BM* (1945), 261. The last five words of line 2 are
arranged as a separate line.

1122

'Tis my first night beneath the Sun
If I should spend it here –
Above him is too low a hight
For his Barometer
Who Airs of expectation breathes
And takes the Wind at prime –
But Distance his Delights confides
To those who visit him

MANUSCRIPT: About 1868 (Bingham 102–67). It is a penciled draft
jotted down on the back of part of a handbill. In line 2 "shall" has been
crossed out and "should" substituted.
PUBLICATION: *BM* (1945), 29. The text is arranged as two quatrains.

1123

A great Hope fell
You heard no noise
The Ruin was within
Oh cunning wreck that told no tale
And let no Witness in

The mind was built for mighty Freight
For dread occasion planned   [*no stanza break*]

How often foundering at Sea
Ostensibly, on Land

A not admitting of the wound
Until it grew so wide
That all my Life had entered it
And there were troughs beside

————

A closing of the simple lid
That opened to the sun
Until the tender Carpenter
Perpetual nail it down –

2. noise] crash   14. lid] Gate
3. Ruin] havoc / damage   16. tender Carpenter] sovreign / un-
13. were] was   suspecting Carpenters
13. troughs] space / room

MANUSCRIPT: The only manuscript is a rough draft (Bingham 107–5)
in pencil, written about 1868 on two sides of a slit-open envelope.
PUBLICATION: *BM* (1945), 115. The first stanza is regularized as a
quatrain. Three suggested changes are adopted:

13. was   16. sovreign [sovereign]
13. room

The line drawn between stanzas 3 and 4 is omitted.

1124

Had we known the Ton she bore
We had helped the terror
But she straighter walked for Freight
So be her's the error –

3] Smiled too brave for the detecting /   4] Till arrested here / [Till] Discov-
   [Smiled too brave for] our detec-   ered here.
   tion

MANUSCRIPT: This unfinished worksheet draft, written in pencil
about 1868, is jotted on the inside of a slit-open envelope (Bingham

107–26). Two words were first suggested as alternatives for "Ton" and then crossed out: "weight" and "Load."

PUBLICATION: *BM* (1945), 135. The suggested changes are rejected.

1125

Oh Sumptuous moment
Slower go
That I may gloat on thee –
'Twill never be the same to starve
Now I abundance see –

Which was to famish, then or now –
The difference of Day
Ask him unto the Gallows led –
With morning in the sky

3. That] Till		8. Ask] to	
3. may] can		8. led] called	
5. Now] Since		9. With] By	
5. I] that			

MANUSCRIPT: About 1868 (Bingham 102–39). It is a penciled worksheet draft jotted down on the inside of a slit-open envelope which ED had addressed in ink: "Mrs Helen Hunt." T. W. Higginson had first met "H. H." at Newport, Rhode Island, in 1866. She visited in Northampton, Massachusetts, and elsewhere in the Connecticut Valley in August 1868. It is quite possible that she met ED at this time. The poem itself, which has no association with Helen Hunt, expresses a mood of jubilation. One may note that late in 1868 news appeared of Charles Wadsworth's impending return to Philadelphia from San Francisco.

PUBLICATION: *BM* (1945), 144. The suggested changes for lines 5 ("Since") and 8 ("called") are adopted. The text is arranged as two quatrains.

1126

Shall I take thee, the Poet said
To the propounded word?
Be stationed with the Candidates
Till I have finer tried –

The Poet searched Philology
And was about to ring
for the suspended Candidate
There came unsummoned in –

That portion of the Vision
The Word applied to fill
Not unto nomination
The Cherubim reveal –

4. finer] vainer / further   6. was] just / when
5. searched] probed   8. There came] Advanced

MANUSCRIPT: About 1868 (Bingham 107–57). It is a penciled work-sheet draft. The first word of line 7 is not capitalized.

PUBLICATION: *BM* (1945), 228. The following suggested changes are adopted:

4. further   6. when
5. probed

1127

Soft as the massacre of Suns
By Evening's Sabres slain

1. massacre] [massacre]s   2. Sabres] Sabre

MANUSCRIPT: About 1868 (Bingham 107–6). This is a worksheet fragment jotted down on a small scrap of paper.

PUBLICATION: *BM* (1945), 317, among the fragments. The suggested changes are rejected.

1128

These are the Nights that Beetles love –
From Eminence remote
Drives ponderous perpendicular
His figure intimate
The terror of the Children   [*no stanza break*]

The merriment of men
Depositing his Thunder
He hoists abroad again –
A Bomb upon the Ceiling
Is an improving thing –
It keeps the nerves ~~in progress~~
Conjecture flourishing –
Too dear the Summer evening
Without discreet alarm –
Supplied by Entomology
With it's remaining charm

4. His] This   11. ~~in progress~~] progressive
5. terror] transport   16. it's] a
6. merriment] jeopardy

MANUSCRIPT: About 1868 (Bingham 107–76). It is a penciled work-sheet draft jotted down on an ink-stained piece of paper. ED began line 13: "Too dear were," then crossed out "were."

PUBLICATION: *BM* (1945), 71. The change made in line 11 is followed, and the suggested change for line 6 is adopted. The text is arranged as four quatrains.

(1129)

Tell all the Truth but tell it slant –
Success in Circuit lies
Too bright for our infirm Delight
The Truth's superb surprise
As Lightning to the Children eased
With explanation kind
The Truth must dazzle gradually
Or every man be blind –

3. bright] bold   7. gradually] moderately

MANUSCRIPT: About 1868 (Bingham 103–10). It is a penciled work-sheet draft written on a scrap of stationery.

PUBLICATION: *BM* (1945), 233. Both suggested changes are rejected. The text is arranged as two quatrains.

1130

That odd old man is dead a year –
We miss his stated Hat.
'Twas such an evening bright and stiff
His faded lamp went out.

Who miss his antiquated Wick –
Are any hoar for him?
Waits any indurated mate
His wrinkled coming Home?

Oh Life, begun in fluent Blood
And consummated dull!
Achievement contemplating thee –
Feels transitive and cool.

5. Wick] Light –   11. thee] this – / here
6. hoar] bleak

MANUSCRIPT: About 1868 (Bingham 97–18). It is a penciled draft.
PUBLICATION: *BM* (1945), 213. The suggested change "this" (line 11)
is adopted.

1131

The Merchant of the Picturesque
A Counter has and sales
But is within or negative
Precisely as the calls –
To Children he is small in price
And large in courtesy –
It suits him better than a check
Their artless currency –
Of Counterfeits he is so shy
Do one advance so near
As to behold his ample flight –

5. small] least   10. advance] obtain
6. large] most   11. ample] gentle –

[793]

MANUSCRIPT: About 1868 (Bingham 102–57). It is a penciled work-sheet fragment jotted down on the back of part of a discarded handbill. On the same sheet is the poem beginning "None who saw it ever told it."

PUBLICATION: *BM* (1945), 302. It is placed among the fragments and arranged as three quatrains with a missing last line. All suggested changes are rejected.

1132

The smouldering embers blush –
Oh Cheek within the Coal
Hast thou survived so many nights?
The smouldering embers smile –
Soft stirs the news of Light
The stolid Rafters glow
One requisite has Fire that lasts
Prometheus never knew –

2. Cheek] *Heart*
3. nights] *years*
5. stirs the news] stir the Flakes
6. Rafters] centres / Hours / instants / *seconds*

7. Fire that lasts] earthly [Fire] / mortal [Fire]
8. never knew] did not know
7–8] This requisite has Fire that lasts It must at first be true –

MANUSCRIPT: About 1868 (Bingham 102–59). It is a penciled work-sheet draft left in a very unfinished state. Line 3 is written:

So many nights hast thou survived

with a "2" placed above "So" and a "1" place above "hast." It is possible that ED wrote the poem upon learning that Charles Wadsworth was leaving his San Francisco pastorate and returning to the East.

PUBLICATION: *BM* (1945), 174. The text is arranged as two stanzas. Three suggested changes are adopted:

2. Heart   6. seconds
3. years

The Snow that never drifts –
The transient, frag[r]ant snow
That comes a single time a Year
Is softly driving now –

So thorough in the Tree
At night beneath the star
That it was Febuary's Foot
Experience would swear –

Like Winter as a Face
We stern and former knew
Repaired of all but Loneliness
By Nature's Alibi –

Were every storm so spice
The Value could not be –
We buy with contrast – Pang is good
As near as memory –

6. beneath] below		13. storm] Gale / snow	
7. Foot] Face / self		13. spice] fair / sweet	
8. world] ~~could~~			

MANUSCRIPT: About 1868 (Bingham 107–70). It is a penciled work-sheet draft.

PUBLICATION: *BM* (1945), 33. All suggested changes except "self" are rejected.

The Wind took up the Northern Things
And piled them in the south –
Then gave the East unto the West
And opening his mouth

The four Divisions of the Earth
Did make as to devour   [*no stanza break*]

While everything to corners slunk
Behind the awful power –

The Wind – unto his Chambers went
And nature ventured out –
Her subjects scattered into place
Her systems ranged about

Again the smoke from Dwellings rose
The Day abroad was heard –
How intimate, a Tempest past
The Transport of the Bird –

2. piled them in] showed them to
3. gave] bent – / bowed
4. his] it's
6. Did make as] Presumed as to
8] Like Worms beneath [the power] – /
   [Like Worms] before [the power –]
9. his] it's

12. ranged] stole
13. rose] curled
14. abroad was heard] resumed abroad
15. intimate a] orderly the
16. Transport] Rapture – / Triumph
16. [The] Riot of the Bird –

MANUSCRIPT: About 1868 (Bingham 102–62). It is a penciled work-sheet draft jotted down in an especially unfinished state on a long strip of paper. On one side (in handwriting other than ED's) is written "Mary H. Warner" and on the other:

"Specimen of Penmanship"
"We six"
four

PUBLICATION: *BM* (1945), 19. One suggested change is adopted:

3. bent

1135

Too cold is this
To warm with Sun –
Too stiff to bended be,
To joint this Agate were a work –
Outstaring Masonry –

How went the Agile Kernel out
Contusion of the Husk
Nor Rip, nor wrinkle indicate
But just an Asterisk.

4. work] feat   5] Beyond machinery –
5. Outstaring] Defying – /
     Appalling – / Abashing

MANUSCRIPT: About 1868 (H 366). It is a penciled worksheet draft.
PUBLICATION: SH (1914), 82. The text is arranged as a nine-line
stanza. The suggested change for line 4 is adopted.

1136

The Frost of Death was on the Pane –
"Secure your Flower" said he.
Like Sailors fighting with a Leak
We fought Mortality.

Our passive Flower we held to Sea –
To Mountain – To the Sun –
Yet even on his Scarlet shelf
To crawl the Frost begun –

We pried him back
Ourselves we wedged
Himself and her between,
Yet easy as the narrow Snake
He forked his way along

Till all her helpless beauty bent
And then our wrath begun –
We hunted him to his Ravine
We chased him to his Den –

We hated Death and hated Life
And nowhere was to go –
Than Sea and continent there is
A larger – it is Woe

[797]

MANUSCRIPT: About 1869 (H 335). It is written in pencil on four sheets and signed "Emily –", and is folded as if enclosed in an envelope. There exists also a transcript made by Sue (H ST 15a) of a variant copy sent to her which is now missing. Six words differ:

2. Secure] Protect	12. Yet] But
7. Yet] But	12. the] a
8. begun] began	15. begun] began

Line 18 reads:

We hated Life & hated Death

It is possible that the transcript variants in lines 8 and 15 are misreadings.

PUBLICATION: *BM* (1945), 54. The text is arranged as five quatrains. It derives from the following transcript made by Mrs. Todd:

The frost of death was on the pane.
"Protect your flower," said he.
Like sailors fighting with a leak
We fought mortality.
Our passive flower we held to sea,
To mountain – to the sun –
Yet even on his scarlet shelf
To crawl, the frost begun.
We pried him back –
Ourselves we wedged
Himself and her between –
But easy as a narrow snake
He forked his way along,
Till all her helpless beauty bent –
And then our wrath begun.
We hunted him to his ravine,
We chased him to his den,
We hated death, and hated life,
And nowhere was to go.
The sea and continent there is
A larger – it is woe!

This transcript presupposes a third autograph copy, now lost. It follows the manuscript copy above in lines 8, 15, 18, and the transcript made by Sue in lines 2, 7, 12. In line 19 the first word "The" is certainly a misreading of "Than". One word is altered:

5. Our] One

The duties of the Wind are few,
To cast the ships, at Sea,
Establish March, the Floods escort,
And usher Liberty.

The pleasures of the Wind are broad,
To dwell Extent among,
Remain, or wander,
Speculate, or Forests entertain.

The kinsmen of the Wind are Peaks
Azof – the Equinox,
Also with Bird and Asteroid
A bowing intercourse.

The limitations of the Wind
Do he exist, or die,
Too wise he seems for Wakelessness,
However, know not I.

MANUSCRIPTS: There are two. The copy reproduced above is written on three sheets in pencil (Bingham 97–13) and signed "Emily." It has been folded as if enclosed in an envelope. It was written about 1869, as was the copy following, also in pencil:

> The Duties of the Wind are few,
> To cast the ships at Sea,
> Establish March, the Floods escort
> And usher Liberty.

This single stanza, signed "Emily –," was sent to Sue. It has been pasted onto the half-title page of a presentation copy of *The Single Hound*, now privately owned (Scull).

PUBLICATION: The first stanza only is in *SH* (1914), 54, where the text derives from the copy to Sue; it is arranged as a five-line stanza. The four-stanza text is in *AB* (1945), 379. The first word of line 8 is arranged as the last of line 7.

A Spider sewed at Night
Without a Light
Upon an Arc of White.

If Ruff it was of Dame
Or Shroud of Gnome
Himself himself inform.

Of Immortality
His Strategy
Was Physiognomy.

MANUSCRIPT: About 1869 (H 238), in pencil. It is addressed "Sue –"
and signed "Emily." A transcript made by ED's cousin, Frances Norcross,
was sent to T. W. Higginson, together with a copy of "The Mushroom,"
and is in BPL (Higg 135a). It is identical in text with the copy to Sue, but
without stanza division.
PUBLICATION: *Poems* (1891), 147, titled "The Spider." The text fol-
lows the Norcross transcript.

1139

Her sovreign People
Nature knows as well
And is as fond of signifying
As if fallible –

MANUSCRIPT: About 1869 (Smith College). This letter-poem, signed
"Emily –", was sent to Sue, probably with a flower. It is introduced with
the phrase: "Rare to the Rare –".
PUBLICATION: Northampton (Mass.) *Daily Hampshire Gazette*, 18
December 1952.

1140

The Day grew small, surrounded tight
By early, stooping Night –
The Afternoon in Evening deep
It's Yellow shortness dropt –   [*no stanza break*]

[800]

The Winds went out their martial ways
The Leaves obtained excuse –
November hung his Granite Hat
Upon a nail of Plush –

MANUSCRIPT: About 1869, in pencil (H 327). It was evidently sent
to Sue and is signed "Emily."
PUBLICATION: *BM* (1945), 40. The text, arranged as two quatrains,
derives from a transcript made by Mrs. Todd.

1141

The Face we choose to miss –
Be it but for a Day
As absent as a Hundred Years,
When it has rode away.

MANUSCRIPT: About 1869, in pencil (H 333). It was evidently sent
to Sue; it is mounted on a leaf with Sue's transcript, to which Sue has
added the signature "Emily."
PUBLICATION: *SH* (1914), 144; also *LL* (1924), 197 – headed "Dear
Sue:" and signed "Emily," with an attributed date of 1855.

1142

The Props assist the House
Until the House is built
And then the Props withdraw
And adequate, erect,
The House support itself
And cease to recollect
The Augur and the Carpenter –
Just such a retrospect
Hath the perfected Life –
A past of Plank and Nail
And slowness – then the Scaffolds drop
Affirming it a Soul.

[801]

MANUSCRIPTS: The fair copy reproduced above (H 347), written about 1869, is in pencil, signed "Emily." It was probably sent to Sue. It is a redaction of the copy in packet 22 (H 122a), written early in 1863:

> The Props assist the House –
> Until the House is Built –
> And then the Props withdraw –
> And adequate – Erect –
>
> The House support itself –
> And cease to recollect
> The Scaffold, and the Carpenter –
> Just such a Retrospect
> Hath the Perfected Life –
> A Past of Plank – and Nail –
> And Slowness – then the Stagings drop –
> Affirming it – A Soul –

4. adequate] conscious and
5. support] sustain
7. Scaffold] Augur
10. Past] time – / state

11. Stagings drop] Scaffolds drop – /
    [Scaffolds] cleave
12. Affirming] pronouncing –

ED adopted two of her suggested changes:

7. Augur   11. Scaffolds

PUBLICATION: *SH* (1914), 28. It derives from the copy to Sue. The spelling "Augur" is corrected to "auger." Three words are altered:

5. support] supports   6. And cease] Ceasing

1143

The Work of Her that went,
The Toil of Fellows done –
In Ovens green our Mother bakes,
By Fires of the Sun.

This unpublished poem (H B 147), written about 1869 in pencil, was probably sent to Sue.

Ourselves we do inter with sweet derision.
The channel of the dust who once achieves
Invalidates the balm of that religion
That doubts as fervently as it believes.

No autograph copy of this poem is known.
PUBLICATION: *Letters* (ed. 1894), 220; (ed. 1931), 206–207; also *LL*
(1924), 271: among the letters to Samuel Bowles, where it is printed, prob-
ably it was written, as prose and conjecturally dated 1869. It is arranged
as verse in *New England Quarterly*, XX (1947), 45.

1145

In thy long Paradise of Light
No moment will there be
When I shall long for Earthly Play
And mortal Company –

MANUSCRIPT: About 1869, in pencil (Bingham 102–29). It is written
on a scrap of stationery.
PUBLICATION: *BM* (1945), 123.

1146

When Etna basks and purrs
Naples is more afraid
Than when she shows her Garnet Tooth –
Security is loud –

MANUSCRIPT: About 1869, in pencil (H 374).
PUBLICATION: *SH* (1914), 9.

1147

After a hundred years
Nobody knows the Place
Agony that enacted there
Motionless as Peace

Weeds triumphant ranged
Strangers strolled and spelled
At the lone Orthography
Of the Elder Dead

Winds of Summer Fields
Recollect the way –
Instinct picking up the Key
Dropped by memory –

2. knows] knew

MANUSCRIPT: About 1869 (Bingham 98–3–2). It is a penciled draft
jotted down on the back of a discarded kitchen memorandum.

PUBLICATION: *Poems* (1891), 229, titled "The Forgotten Grave." The
suggested change is rejected.

1148

After the Sun comes out
How it alters the World –
Waggons like messengers hurry about
Yesterday is old –

All men meet as if
Each foreclosed a news –
Fresh as a Cargo from Batize
Nature's qualities –

4] Liverpool is old –   5. meet] pass – / haste
5] Men express as if

MANUSCRIPT: This poem is unpublished. The copy (H 224), written
about 1869, is a penciled worksheet draft jotted down on a sheet of paper
that had been addressed "Mrs Nash –." Emeline (Kellogg) Nash, a friend
since school days, lived in Amherst. There is no reason to believe the poem
and the address have any connection.

I noticed People disappeared
When but a little child –
Supposed they visited remote
Or settled Regions wild –
Now know I –
                    or ~~I know now~~
              They both visited
And settled Regions wild
But ~~vaster—that~~
          ~~vaster~~
              did because they died
A Fact witheld the little child –
    a

MANUSCRIPT: About 1869 (Bingham 98–3–13). It is an unfinished worksheet draft in pencil, written on two scraps pinned together.

PUBLICATION: *Poems* (1891), 201. The text is arranged as two quatrains. The first stanza follows the first four lines of the manuscript. Stanza 2 reads:

> Now know I they both visited
> And settled regions wild,
> But did because they died, — a fact
> Withheld the little child!

How many schemes may die
In one short Afternoon
Entirely unknown
To those they most concern –
The man that was not lost
Because by accident
He varied by a Ribbon's width
From his accustomed route –
The Love that would not try
Because beside the Door   [*no stanza break*]

It must be competitions
Some unsuspecting Horse was tied
Surveying his Despair

5. lost] wrecked / robbed / killed   10. beside] before

MANUSCRIPT: This penciled worksheet draft (Bingham 104–19) was
written about 1869 on a small scrap of paper. It is in a very unfinished
state. Line 11, for instance, seems not to be an alternative reading for
either line 10 or line 12 — or for any other — yet it is meaningless as it
stands. Preceding it, crossed out, is "some." A trial line 6, crossed out,
reads:

Because he was detained

Preceding line 13 is "that," crossed out. In the margin, written some five
years later, is the first line of stanza 4 of the poem beginning "Not with a
Club, the Heart is broken:"

Shame need not crouch

PUBLICATION: BM (1945), 282. The text eliminates line 11. It adopts
the suggested change "robbed" in line 5, and is arranged as three quatrains.

1151

Soul, take thy risk,
With Death to be
Were better than be not
With thee

1. risk] [risk]s / chance

MANUSCRIPT: About 1869, in pencil (Bingham 105–7). These lines
are on a small scrap of paper on the reverse of which is a penciled drawing
of a tombstone half hidden in tall grass.

PUBLICATION: BM (1945), 317. The suggested change "risks" is
adopted. The last two words of line 3 are printed as the first of line 4. It is
placed among the fragments.

Tell as a Marksman – were forgotten
Tell – this Day endures
Ruddy as that coeval Apple
The Tradition bears –

Fresh as Mankind that humble story
Though a statlier Tale
Grown in the Repetition hoary
Scarcely would prevail –

Tell had a son – The ones that knew it
Need not linger here –
Those who did not to Human Nature
Will subscribe a Tear –

Tell would not bare his Head
In Presence
Of the Ducal Hat –
Threatened for that with Death – by Gessler –
Tyranny bethought

Make of his only Boy a Target
That surpasses Death –
Stolid to Love's supreme entreaty
Not forsook of Faith —

Mercy of the Almighty begging –
Tell his Arrow sent –
God it is said replies in Person
When the cry is meant

2. this Day] till now
4. The Tradition] Heroism
5. Fresh] New
6. Though] While
7. in] by
8. would] could
9. knew] heard
10. linger] tarry
11. who did] that do
12. Will] Would
20. supreme] sublime
21. forsook] forgot
22. Mercy] Power
22. begging] asking

MANUSCRIPT: About 1869 (Bingham 104–42). It is a penciled work-sheet draft on two pieces of paper pinned together.

PUBLICATION: *BM* (1945), 129–130. The suggested change for line 8 is adopted and the "do" of line 11. The text is arranged as six quatrains.

1153

Through what transports of Patience
I reached the stolid Bliss
To breathe my Blank without thee
Attest me this and this –
By that bleak exultation
I won as near as this
Thy privilege of dying
Abbreviate me this

4] Remit me this and this

MANUSCRIPT: About 1874 (Bingham 104–71). It is a penciled work-sheet draft jotted down on the inside of a fragment of envelope.

PUBLICATION: *BM* (1945), 174. The text is arranged as two quatrains. The suggested change is rejected.

1154

A full fed Rose on meals of Tint
A Dinner for a Bee
In process of the Noon became –
Each bright Mortality
The Forfeit is of Creature fair
Itself, adored before
Submitting for our unknown sake
To be esteemed no more

MANUSCRIPT: About 1870, in pencil (H 225). The copy is addressed "Sue" and signed "Emily – ."

The poem is published here for the first time.

Distance – is not the Realm of Fox
Nor by Relay of Bird
Abated – Distance is
Until thyself, Beloved.

MANUSCRIPT: About 1870 (Morgan Library), in pencil, signed
"Emily – " It probably was sent to Sue.
PUBLICATION: *SH* (1914), 126. Lines 2–4 are altered to read:

> Nor by relay as Bird;
> Abated, Distance is until
> Thyself, Beloved!

1156

Lest any doubt that we are glad that they were born Today
Whose having lived is held by us in noble Holiday
Without the date, like Consciousness or Immortality –

MANUSCRIPT: It is in the handwriting of late 1870. It is a penciled greet-
ing (H B 33), signed "Emily – ," evidently sent to Sue on her fortieth birth-
day, 19 December 1870. The note in *FF* reads: "To Sue with flowers on
her birthday." For another greeting sent to Sue on her fiftieth birthday, see
"Birthday of but a single pang."
PUBLICATION: *FF* (1932), 225. It is arranged as three three-line stanzas.
One word is altered:

3. or] Of

1157

Some Days retired from the rest
In soft distinction lie
The Day that a Companion came
Or was obliged to die

MANUSCRIPTS: There are two, both in pencil. One may have been sent
to Sue. The one here reproduced (H 317) was written about 1870. The

other (H 318) was written about 1872, and is identical except for a period at the end.

PUBLICATION: *SH* (1914), 43.

1158

Best Witchcraft is Geometry
To the magician's mind –
His ordinary acts are feats
To thinking of mankind.

MANUSCRIPTS: The lines above were written about 1870, in pencil (H 252b). Another version of the first two lines only, also in pencil (H B 23), was sent about the same time to Sue and is signed "Emily –":

Best Witchcraft is Geometry
To a Magician's eye –

PUBLICATION: Only the two lines sent to Sue have been published, *FF* (1932), 145 and 242.

1159

Great Streets of silence led away
To Neighborhoods of Pause –
Here was no Notice – no Dissent
No Universe – no Laws –

By Clocks, 'twas Morning, and for Night
The Bells at Distance called –
But Epoch had no basis here
For Period exhaled.

MANUSCRIPTS: There are two fair copies, identical in text, both written about 1870. The copy reproduced above (Bingham 98–3–9) shows minor differences in form from the copy to Sue (H 260), which is in pencil, signed "Emily –".

Great Streets of Silence led away
To Neighborhoods of Pause –
Here was no Notice – no Dissent –
No Universe – no Laws –

[810]

By Clocks – 'twas Morning
And for Night
The Bells at distance called –
But Epoch had no basis here –
For Period exhaled –

A third copy, now lost, evidently was sent to the Norcross cousins, for among the letters to them is one which is said to have concluded with these lines: *Letters* (ed. 1931), 239. The letter was written in the spring of 1870.

PUBLICATION: *Poems* (1891), 225, titled "Void." It follows the text and form of the packet copy.

1160

He is alive, this morning –
He is alive – and awake –
Birds are resuming for Him –
Blossoms – dress for His Sake.
Bees – to their Loaves of Honey
Add an Amber Crumb
Him – to regale – Me – Only –
Motion, and am dumb.

MANUSCRIPT: This unpublished poem (H 263) is in pencil, endorsed "Mr Bowles –" and signed "Emily." It is in the handwriting of about 1870. Samuel Bowles was not infrequently in Amherst. During June 1870 he and Mrs. Bowles were overnight guests in the home of Edward Dickinson. The fact that the note was still among the papers in the Dickinson homestead at the time of ED's death and for many years thereafter could mean that it was never delivered; more probably Bowles failed to take it with him.

1161

Trust adjusts her "Peradventure" –
Phantoms entered "and not you."

MANUSCRIPT: September 1870 (BPL Higg 65). The lines are incorporated in a letter to T. W. Higginson, written after his first visit to her in August. They follow the sentence:

I remember your coming as serious sweetness placed now with the Unreal.

PUBLICATION: *Letters* (ed. 1931 only), 288.

1162

The Life we have is very great.
The Life that we shall see
Surpasses it, we know, because
It is Infinity.
But when all Space has been beheld
And all Dominion shown
The smallest Human Heart's extent
Reduces it to none.

MANUSCRIPT: The poem is incorporated in a letter to Mrs. Holland written in October 1870 (H H 24).
PUBLICATION: The copy reproduced above is in *LH* (1951), 85. The identical text, printed as two quatrains, is in *BM* (1945), 241, derived from an unknown source.

1163

God made no act without a cause,
Nor heart without an aim,
Our inference is premature,
Our premises to blame.

These lines are incorporated in a letter (now lost) to the Norcross cousins. The text above reproduces that in *Letters* (ed. 1894), 262; (ed. 1931), 241; also *LL* (1924), 273. The letter there is dated 1870.

1164

Were it to be the last
How infinite would be
What we did not suspect was marked –
Our final interview.

[812]

This unpublished poem is incorporated in a letter to Mrs. Joseph A. Sweetser, ED's "Aunt Katie." It was written on the occasion of the death of the Sweetsers' son, Henry E. Sweetser, 17 February 1870. The manuscript is privately owned (Esty).

1165

Contained in this short Life
Are magical extents
The soul returning soft at night
To steal securer thence
As Children strictest kept
Turn soonest to the sea
Whose nameless Fathoms slink away
Beside infinity

MANUSCRIPTS: There are three autograph copies, all written about 1870. They are in pencil and cover both sides of a small sheet of stationery (Bingham 104–9). The copy reproduced above is the only completed version. The two rough drafts have many suggested changes set down between the lines and in the margins. The least finished evidently attempted a poem of twelve lines:

Contained in this short Life
Were wonderful extents
Discernible to not a friend
Except Omnipotence
A friend too straight to stoop
Too distant to be seen
Come unto me enacted how
With Firmaments between
The soul came home from trips
That would to sense have dazzled

1. Contained] Combined / Comprised
2. Were wonderful] Are magical /
   [Are] Terrible / [Are] miraculous / [Are] tenderest –
2] Were exquisite extents
6. distant] subtle
7. enacted] accomplished

8. Firmaments] Centuries
9. from trips] to sleep
9. trips] towns / scenes
10. would to sense] Un to sense –
10] Unmanifest to sense / Unwitnessed of the sense / As doth the tired sense

[813]

The second rough draft, a poem of eight lines, is the one on which ED drew for her finished copy:

> Contained in this short Life
> Are magical extents
> The soul returning soft at night
> To steal securer thence
> As children strictly kept
> Take sooner to the sea
> Whose waters are the brawling Brook
> To thine Infinity

1. short] plain
2. magical] exquisite
3. soft at night] still by Dawn / loth
   [by Dawn]
4. securer] at sunrise
5. strictly] strictest
6. Take] Turn

6. sooner [soon]est / [soon]er
7. brawling] nameless
8] Beside Infinity
7–8] Whose nameless fathoms slink
   away
      Beside infinity

PUBLICATION: *BM* (1945), 265. It is printed as two eight-line stanzas. Stanza 1 follows the text of the finished copy. Stanza 2 follows the text of the first eight lines of the first rough draft with selection of "Are terrible extents" for line 2. All three autographs are reproduced in facsimile in *BM*, xiii–xiv.

1166

> Of Paul and Silas it is said
> They were in Prison laid
> But when they went to take them out
> They were not there instead.
>
> Security the same insures
> To our assaulted Minds –
> The staple must be optional
> That an Immortal binds.

MANUSCRIPT: About 1870, in packet 94–4 (Bingham). The imprisonment of Paul and Silas is told in Acts xvi. 23–40. ED errs in saying "They were not there" when, the prison being rent, the jailors went to fetch them; they had in fact remained. She confuses the account with one related earlier (Acts v. 18–23) wherein "the apostles" were released from imprisonment by angels.

PUBLICATION: *BM* (1945), 120.

1167

Alone and in a Circumstance
Reluctant to be told
A spider on my reticence
Assiduously crawled

And so much more at Home than I
Immediately grew
I felt myself a visitor
And hurriedly withdrew

Revisiting my late abode
With articles of claim
I found it quietly assumed
As a Gymnasium
Where Tax asleep and Title off
The inmates of the Air
Perpetual presumption took
As each were special Heir –
If any strike me on the street
I can return the Blow –
If any take my property
According to the Law
The Statute is my Learned friend
But what redress can be
For an offense nor here nor there
So not in Equity –
That Larceny of time and mind
The marrow of the Day
By spider, or forbid it Lord
That I should specify.

1. in] of
4. Assiduously] deliberately / deter-
   minately/ impertinently
7. a] the
8. hurriedly] hastily

12. As] for
14. inmates] Peasants
15. presumption] complacence
16. special] lawful / only
19. take] seize

MANUSCRIPT: About May or June 1870, in pencil (Bingham 107–11). This may have been intended as a poem of seven quatrains, but line spaces are not indicated after the second stanza. In line 23 ED had first written "not anywhere," then crossed it out and substituted "nor here nor there." Pasted onto the center of the front half of the half-sheet of notepaper on which the poem is written there is an unused three-cent postage stamp of the issue of 1869. Beneath one side of the stamp are two small strips clipped from *Harper's Magazine* for May 1870. One bears the name "George Sand" and the other "Mauprat" — the title of the novel by George Sand published in 1836. The poem was written after the stamp and strips were pasted onto the sheet, for the lines accommodate themselves to the occupied space. Such deliberateness would suggest that the poem is autobiographical; that "in a circumstance reluctant to be told" ED had been guided to *Mauprat* and had found the book a "larceny of time and mind."

PUBLICATION: *BM* (1945), 102–103. It is printed as a seven-stanza poem. The suggested changes for lines 4 ("deliberately"), 7, 16 ("lawful"), and 19 are adopted.

1168

As old as Woe –
How old is that?
Some eighteen thousand years –
As old as Bliss
How old is that
They are of equal years

Together chiefest they are found
But seldom side by side
From neither of them tho' he try
Can Human nature hide

4. Bliss] Joy –
5] The age of that
7. chiefest] chiefly

8. But] Tho
10. Can] may

MANUSCRIPT: This unfinished draft (Bingham 107–13) is written in pencil on the inside of a slit-open envelope bearing the address "Mrs. Helen Hunt" in ED's hand. It may be roughly dated 1870. The suggested change for line 5 is preceded by the word "or."

PUBLICATION: *BM* (1945), 288. The suggested change for line 7 is adopted. The text is arranged as two quatrains.

1169

Lest they should come – is all my fear
When sweet incarcerated here

MANUSCRIPT: About 1870 (Bingham 109–4). It is a penciled fragment jotted down on a very small scrap of paper.

PUBLICATION: *BM* (1945), 318. It is placed among the fragments.

1170

Nature affects to be sedate
Upon occasion, grand
But let our observation shut
Her practices extend

To Necromancy and the Trades
Remote to understand
Behold our spacious Citizen
Unto a Juggler turned –

1. affects] was known   6. Remote] astute / obscure
3. shut] *halt*   7. our] my / this
4. practices] qualities

MANUSCRIPT: About 1870 (Bingham 102–34). It is a penciled work-sheet draft jotted down on both sides of a small scrap of paper.

PUBLICATION: *BM* (1945), 50. The suggested change for line 3 is adopted.

On the World you colored
Morning painted rose –
Idle his Vermillion
Aimless crept the Glows
Over Realms of Orchards
I the Day before
Conquered with the Robin –
Misery, how fair
Till your wrinkled Finger
Shored the sun away
Midnight's awful Pattern
In the Goods of Day –

4. crept] stole   10. Shored] pushed

MANUSCRIPT: About 1870 (Bingham 107–53). It is a penciled work-sheet draft.
PUBLICATION: *BM* (1945), 170. The suggested change for line 10 is adopted. The text is arranged as three quatrains.

The Clouds their Backs together laid
The North begun to push
The Forests galloped till they fell
The Lightning played like mice

The Thunder crumbled like a stuff
How good to be in Tombs
Where Nature's Temper cannot reach
Nor missile ever comes

4. played] skipped   8. missile] vengeance
6. good] safe / firm / calm

MANUSCRIPT: About 1870 (Bingham 98–3–29). It is a penciled work-sheet draft jotted down on a scrap of stationery. In line 7 ED crossed out "could" and substituted "can." In line 4 she underlined "played," her original word, not her alternate "skipped," perhaps trying to avoid a resemblance to Psalms 114.4: The mountains skipped like rams.

PUBLICATION: *Poems* (1890), 125, titled "Refuge." The stanza division is not retained. The suggested changes for lines 4 and 8 are adopted. The suggested change "safe" (line 6) is altered thus:

How good to be safe in tombs

1173

The Lightning is a yellow Fork
From Tables in the sky
By inadvertent fingers dropt
The awful Cutlery

Of mansions never quite disclosed
And never quite concealed
The Apparatus of the Dark
To ignorance revealed.

4. awful] solemn

MANUSCRIPT: About 1870 (Bingham 102–68). It is a rough penciled draft.

PUBLICATION: *BM* (1945), 17–18. The suggested change is rejected.

1174

There's the Battle of Burgoyne –
Over, every Day,
By the Time that Man and Beast
Put their work away
"Sunset" sounds majestic –
But that solemn War
Could you comprehend it
You would chastened stare –

1. There's] That's

MANUSCRIPT: About 1870 (Bingham 107–75). It is a penciled work-sheet draft jotted down on the inside of a slit-open envelope.

PUBLICATION: *BM* (1945), 21. The suggested change is adopted. The text is arranged as two quatrains.

1175

We like a Hairbreadth 'scape
It tingles in the Mind
Far after Act or Accident
Like paragraphs of Wind

If we had ventured less
The Gale were not so fine
That reaches to our utmost Hair
It's Tentacles divine.

1. We] I   6. Gale] *Breeze*
5. we] I   8. Tentacles] Resonance

MANUSCRIPT: About 1870 (Bingham 107–86). It is a penciled work-sheet draft. ED suggested "articles" in place of "paragraphs" (line 4), but crossed it out.
PUBLICATION: *BM* (1945), 121. The suggested change for line 6 is adopted.

1176

We never know how high we are
Till we are asked to rise
And then if we are true to plan
Our statures touch the skies –

The Heroism we recite
Would be a normal thing
Did not ourselves the Cubits warp
For fear to be a King –

2. asked] called   6. normal] daily
3. plan] growth

MANUSCRIPT: About 1870 (Bingham 105–11). It is a penciled draft.
PUBLICATION: *Poems* (1896), 27, titled "Aspiration." The suggested changes for lines 2 and 6 are adopted.

Date Due